Lecture Notes in Computer Science

Lecture Notes in Artificial Intelligence 15152

Founding Editor

Jörg Siekmann

Series Editors

Randy Goebel, *University of Alberta, Edmonton, Canada*
Wolfgang Wahlster, *DFKI, Berlin, Germany*
Zhi-Hua Zhou, *Nanjing University, Nanjing, China*

The series Lecture Notes in Artificial Intelligence (LNAI) was established in 1988 as a topical subseries of LNCS devoted to artificial intelligence.

The series publishes state-of-the-art research results at a high level. As with the LNCS mother series, the mission of the series is to serve the international R & D community by providing an invaluable service, mainly focused on the publication of conference and workshop proceedings and postproceedings.

Daniela Briola · Rafael C. Cardoso · Brian Logan
Editors

Engineering Multi-Agent Systems

12th International Workshop, EMAS 2024
Auckland, New Zealand, May 6–7, 2024
Revised Selected Papers

 Springer

Editors
Daniela Briola ⓘ
University of Milano-Bicocca
Milan, Italy

Rafael C. Cardoso ⓘ
University of Aberdeen
Aberdeen, UK

Brian Logan ⓘ
Utrecht University
Utrecht, The Netherlands

ISSN 0302-9743   ISSN 1611-3349 (electronic)
Lecture Notes in Artificial Intelligence
ISBN 978-3-031-71151-0   ISBN 978-3-031-71152-7 (eBook)
https://doi.org/10.1007/978-3-031-71152-7

LNCS Sublibrary: SL7 – Artificial Intelligence

This Springer imprint is published by the registered company Springer Nature Switzerland AG
The registered company address is: Gewerbestrasse 11, 6330 Cham, Switzerland

If disposing of this product, please recycle the paper.

Preface

A key unifying theme underlying artificial intelligence is the idea of intelligent software agents able to reason, act, interact, and learn. This metaphor has stimulated much research in AI and in Autonomous Agents and Multi-Agent Systems, giving rise to research in agent-oriented software engineering, programming multi-agent systems, and declarative agent languages and technologies.

History

The International Workshop on Engineering Multi-Agent Systems (EMAS) was formed in 2013 as a merger of three long-running workshops: Agent-Oriented Software Engineering (AOSE), Programming Multi-Agent Systems (ProMAS), and Declarative Agent Languages and Technologies (DALT). This merger established EMAS as a reference venue for work that is broadly concerned with the engineering of agents and multi-agent systems.

Since its inception, EMAS has been co-located with the International Conference on Autonomous Agents and Multi-Agent Systems (AAMAS). EMAS 2013 took place in St. Paul (with post-proceedings published as Springer LNCS/LNAI volume 8245), EMAS 2014 in Paris (LNCS/LNAI 8758, and a special issue in the International Journal of Agent-Oriented Software Engineering, IJAOSE Vol. 5 No. 2/3, 2016), EMAS 2015 in Istanbul (LNCS/LNAI 9318, and a special issue in IJAOSE Vol. 6 No. 2, 2018), EMAS 2016 in Singapore (LNCS/LNAI 10093, and a special issue in IJAOSE Vol. 6 No. 3/4, 2018), EMAS 2017 in São Paulo (LNCS/LNAI 10738), EMAS 2018 in Stockholm (LNAI 11375, and a report in Software Engineering Notes), EMAS 2019 in Montreal (LNAI 12058), EMAS 2020 in Auckland (LNAI 12589), EMAS 2021 in London (LNAI 13190), EMAS 2022 in Auckland (a special issue is to appear in AMAI), and EMAS 2023 in London (LNAI 14378). From 2020 to 2022, because of the COVID-19 pandemic, AAMAS and its co-located workshops (including EMAS) were organised as online events in a fully virtual format. Since EMAS 2023 (including EMAS 2024), the workshops have been held in person.

Topics

Despite the substantial body of knowledge and expertise developed in the design and development of Multi-Agent Systems (MAS), the systematic development of large-scale and open MAS still poses many challenges. Even though various languages, models, techniques, and methodologies have been proposed in the literature, researchers and developers are still faced with fundamental questions affecting MAS engineering, such as:

- How to specify, design, implement, verify, test, and validate large-scale and open MAS?
- How to ensure and control the global behaviour of decentralised, large-scale, and open MAS?
- How to express the requirements for MAS and how to translate these requirements into agent goals?
- Which (multi-)agent architectures and languages are most suitable for MAS in different domains?
- How to seamlessly integrate AI and machine learning techniques into design/programming languages and tools for agent-based systems?
- How to engineer agent and multi-agent systems that are secure and protect the privacy concerns of users?
- How to scale to the complexity of real-world application domains?
- What are the implications of MAS engineering in the context of continuous development and deployment?
- How can MAS be applied in specific application areas, such as Cyber-Physical Systems and Internet-of-Things?
- How to seamlessly integrate MAS engineering with mainstream software engineering models, languages, frameworks, and tools?
- Which processes and methodologies can integrate the above and provide a disciplined approach to the engineering of MAS?

EMAS 2024

EMAS 2024 was held in person as a 2-day workshop.[1] We received a total of 18 submissions, each of which was reviewed (single-blind) by three reviewers. In total, 15 papers were accepted for presentation at the workshop (8 regular papers, 6 short papers, and 1 student paper). After the workshop, authors of all accepted papers were invited to submit a revised and extended version of their paper to the post-proceedings. A total of 13 submissions were received. Each submission underwent an additional reviewing phase by the same reviewers as in the previous phase (single-blind, three reviewers per paper). Out of the 13 submissions submitted to the post-proceedings, 11 were accepted (7 regular papers and 4 short papers).

EMAS 2024 provided a forum for researchers and practitioners in the domains of agent-oriented software engineering, programming multi-agent systems, declarative agent languages and technologies, artificial intelligence, and machine learning to present and discuss their research and emerging results in engineering MAS. The overall purpose of the workshop is to facilitate the cross-fertilisation of ideas and experiences in the various fields to:

- Enhance our knowledge of the theory and practice of engineering intelligent agents and multi-agent systems, and advance the state of the art;
- Demonstrate how MAS methodologies, architectures, languages, and tools can be used in the engineering of deployed large-scale and open MAS;

---

[1] The complete workshop programme and all slides used in the presentations are available online at: https://emas.in.tu-clausthal.de/2024/program/ (Accessed 8 July 2024).

- Define new directions for engineering MAS by drawing on results and recommendations from related research areas;
- Encourage PhD and Masters students to become involved in and contribute to the area.

We reintroduced awards in EMAS 2024. The best paper award went to the authors Martina Baiardi, Samuele Burattini, Giovanni Ciatto, Danilo Pianini, Alessandro Ricci, and Andrea Omicini for their paper "On the external concurrency of current BDI frameworks for MAS". A certificate of appreciation was presented to Dennis Maecker, Henning Gösling, and Timon Sachweh for their significant contribution in submitting 4 papers to EMAS 2024.

Additionally, we held a community discussion session to talk about possible improvements and optimisations. We discussed topics such as the invitation policy and publication date of the post-proceedings, planning future editions of the workshop, future trends in engineering multi-agent systems, and real-world applications.

We look forward to the next edition of the EMAS workshop.

July 2024   Daniela Briola
                                                          Rafael C. Cardoso
                                                             Brian Logan

Organisation

Program Committee

Natasha Alechina	Utrecht University, Netherlands
Matteo Baldoni	Università di Torino, Italy
Cristina Baroglio	Università di Torino, Italy
Olivier Boissier	Mines Saint-Étienne, France
Rafael Bordini	PUCRS, Brazil
Maiquel de Brito	Federal University of Santa Catarina, Brazil
Moharram Challenger	University of Antwerp, Belgium
Amit Chopra	Lancaster University, UK
Andrei Ciortea	University of St. Gallen, Switzerland
Rem Collier	UCD, Ireland
Stefania Costantini	Univ. dell'Aquila, Italy
Davide Dell'Anna	Utrecht University, Netherlands
Louise A. Dennis	University of Manchester, UK
Babak Esfandiari	Carleton University, Canada
Angelo Ferrando	University of Modena and Reggio Emilia, Italy
Lars-Ake Fredlund	Universidad Politécnica de Madrid, Spain
Stéphane Galland	Université de Technologie de Belfort-Montbéliard, France
Jorge Gomez-Sanz	Universidad Complutense de Madrid, Spain
Zahia Guessoum	Université de Reims Champagne-Ardenne, France
James Harland	RMIT University, Australia
Vincent Hilaire	Université de Technologie de Belfort-Montbéliard, France
Jomi Fred Hübner	Federal University of Santa Catarina, Brazil
Yves Lespérance	York University, Canada
Philippe Mathieu	University of Lille, France
Viviana Mascardi	University of Genoa, Italy
Simon Mayer	University of St. Gallen, Switzerland
Felipe Meneguzzi	University of Aberdeen, UK
Roberto Micalizio	Università di Torino, Italy
Jörg P. Müller	TU Clausthal, Germany
Luis Gustavo Nardin	Mines Saint-Étienne, France
Alessandro Ricci	University of Bologna, Italy
Sebastian Rodriguez	RMIT University, Australia
Luca Sabatucci	ICAR-CNR, Italy

Amal El Fallah Seghrouchni	Sorbonne Université, France
Valeria Seidita	Università degli Studi di Palermo, Italy
Viviane Torres da Silva	IBM, Brazil
Gerhard Weiss	University of Maastricht, Netherlands
Michael Winikoff	Victoria University of Wellington, New Zealand
Yi Yang	KU Leuven, Belgium
Vahid Yazdanpanah	University of Southampton, UK
Neil Yorke-Smith	Delft University of Technology, Netherlands
Rym Zalila-Wenkstern	University of Texas at Dallas, USA

Program Committee Chairs

Daniela Briola	University of Milano-Bicocca, Italy
Rafael C. Cardoso	University of Aberdeen, UK
Brian Logan	Universiteit Utrecht, The Netherlands, and University of Aberdeen, UK

Steering Committee

Matteo Baldoni	Università degli Studi di Torino, Italy
Rafael Bordini	PUCRS, Brazil
Mehdi Dastani	Utrecht University, The Netherlands
Jürgen Dix	Technische Universität Clausthal, Germany
Amal El Fallah Seghrouchni	Sorbonne Université, France
Brian Logan	Universiteit Utrecht, The Netherlands, and University of Aberdeen, UK
Jörg P. Müller	Technische Universität Clausthal, Germany
Alessandro Ricci	Università di Bologna, Italy
Danny Weyns	Katholieke Universiteit Leuven, Belgium
Michael Winikoff	Victoria University of Wellington, New Zealand
Rym Zalila-Wenkstern	University of Texas at Dallas, USA

Invited Talks

Our intent was to invite one speaker from a related community, and another speaker from within the EMAS community. This was achieved by inviting Stephen Cranefield for his work with the Coordination, Organizations, Institutions, Norms, Ethics for Governance of Multi-Agent Systems (COINE) community, and Sebastian Rodriguez for his work in the EMAS community. Invited speakers were asked to provide their perspectives on the state of the art in the theory and practice of engineering multi-agent systems.

Engineering Social Order in Multi-agent Systems

Stephen Cranefield

University of Otago, New Zealand

One of my long-standing research interests is to develop practical techniques for agents to understand the social constraints they and other agents are operating under, so they can coordinate more effectively without relying on centralised infrastructure. I will begin this talk with a brief overview of my prior work on monitoring social expectations, learning norms from observation, following social practices and proposing and executing group plans. I will then discuss recent work on a practical technique for recognising common belief, which is an important enabler of efficient coordination within groups. Our approach is based on philosopher David Lewis's account of common knowledge (which is really about warranted common belief). It considers the common case where (i) a publicly observable "state of affairs" A (which we view as a set of percepts) indicates to an agent that some proposition P holds, and (ii) through reasoning about shared background knowledge and standards of reasoning, the agent can infer that other agents should also believe P. Prior work does not provide a precise and satisfactory definition of the nature of indication, nor does it explain how agents reason about shared knowledge and reasoning standards. We propose specific mechanisms based on theory-of-mind (ToM) rules in a forward-chaining rule engine. We prove that only two levels of ToM modelling is required to recognise the existence of common belief. The approach is implemented using the Prolog Forward Chaining (Pfc) library and can be used in conjunction with the Jason agent platform. We illustrate the approach in a scenario from classical Athens of decision-making requiring common belief of the information on a public monument.

Agile Approach for Agent Oriented Software Engineering

Sebastian Rodriguez

RMIT University, Australia

The agile software development life cycle is widely used in industry today due to its highly flexible and iterative processes that facilitate rapid prototyping. In this talk, we advocate to close the gap between mainstream software engineering and agent technology by adopting and adapting well-known and accepted techniques. We introduce an agile approach to capturing requirements in agent systems via user and system stories and translating these requirements into goal-oriented agent models. We cover how to define test cases to verify the expected system behaviour following a Behaviour-Driven Development (BDD) approach. We leverage a range of state-of-the-art development tools, inheriting the rich set of features they provide. Finally, we discuss future directions and opportunities.

Contents

SPARKIT: A Mind Map-Based MAS
for Idea Generation Support

Masaki Ishizaka[1(✉)], Akihito Taya[2], and Yoshito Tobe[1]

[1] Grad. Sch. Aoyama Gakuin University, Sagamihara, Japan
{zacker,y.tobe}@rcl-aoyama.jp
[2] The University of Tokyo, Meguro, Japan
taya-a@iis.u-tokyo.ac.jp

Abstract. Innovative solutions to societal challenges require the generation of creative ideas. Collaboration between humans and multi-agent systems (MAS) is a promising approach for idea generation, yet fostering creative discussions remains a challenge. This paper proposes Synergistic Platform for Advancing and Reinforcing Knowledge through Interactive Tools (SPARKIT) and SPARK-flow leveraging mind maps to facilitate idea generation within a MAS framework. SPARKIT supports idea generation with two types of large language model (LLM)-based agents: Debater Agents and the Moderator Agent. Debater Agents offer varied perspectives from their expertise, while the Moderator Agent structures discussions into a mind map to enhance user-agent collaboration. SPARK-flow is designed to stimulate creative idea generation by orchestrating discussions among these agents. A distinctive aspect of SPARKIT and SPARK-flow is that the agents facilitate the discussion and its structuring into a mind map, reducing the user's burden compared to existing methods. This paper compares different methods of discussion using language models and reveals that the impact of the discussion method on the creativity of ideas is consistent between humans and language models, with mind maps significantly enhancing creativity.

Keywords: Idea Generation · Mind Mapping · Human-Agent Interaction · Agent-based Discussion

1 Introduction

Addressing complex social challenges requires concrete and feasible solutions. However, especially in the early stages of idea generation, limited perspectives due to a lack of information and knowledge boundaries are major challenges. Research is progressing on digital tools [3,4,25,35] and agent-based systems [13, 26] that support idea generation by providing users with extensive information. Nonetheless, since feedback from these systems depends on user input, they can be challenging for users without specific ideas on the topic to use effectively.

Idea generation requires organizing information. Mind maps are recognized as an effective tool for visually organizing thoughts and findings. [30,32,38].

© The Author(s), under exclusive license to Springer Nature Switzerland AG 2025
D. Briola et al. (Eds.): EMAS 2024, LNAI 15152, pp. 1–22, 2025.
https://doi.org/10.1007/978-3-031-71152-7_1

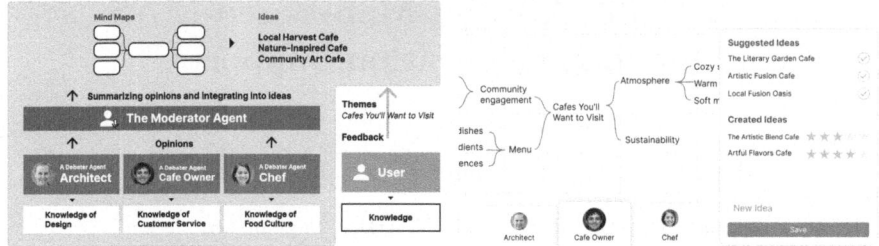

(a) SPARKIT Architecture.   (b) SPARKIT Interface.

Fig. 1. SPARKIT: A system for facilitating discussions through mind maps, involving Debater Agents, the Moderator Agent, and user interaction

Furthermore, combining concepts is crucial for generating creative ideas [10, 11, 23]. While mind maps help in understanding the relationships between concepts, existing tools [7, 12] primarily focus on their creation and do not sufficiently support the derivation and refinement of specific ideas from them.

This paper proposes Synergistic Platform for Advancing and Reinforcing Knowledge through Interactive Tools (SPARKIT), a system that supports idea generation through discussions involving multiple agents and users, facilitated by mind maps. SPARKIT uses two types of large language model (LLM)-based agents: Debater Agents and the Moderator Agent. When a user inputs a theme to address a specific problem, these agents generate mind maps and develop solution-oriented ideas. For instance, when a user planning to open a new café enters the theme "Cafés You'd Love to Visit," SPARKIT offers specific ideas and inspiration for café concepts, as shown in Fig. 1. Debater Agents provide varied perspectives with expertise dynamically assigned through prompts. The Moderator Agent summarizes discussions into mind maps and suggests concrete ideas. SPARKIT incorporates users' opinions and preferences through mind maps and ideas, guiding discussions toward user objectives. The primary objective of SPARKIT is to assist users in generating innovative ideas by providing diverse perspectives through unique agent viewpoints.

To obtain creative ideas, it is beneficial to discuss with multiple people who have different perspectives. However, too many opinions can cause the discussions to diverge and make it difficult to converge. In this study, we design SPARK-flow, a method within the SPARKIT that uses mind maps to balance divergent and convergent thinking in agent discussions. SPARK-flow draws inspiration from existing research on methods of discussion for creative idea generation [2, 18, 21, 34], integrating them into discussions among multi-agent systems. Section 2 describes the characteristics of creative ideas and existing research on methods of discussion. Section 3 explores how to apply these methods to multi-agent discussions, and Sect. 4 analyzes the impact of each method on the generated ideas. Our contributions are as follows:

1. We propose SPARKIT, a system that leverages multiple LLM-based agents with different expertise and utilizes mind mapping to support idea generation for users.
2. We design SPARK-flow, a method that extracts discussion topics and organizes them into a mind map, enabling creative idea generation through iterative discussions among agents.
3. We demonstrate the effectiveness of SPARK-flow by evaluating it based on five aspects of discussion methods and analyzing the generated mind maps to reveal the factors in creative idea generation.

2 Related Work

2.1 Mind Map-Based Idea Generation

Mind maps are tools that place a core theme at the center, with related keywords branching out successively. This approach is beneficial for organizing thoughts in a structured manner. Mind maps were proposed by Tony Buzan [6] and are used in a wide range of fields, not limited to idea generation, but also in education [33], language acquisition [30], and more. Employing mind maps for brainstorming has been shown to enhance creativity [38] and increase the number of ideas compared to using bullet points [31]. Furthermore, deeper engagement in mind mapping tends to yield more unique ideas [24], supporting the theory that creativity thrives on integrating new elements into existing frameworks [11].

Tools for automatically creating mind maps have been proposed, such as methods that present technology and idea relationships using patent databases [25], aggregate crowd-sourced ideas into mind maps [7], and alternate mind map creation between humans and computers [12]. Although these tools ease mind map generation, they do not support the crucial steps of extracting and organizing ideas from the created mind maps. In contrast, SPARKIT not only generates mind maps but also offers support to utilize the information for the creation and refinement of specific ideas.

2.2 Enhancing Idea Generation with Digital Tools

Several systems have been proposed to support idea generation by presenting keywords [3] or images [35] related to the conversation topic. These methods stimulate users based on the conversation's content, thereby increasing the number of ideas. Nonetheless, the support becomes ineffective when the user stops speaking, as feedback is triggered by the user's utterances.

Cloud-based methods allowing numerous participants to share ideas in real-time can prevent discussion stagnation and have been shown to foster increasingly creative ideas over time [4]. However, these methods face challenges such as gathering participants and integrating diverse opinions.

The advent of LLM has introduced new possibilities for idea generation support. Tools that facilitate idea generation in a conversational format [13] and those that autonomously generate concepts [26] have been gaining attention. However, language models require user input to generate output, which means users must take the lead in the process. Additionally, the novelty and diversity of ideas generated by language models are often inferior to those obtained through crowdsourcing [26].

SPRKIT enables the generation of diverse ideas through discussions among multiple agents. Moreover, by structuring the content of discussions into mind maps, the system autonomously promotes the discussion, reducing the burden on users in generating ideas.

2.3   Activation of Idea Generation

Brainstorming is widely acknowledged as a method that fosters creativity. However, it has been observed that the efficiency of idea generation varies according to the structure of the brainstorming session. According to Al-Samarraie et al., group brainstorming, where participants interact simultaneously, is effective in producing a multitude of ideas. However, the number of ideas generated per person is less compared to the format where participants think of ideas individually [2]. Furthermore, it has been shown that for generating creative ideas, it is crucial to iteratively generate ideas within a short time [15], to engage in more associations [5], and to evaluate ideas when creating them iteratively [21].

The integration of concepts is a critical attribute of creative ideas. While directly combining different concepts has a limited impact on creativity, it has been demonstrated that adding new ideas based on already combined ideas enhances creativity [10,11,23]. Therefore, exposing users to ideas from diverse domains beforehand is considered effective [34]. SPARKIT leverages Debater Agents with diverse roles to provide users with multiple perspectives, facilitating rapid and iterative idea generation through the combination of these insights.

2.4   Evaluation of Idea

The creativity of ideas is evaluated using indicators such as novelty and usefulness [28,29,34]. According to Diedrich et al., novelty contributes more significantly to predicting creativity than usefulness, and in ideas with high novelty, usefulness contributes more substantially to creativity [14]. Kern et al. evaluated the responses to the Alternative Uses Test (AUT) using GPT-4 [1] in terms of novelty, feasibility, and value, with a notable positive correlation observed in the assessment of novelty compared to human evaluations [22]. Furthermore, it was demonstrated that the alignment between evaluations of GPT-4 and human evaluations strengthens as the agreement among human evaluators increases [27]. According to Hackl et al., multiple evaluations of macroeconomics test answers by GPT-4 resulted in an Intraclass Correlation Coefficient (ICC) of 0.999, indicating the reliability evaluation of GPT-4 [20]. These findings suggest that GPT-4 can consistently evaluate the creativity of ideas similarly to human evaluators. Therefore, this paper employs GPT-4 to assess the creativity of ideas generated by SPARKIT.

3   SPARKIT

SPARKIT is a system that supports idea generation through discussions among multiple agents, facilitated by mind maps. We implement SPARKIT as a web application. Users can edit the generated mind maps and provide feedback to the agents by evaluating the generated ideas, as shown in Fig. 1(b). To generate creative ideas, it is helpful to discuss with people from different perspectives. However, such discussion is not possible with only a single user. Moreover, too many opinions may cause the discussion to diverge, making it difficult to converge. To address this challenge, SPARKIT employs two types of agents: Debater Agents and the Moderator Agent, and conducts discussions using a method called SPARK-flow.

3.1   Debater Agents

Debater Agents are language models assigned roles, such as "architect," through prompts and present opinions based on those roles. By establishing specific roles, language models can generate opinions based on the knowledge associated with those roles. This approach enables the production of more detailed responses than those possible without such role settings [37]. Additionally, by engaging multiple agents in discussions, even if the responses generated by the language model are initially incorrect, iterating through discussions can lead to improved and more accurate answers [16].

3.2   The Moderator Agent

Presenting the opinions generated by the Debater Agents directly to the user can lead to a proportional increase in text volume with the number of agents. This can make it difficult for users to grasp the content. To mitigate this, the Moderator Agent summarizes the discussion into a mind map, offering the following three advantages: (1) **Reduction of text volume by eliminating redundancies** This helps to control the increase in text volume associated with the rise in the number of agents, thereby reducing the cognitive load on the user. (2) **Visualization of the relationships between concepts** This representation facilitates the combination of concepts [30, 32, 33]. (3) **Clustering topics** By clustering topics, it becomes easier to identify topics of interest, which can facilitate the generation of ideas that meet the user's requirements. Additionally, supplying the mind map as a prompt to the language model enhances response performance [36]. By summarizing the discussion in a mind map, the Moderator Agent not only facilitates discussions among the agents but also aids in idea generation by organizing and presenting the discussion points to the user.

3.3   SPARK-Flow

SPARK-flow is a mechanism within SPARKIT that orchestrates the flow of discussion among agents. SPARK-flow aims to: (1) generate creative ideas through

6   M. Ishizaka et al.

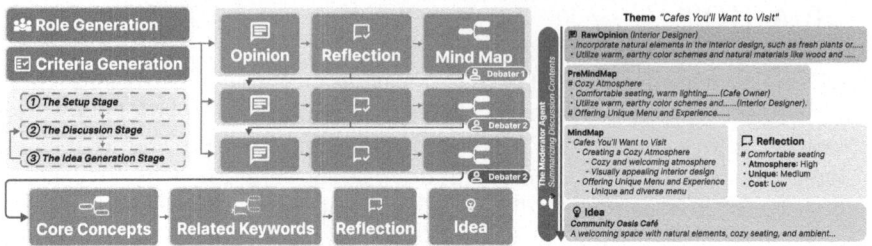

Fig. 2. SPARK-flow

the synergy of agent interactions and (2) create mind maps to present the discussion in an understandable format for users.

SPARK-flow consists of three main stages: the Setup Stage, the Discussion Stage, and the Idea Generation Stage. In the Setup Stage, the agents participating in the discussion are determined. In the Discussion Stage, Debater Agents engage in discussions on the theme. The Idea Generation Stage then focuses on generating ideas based on the content of these discussions. SPARK-flow repeats the Discussion Stage and Idea Generation Stage in cycles, each referred to as a *round*. Figure 2 illustrates the flow of the discussion and also shows the input-output relationships at each step, with inputs being conveyed to the agents using prompts.

The Setup Stage begins with the assignment of roles to Debater Agents $\mathcal{D} = \{p_{d_1}, p_{d_2}, \ldots, p_{d_{N_{\text{Roles}}}}\}$. The participants in the discussion have a significant impact on the ideas generated. If the role is not suitable for the theme, it can lead to forcibly connecting the theme and knowledge, resulting in the generation of ideas that lack relevance to the theme. To address this, we prompt the language model p to generate roles that are expected to yield creative ideas for the theme. In terms of the number of agents, it has been confirmed that increasing the number of agents beyond 3 to 4 leads to a deterioration in accuracy or a plateauing effect [9,16]. Therefore, we set the number of agents $N_{\text{Roles}} = 3$.

While the amount of information generated increases in proportion to the number of agents, some of it does not contribute to creative ideas. It is essential to filter out irrelevant information to maintain a manageable volume of data for consideration. To address this, SPARK-flow produces N_{Criteria} evaluation criteria $\mathcal{C}$, used in later steps to assess items and determine their inclusion in mind maps or ideas. In subsequent steps, the generated content is evaluated based on these criteria, which are used as a basis for deciding whether to include them in the mind map or ideas.

The Discussion Stage begins once the Setup Stage is completed. Debater Agent p_{d_i} generates opinions O_i (*RawOpinion*) based on the assigned role and the theme. Debater Agents are instructed to generate RawOpinion in bullet point format, as shown in Fig. 2, to enable a wider range of independent perspectives than in conversational sentence format.

Algorithm 1. The Discussion Stage in SPARK-flow

Require: *theme*, N_{Roles}, N_{Criteria}

Ensure: M

  $M \leftarrow$ None;

  $E \leftarrow$ None;

  $\mathcal{D} \leftarrow$ empty list;

  $\mathcal{C} \leftarrow$ empty list;

  for $i = 1$ to N_{Roles} **do**

    $d_i \sim p(\text{role}|\text{theme})$;

    Append p_{d_i} to $\mathcal{D}$;

  end for

  for $i = 1$ to N_{Criteria} **do**

    $c_i \sim p(\text{criterion}|\text{theme})$;

    Append c_i to $\mathcal{C}$;

  end for

  for all d_i in $\mathcal{D}$ **do do**

    $O_{d_i} \sim p_{d_i}(\text{o}|\text{theme}, M, E)$;

    $P_{d_i} \sim p_m(\text{g}|\text{theme}, M, O_{d_i})$;

    $E_{d_i} \sim p_m(\text{e}|\text{theme}, P_{d_i})$;

    $M_{d_i} \sim p_m(\text{m}|\text{theme}, M, P_{d_i}, E_{d_i})$;

    $M \leftarrow M_{d_i}$;

    $E \leftarrow E_{d_i}$;

  end for

  return M

Directly incorporating the opinions of Debater Agents into a mind map can lead to a complex and bloated mind map because language models attempt to include all elements. To address this issue, the Moderator Agent p_m performs two steps before generating the mind map M_{d_i} (*MindMap*). First, the Moderator Agent generates a clustered representation of the opinions, called *PreMindMap* P_{d_i}, by extracting common elements from the opinions of the Debater Agents. The elements contained in the MindMap and PreMindMap are referred to as *nodes*. Although the formats of the MindMap and PreMindMap are similar, as shown in Fig. 2, the text within the nodes of the PreMindMap uses the content of RawOpinion directly, while in the MindMap, these are summarized. This allows the Moderator Agent to decide on the content to be included in the MindMap by considering more information. Next, in the reflection step, the Moderator Agent p_m evaluates each node in P_{d_i} based on $\mathcal{C}$ to generate evaluations E_{d_i}, determining the priority for inclusion in the MindMap M_{d_i}. These two steps allow only the elements with a high potential for contributing to idea generation to remain in the mind map M_{d_i}.

After each Debater Agent generates an opinion, the Idea Generation Stage begins. The Moderator Agent selects nodes from the mind map to represent the core concept of an idea and chooses other nodes to combine with it, leveraging the benefits of concept combination using the mind map. Finally, the selected nodes are combined with the core concept based on the evaluation of the reflection step, resulting in the generation of new ideas.

By structuring the flow of discussion, SPARK-flow extracts elements from the discussion content that contribute to creative ideas and organizes them into ideas using a mind map.

3.4   Divergent and Convergent Thinking

According to Guilford, productive thinking can be categorized into two types: divergent and convergent thinking [19]. In divergent thinking, the ability to think in various directions is crucial, with traits such as fluency, flexibility, and originality being emphasized in creativity. On the other hand, convergent thinking is the process of consolidating thoughts into a unique answer. It is stated that divergent and convergent thinking do not occur entirely separately but often coexist.

SPARK-flow encourages divergent thinking by allowing Debater Agents to freely express opinions based on their role. The participation of multiple agents with diverse knowledge in the discussion enables thinking in more varied directions. Convergent thinking in SPARK-flow corresponds to the process of organizing these opinions into a mind map and generating ideas. To replicate the impact of convergent thinking on the subsequent process, the mind map generated during convergence is referenced by the Debater Agents when generating opinions. Additionally, this enables Debater Agents to reference the opinions of others, allowing them to supplement or develop the opinions of other agents.

Research has consistently shown that creative ideas are combinations of new elements or ideas with established technological components or methodologies [10, 11, 23]. In SPARK-flow, we apply this concept by summarizing the content of discussions into mind maps, which encourages the structural discovery of new relevancies and combinations. During idea generation, keywords are selected from the mind map, and related keywords are chosen to form new ideas. This approach enables the generation of new ideas unconstrained by existing concepts and the utilization of language model knowledge to make the ideas more concrete.

3.5   Reflection

The studies [17, 21] have consistently demonstrated the impact of evaluating ideas during the productive thinking phase. It has been found that a single evaluation of ideas can enhance the quality of subsequent ideas. To leverage the benefits of reflection, SPARK-flow implements reflection before mind mapping and idea generation, and references the results in later steps to enhance creativity. Additionally, SPARK-flow adopts multiple evaluation criteria. This approach encourages the generation of higher-quality ideas, even if the evaluation is low from some perspectives, by combining them with other elements.

Users can participate in the reflection step because all processes are conducted in natural language. By evaluating the generated ideas and opinions, users can clarify the ideas they are seeking, and the results affect the later process of SPARK-flow. This is expected to lead to the creation of ideas that meet the users' needs.

3.6 Settings of Experiments

Dataset. In this experiment, SPARK-flow was executed with 30 to 50 themes generated by OpenAI's Chat Completions API (gpt-3.5-turbo). The cosine similarity between themes, calculated using embeddings from the Universal Sentence Encoder [8], averaged 0.56 with a standard deviation of 0.036, suggesting moderate diversity among the themes. In each step, specific prompts are given to the language model to execute SPARK-flow. The Debater Agents and the Moderator Agent were powered by gpt-3.5-turbo, each sequentially assuming three roles for opinion presentation. To eliminate the influence of roles and evaluation criteria, the comparative experiments utilized pre-generated common roles and three evaluation criteria ($N_{Criteria} = 3$). As a baseline method, we employ a technique that prompts gpt-3.5-turbo to generate creative ideas based on a given theme. In this paper, we refer to this approach as *Simple*. Simple has two variations: *Simple(w/ role)* and *Simple(w/o role)*, generating ideas based on a specific role and theme, and the theme alone, respectively.

Idea Evaluation. To compare the effectiveness of different idea generation methods, ideas from each method were presented to OpenAI's Chat Completion API (gpt-4). The model was asked to select the more creative idea between pairs of ideas generated by different methods. By ensuring the source of the ideas was unidentifiable, we enabled an objective evaluation. It is known that explicitly asking for the rationale behind the evaluation improves the accuracy of the assessment [22]. Therefore, in this paper, GPT-4 not only selected ideas but also generated reasons for its choices. Approximately three ideas per theme and round are compared, and the win rate for each method is calculated based on these comparison results. A one-sample t-test was conducted on win rates of all themes to test the null hypothesis that there is no difference in the quality of ideas generated by the two methods. If the null hypothesis is rejected and the win rate of one method exceeds 50%, that method is considered superior. In addition to a comparison involving modifications to SPARK-flow, a common evaluation was conducted by comparing ideas from multiple methods against those generated by the baseline method, Simple(w/o role).

4 Experiments and Results

4.1 Comparative Evaluation of SPARK-Flow and Simple Method in Idea Generation

This experiment aims to evaluate whether the ideas generated by SPARK-flow exhibit superior quality compared to those produced by a conventional method.

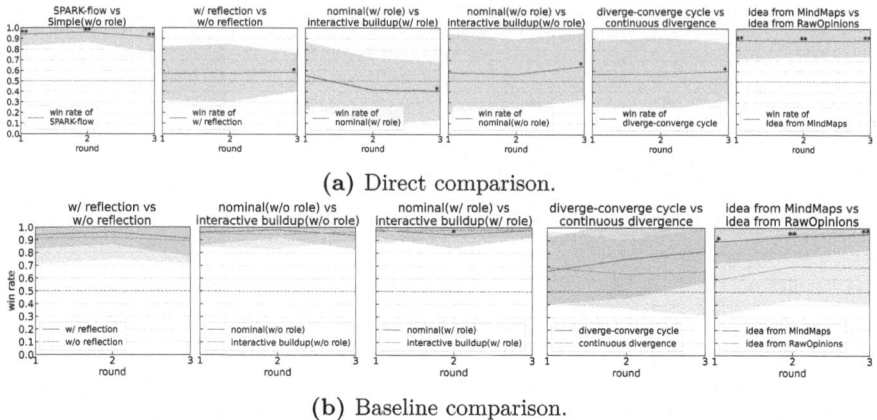

(a) Direct comparison.

(b) Baseline comparison.

Fig. 3. (a) Win rates for two methods over rounds, tested against a 50% baseline with p-values. (b) Win rate trajectories against Simple(w/o role) as baseline, with p-values assessing differences. The symbols * and ** indicate p < 0.05 and p < 0.001, respectively

We compared the ideas generated by SPARK-flow with those generated by Simple(w/o role).

Figures 3 and Table 1 show the evolution of the win rate per round and the win rate, along with the percentage of themes with a win rate exceeding 50% in the final round, respectively. The win rate of SPARK-flow against Simple(w/o role) was 91.3% (p < 0.01), and since the win rate exceeded 50% in 96.7% of all themes, it was demonstrated that the ideas generated by SPARK-flow are more creative than those generated by Simple, regardless of the theme. Furthermore, when evaluating the impact of the presence or absence of roles on the creativity of ideas, the win rate of Simple(w/o role) against Simple(w/ role) was 55.1% (p=0.1), suggesting that the use of roles contributes to the generation of creative ideas.

4.2   Reflection Improves the Creativity of Ideas

In this experiment, we investigated the impact of reflection on the quality of ideas generated using a language model for ideation. The experiment compared the effects of the presence or absence of reflection and reference to the evaluation.

The results of this experiment suggest the potential for reflection to improve the quality of idea generation. The win rate when reflection was performed was statistically significant at 58.4% (p < 0.05), and given its low dependency on the theme, reflection is considered to play an important role in the idea generation process. In idea-generation systems utilizing language models, encouraging user reflection is key to leading to higher-quality ideas. These results indicate that SPARK-flow enables the generation of ideas through discussions among agents that cannot be obtained by a single agent.

Table 1. Win rates for Method A in direct comparisons against Method B across various themes

Method A	Method B	N_{Theme}	$N_{Compare}$	>50% Win Rate Theme Raio[%]
SPARK-flow	Simple(w/o role)	30	450	96.7
w/reflection	w/o reflection	50	750	68.0
nominal(w/role)	interactive buildup(w/ role)	50	450	32.0
nominal(w/o role)	interactive buildup(w/o role)	31	279	71.0
diverge-converge cycle	continuous divergence	50	450	66.0
idea from MindMaps	idea from RawOpinions	30	450	96.7

4.3   Comparing Nominal and Interactive Buildup Groups in Agent-Based Idea Generation

In the discussion methods for idea generation, Girotra et al. suggest that groups that discuss collectively from the beginning, termed "nominal groups," are less effective in generating superior ideas compared to groups that engage in individual thinking followed by group discussion, which they refer to as "interactive buildup" [18]. This experiment aims to verify whether this insight is also applicable to discussions involving language models. When Debater Agents generate opinions, in the nominal group scenario, they do not reference the opinions of others, whereas, in the interactive buildup scenario, they continuously form opinions while referencing the opinions of others. Furthermore, when generating ideas, all opinions are referenced and aggregated into the final idea. Additionally, the impact of roles was considered, and comparisons were made in the absence of roles.

With roles, the interactive buildup showed superior results, with a win rate of 59.3% (p<0.05), which is a trend opposite to that of [18]. In contrast, without roles, the nominal group showed a better win rate of 59.9% (p<0.05), consistent with the results of [18].

Assigning roles to language models can be assumed to bias their outputs. Therefore, in an interactive buildup with roles, opinions can be presented from different perspectives. Furthermore, the experiment by [18] demonstrated that interactive buildup facilitates the formation of ideas through the accumulation of others' opinions. Similarly, observations confirm that discussions utilizing language models also enable the supplementation of opinions presented by specific roles with insights from different viewpoints. On the other hand, when agents are not assigned roles, they tend to answer the given task more correctly, resulting in a lack of diversity in the discussion. Furthermore, discussions by language models differ from those by humans in that they do not experience stagnation. Given this characteristic, it is expected that interactive buildup among agents with roles will provide the most beneficial impact by offering users diverse perspectives in idea generation.

4.4   Balancing Divergence and Convergence

In this experiment, we investigated how the balance between divergence and convergence in discussions among debating agents influences the quality of idea generation. In actual communication, discussions often oscillate between divergent modes, similar to brainstorming, and convergent modes, which involve detailed opinions and feedback. The effectiveness of these approaches in ideation using language models is still not fully understood. In standard interactions with existing language models, the user typically controls the direction of the discussion. However, there remain challenges in facilitating efficient and independent debates between agents. Our experiment specifically examined the role of agent collaboration in managing this balance for enhanced idea generation.

To compare the balance of divergence and convergence, we divided into two groups: (1) employing alternating divergence and convergence and (2) continuously diverging. The first group's agents would reflect and consolidate opinions in a mind map after each discussion, while the latter group's agents would immediately proceed to the next discussion without this consolidation step. To align the two groups, ideas were generated from opinions, not mind maps. We focused on the impact of divergence and convergence on discussion content, selecting ideation keywords exclusively from the compiled mind maps, and deliberately not generating related keywords using the language model's knowledge.

The results of the experiment revealed a notable trend: the group alternating between divergence and convergence showed an improvement in idea quality over time. This was evidenced by a statistically significant advantage in idea quality compared to a simpler approach without these dynamics (win rate: 72.3%, $p = 4.00 \times 10^{-6}$). On the contrary, the group engaging in continuous divergence demonstrated a decrease in idea quality over time, with a lower win rate of 66.3% ($p = 5.50 \times 10^{-2}$) compared to the Simple(w/o role).

The findings highlight the increasing significance of the convergence process as discussions progress. Furthermore, the large variance in win rates compared to Simple (w/o) for both methods indicates that generating ideas from opinions, rather than from a mind map, leads to unstable idea quality. This suggests the importance of organizing information from discussions into a mind map before generating ideas.

4.5   Enhancing Idea Generation Through Mind Mapping

The comparative analysis conducted in this experiment focused on the use of mind maps for idea generation versus the method of directly referencing the opinions of Debater Agents. The aim was to assess how different methods of summarizing discussion content affect the quality of the generated ideas. Exceptionally, in the Idea Generation Stage, keyword generation related to the discussion topics was omitted to maintain consistency with the original SPARK-flow, except for this alteration. When referencing opinions directly, all opinions presented by the Debater Agents up to that point were considered.

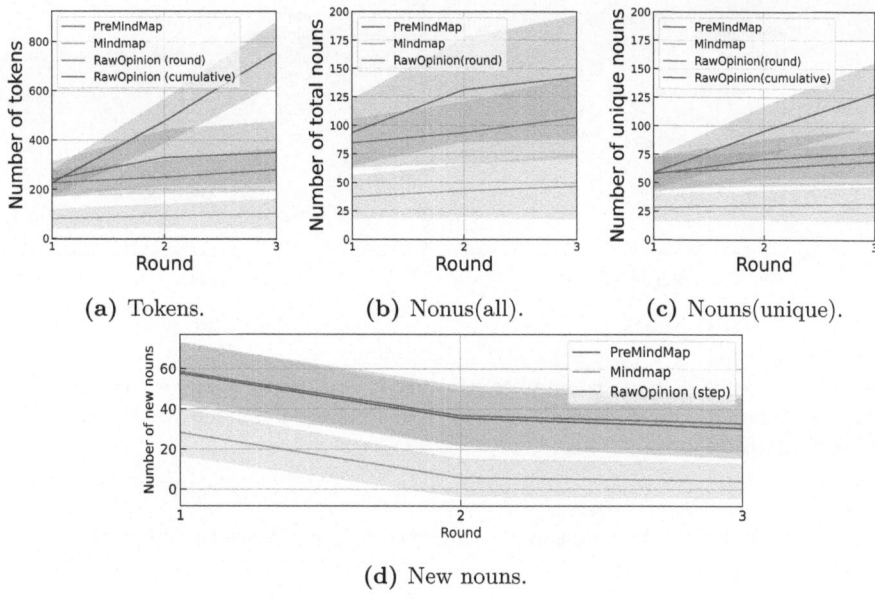

(a) Tokens.   (b) Nonus(all).   (c) Nouns(unique).

(d) New nouns.

Fig. 4. Sequential evolution of tokens and nouns in mind maps over three rounds. (a) Token counts per round, (b) Total noun counts, including repetitions, (c) Count of unique nouns, excluding repetitions, (d) New nouns not previously appearing. The 'RawOpinion (round)' indicates new elements per round, and 'Opinion (cumulative)' shows the aggregate up to each round

Idea generation using mind maps demonstrated a significantly higher win rate (89.3%, $p<0.05$) compared to the method of direct opinion reference. Moreover, the variance in win rates, when compared to Simple(w/o role), indicated a variance of 12.3% for ideas generated from mind maps, as opposed to 28.6% for those derived from direct opinion referencing. This disparity suggests that mind maps are more effective in consistently yielding creative ideas.

The enhancement in idea quality attributable to mind maps is linked to a reduction in information volume and the facilitation of concept association. Figure 4 shows the transition in the number of tokens and nouns in mind maps and opinions for each round. Direct referencing led to a per-round increase of approximately 200 tokens, while the increase for mind map-contained tokens was limited to about 30 tokens. This disparity underscores the efficiency of mind maps in organizing information, thereby reducing the volume of necessary information and stabilizing idea creativity. Figure 6 analyzes the hierarchical structure of nodes in the mind map and the relationships between nodes. As the hierarchy deepens, the similarity between nodes with the same parent increases, while the similarity between nodes with different parents decreases. This indicates that using a mind map makes it easier to combine related concepts with structural hints, facilitating the generation of new ideas. The ease of combining

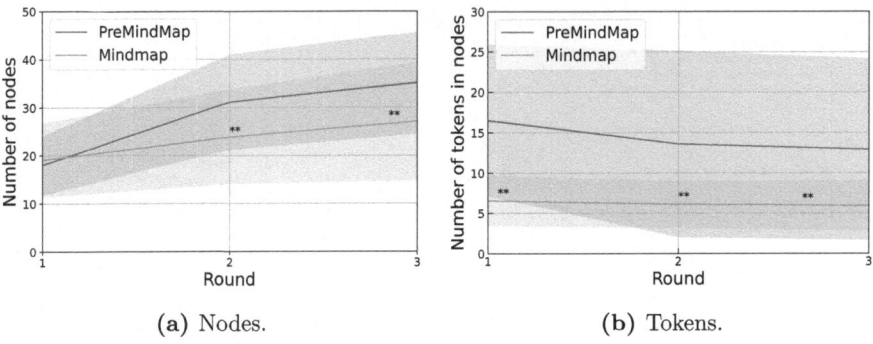

(a) Nodes.   (b) Tokens.

Fig. 5. (a) Trends in node counts across rounds, with t-test p-values for differences between Mindmap and PreMindMap. (b) Token counts per node, with significance tested similarly to (a)

concepts considering their distance is believed to contribute to the originality of ideas.

4.6   Integrating Debater Agent Opinions Into a Mind Map

This study analyzes how opinions generated by Debater Agents in SPARK-flow are organized into a mind map. Figure 4(a) shows an increasing trend in the number of tokens for RawOpinion, PreMindMap, and MindMap across successive rounds, indicating that the amount of information grows with each round. This trend can be attributed to the Debater Agents referencing the opinions of previous agents and generating opinions with an increased amount of information based on those references.

While PreMindMap and MindMap are structurally similar, there is a significant difference in their token counts. The token count for PreMindMap is approximately 300, whereas, for MindMap, it is about 100. This indicates that SPARK-flow references a large amount of information before summarizing it into the MindMap.

As shown in Fig. 5, the comparison between the number of nodes in the MindMap and the PreMindMap indicates that the number of nodes in the MindMap is maintained from the PreMindMap. However, as demonstrated in Fig. 5(b), the amount of text contained in each node is reduced. This organization of information contributes to the efficiency of presenting information to the user and the handling of necessary information during idea creation. Presenting the RawOpinion directly to the user would require referencing the output content of all Debater Agents. This leads to a tendency towards information overload, with an increase of approximately 300 tokens per round, as shown in Fig. 4(a). In contrast, the MindMap limits the increase in token count to about 100, facilitating easier handling of information.

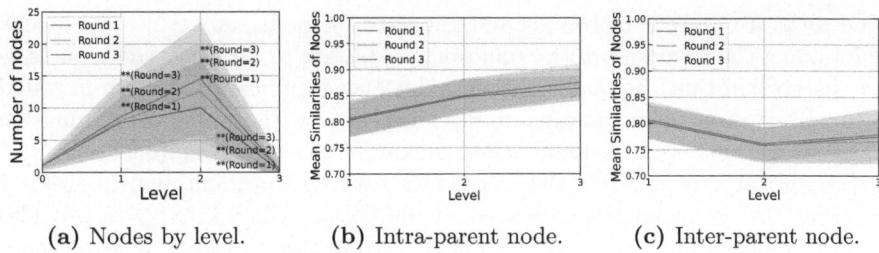

(a) Nodes by level.   **(b)** Intra-parent node.   **(c)** Inter-parent node.

Fig. 6. (a) Number of nodes per Level in mind maps, with p-values from t-tests comparing node counts of preceding Levels. The symbols * and ** indicate $p < 0.05$ and $p < 0.001$, respectively. (b) Similarity between nodes sharing the same parent, and (c) similarity between nodes with different parents, respectively

Figure 4(c) shows the round-by-round transition of the number of unique nouns, revealing that the number of unique nouns increases with each round for both methods. This suggests that the generation of opinions by multiple Debater Agents is increasing the number of concepts considered. Furthermore, when comparing the difference between the total number of nouns shown in 4(b) and the number of unique nouns, the magnitude of this difference is smaller for MindMap than for RawOpinion, indicating that MindMap significantly reduces the duplication of concepts contained in RawOpinion. Additionally, as shown in Fig. 4(d), the number of newly introduced nouns is proportional between RawOpinion and MindMap. This explains why the token count in MindMap does not increase significantly, suggesting that the number of concepts presented by Debater Agents decreases and the information selected is narrowed down.

4.7 Structural Analysis of Mind Maps

Creative ideas are characterized by the integration of new concepts with existing combinations [10,11,23]. Additionally, as demonstrated in Sect. 4.5, utilizing mind maps facilitates the generation of creative ideas. This section investigates how the use of mind maps, through the analysis of their structural characteristics, contributes to the generation of creative ideas.

In this study, we introduce a hierarchical structure for analyzing mind maps, where the root node is arbitrarily designated as $Level = 0$. This categorization facilitates our examination of the distribution and similarity of nodes across different levels. Findings reveal a notable peak in the number of nodes at $Level = 2$, as depicted in Fig. 6(a), followed by a substantial decrease at $Level = 3$, where the presence of nodes is markedly sparse. While the number of nodes at $Level = 2$ increases with each round, there is no significant change in the number of nodes at $Level = 1$. Comparing the embedding vectors of the text in nodes at $Level = 1$ across rounds, the average cosine similarity between the most similar nodes is 0.99 with a standard deviation of 9.6×10^{-5}, indicating that the content of nodes at $Level = 1$ remains consistent across rounds. This suggests a strategy by the Moderator Agent during the creation of mind maps to reference mind maps from previous rounds and not alter the nodes at Level = 1, thereby maintaining the structure of the mind map. This approach likely contributes to the observation that the quality of ideas does not significantly vary from round to round, offering the advantage of providing users with organized information that does not undergo drastic changes, making it easier to comprehend.

Semantically interpreting the hierarchical structure of mind maps, Level = 1 represents broad perspectives related to the theme, while Level = 2 provides detailed opinions on those perspectives. The transition in the number of nodes across rounds reflects that in SPARK-flow generated mind maps, broad perspectives are formed in the initial rounds, followed by the addition of specific opinions in subsequent rounds. The analysis of the number of tokens in nodes presented in Fig. 6 reveals that, regardless of the Level, there is no significant difference in the number of tokens contained in nodes, with an average of 5 tokens. This indicates that each node in the mind map consists of sentences of a certain length, rather than just words.

By comparing the similarity of embedding vectors of node texts, as shown in Figs. 6(b) and 6(c), it is evident that nodes sharing the same parent node exhibit high similarity, while nodes with different parent nodes show low similarity. This suggests that combining nodes with the same parent node corresponds to combining closely related concepts, while combining nodes with different parent nodes involves merging distant concepts, indicating that the structure of mind maps is an effective tool for generating creative ideas.

5   Conclusion and Future Work

In conclusion, this study introduced the SPARKIT system and its algorithm, SPARK-flow, aimed at enhancing idea generation. The experimental results have shown that SPARKIT outperforms simpler methods in generating superior ideas, and the use of language models for idea generation aligns well with human-generated ideas in various aspects. The employment of mind maps was particularly highlighted for its ability to improve the quality of ideas. However, while the results are promising, there are concerns about the reproducibility of results due to differences in the LLMs used. This issue can be addressed by fixing the model or using open-source models.

For future work, we envision further enhancing the capabilities of language models through the application of reinforcement learning, as well as forming multiple agent groups to promote idea generation from diverse perspectives. This approach is expected to yield more creative and user-centric ideas.

Appendix

Promptes

In this section, we provide examples of the prompts used in experiments. These prompts are critical for understanding the input that was provided to the language model (Table 2).

Table 2. Prompt Templates

Prompt Name	Value
role generation	We are looking to generate interesting ideas about the theme {**theme**}. For this theme, please list professions or roles that are expected to provide interesting opinions, in the following format. - <Role 1>: Reason - <Role 2>: Reason ...
criteria generation	We are discussing to generate interesting ideas about the theme {**theme**}. To generate interesting ideas about this theme, please state the criteria for evaluating ideas in the following format - <Criterion 1> - <Criterion 2> ...
opinion generation	We are discussing to generate interesting ideas about the theme {**theme**}. Below is a summary of the discussion content from the perspective of other agents. {mindmap} Below is a summary of the discussion content from the perspective of other agents. # {role} {view} Below is a reflection of the discussion content so far. {evaluation} Please list interesting ideas and opinions in bullet points from the perspective of the role {**role**} regarding other agents' views
premindmap	We are discussing to generate interesting ideas about the theme {**theme**}. Below is a mindmap summarizing the discussion content of other agents.

(*continued*)

Table 2. (*continued*)

Prompt Name	Value

	{mindmap_ref}
	
	 Below is a new opinion from the perspective of **{role}**
	
	 {view}
	
	 Please group the new opinions with the existing discussion content in the following format
	
	 ```- <Common points of Elements 1, 2...>```
	``` - <Element 1>```
	``` - <Element 2>```
	``` ...```

reflection	We are discussing to generate interesting ideas about the theme **{theme}**. Below is a summary of the discussion content
	
	 {views}
	
	 Please evaluate views based on the criteria **{criteria}** and determine their priority
	
	 ```# Evaluation Format```
	```- <Element>: {criteria} [High/Medium/Low]```
	```- <Element>: High Low Medium```
	```...```

mind map generation	We are discussing to generate interesting ideas about the theme **{theme}**. Below are the opinions from the discussion:
	
	 {premindmap}
	
	 Below evaluations are done based on the criteria **{criteria}**
	
	 {reflection}
	
	 The evaluations are done in the following format
	
	 ```- <Element>: {criteria} [High/Medium/Low]```
	```- <Element>: High Low Medium```
	```...```
	
	 {mindmap_ref}
	
	 Based on these evaluations and priorities, please create a mindmap from the discussion content for easy reference, as shown below

(*continued*)

Table 2. (*continued*)

Prompt Name	Value

	```- {theme}```
	    ```- <Commonalities between Elements 1, 2...>```
	        ```- Element 1```
	        ```- Element 2```
	        ```...```
	
	When including elements in the mindmap, please summarize each element in a word for clarity

core concept selection	We are discussing to generate interesting ideas about the theme **{theme}**. Below is the mindmap organizing the discussion content.
	
	```{mindmap}```
	
	Below is the evaluation of the discussion content so far.
	
	```{evaluation}```
	
	The Format of the evaluation is as follows
	
	```- <Element>: {criteria} [High/Medium/Low]```
	```- <Element>: High Low Medium```
	```...```
	
	Please select one especially important or interesting topic from the mind map.
	
	```Topic: <Topic selected from the mind map>```
	```Reason: <Reasons and how it relates to the theme>```

related keywords selection	Please select related topics from the mind map to generate interesting ideas about the theme **{theme}**.
	
	```<Topic 1>: <Reason and how it relates to the theme>```
	```<Topic 2>: ...```
	```...```

reflection in idea generation	Evaluate each element from the perspective of the **{criteria}**.

idea generation	Combine the selected elements to generate an idea about the theme of **{theme}**.
	
	```Idea: <Idea Title>```
	```Description: <Provide a brief summary in 2-3```
	```sentences explaining the nature of the idea,```
	
	```its background, and why it is compelling.>```

(*continued*)

Table 2. (continued)

Prompt Name	Value
idea evaluation	Which of the following ideas does a better job of capturing the essence of an **{theme}** while remaining unique and engaging? An excellent idea should be both imaginative and relevant to the theme. Theme: {theme} Idea A: {idea_a}: {description_a} Idea B: {idea_b}: {description_b} FIRST provide a one-sentence comparison of the two ideas, explaining which you prefer and why. SECOND, on a new line, state only "A" or "B" to indicate your choice. Your response should use the format: Preferred: <"A" or "B">

Themes

In this section, we present subset of themes used in experiments (Table 3).

Table 3. Examples of Themes

ID	Theme
1	The impact of automation on legal industry
2	Exploring the future of food production and agriculture
3	The fusion of art and science
4	Enhancing access to quality mental healthcare in low-resource settings
5	The impact of automation on job displacement and retraining the workforce
6	Mental health and self-care practices
7	Nurturing innovation and creativity in the film and entertainment industry
8	Space exploration and colonization
9	Promoting peace and conflict resolution in global affairs
10	The importance of lifelong learning
11	Mental health stigma and promoting awareness and support
12	Innovative approaches to waste reduction and recycling
13	The role of AI in personalized customer experience and recommendation systems
14	Artificial intelligence in everyday life
15	Using gaming to tackle real-world problems
16	Innovations in sustainable fashion materials
17	The psychology of resilience in the face of change
18	The impact of technology on the live music and concert industry
19	The impact of AI on financial markets and investment strategies
20	Nurturing entrepreneurship and supporting small businesses
21	Building resilient communities and disaster preparedness measures
22	Strategies for promoting digital literacy and bridging the digital divide
23	The role of music in shaping cultural identity

References

1. Achiam, J., et al.: GPT-4 technical report. arXiv preprint arXiv:2303.08774 (2023)
2. Al-Samarraie, H., Hurmuzan, S.: A review of brainstorming techniques in higher education. Thinking Skills Creat. **27**, 78–91 (2018)
3. Andolina, S., Klouche, K., Cabral, D., Ruotsalo, T., Jacucci, G.: Inspirationwall: supporting idea generation through automatic information exploration. In: Proceedings of the 2015 ACM SIGCHI Conference on Creativity and Cognition, pp. 103–106 (2015)
4. Andolina, S., Schneider, H., Chan, J., Klouche, K., Jacucci, G., Dow, S.: Crowdboard: augmenting in-person idea generation with real-time crowds. In: Proceedings of the 2017 ACM SIGCHI Conference on Creativity and Cognition, pp. 106–118 (2017)
5. Benedek, M., Neubauer, A.C.: Revisiting mednick's model on creativity-related differences in associative hierarchies: evidence for a common path to uncommon thought. J. Creat. Behav. **47**(4), 273–289 (2013)
6. Buzan, T., Buzan, B.: The Mind Map Book. Pearson Education, Boston (2006)
7. Camburn, B., et al.: Computer-aided mind map generation via crowdsourcing and machine learning. Res. Eng. Design **31**, 383–409 (2020)
8. Cer, D., Yang, Y., Kong, S.y., Hua, N., Limtiaco, N., St. John, R., Constant, N., Guajardo-Cespedes, M., Yuan, S., Tar, C., Strope, B., Kurzweil, R.: Universal sentence encoder for English. In: Blanco, E., Lu, W. (eds.) Proceedings of the 2018 Conference on Empirical Methods in Natural Language Processing: System Demonstrations, pp. 169–174. Association for Computational Linguistics, Brussels, Belgium (Nov 2018). https://doi.org/10.18653/v1/D18-2029. https://aclanthology.org/D18-2029
9. Chan, C.M., et al.: Chateval: towards better llm-based evaluators through multi-agent debate. arXiv preprint arXiv:2308.07201 (2023)
10. Chan, J., Dow, S.P., Schunn, C.D.: Do the best design ideas (really) come from conceptually distant sources. In: Engineering a Better Future: Interplay between Engineering, Social Sciences, and Innovation, p. 111 (2018)
11. Chan, J., Schunn, C.D.: The importance of iteration in creative conceptual combination. Cognition **145**, 104–115 (2015)
12. Chen, T.J., Krishnamurthy, V.R.: Investigating a mixed-initiative workflow for digital mind-mapping. J. Mech. Des. **142**(10), 101404 (2020)
13. Di Fede, G., Rocchesso, D., Dow, S.P., Andolina, S.: The idea machine: LLM-based expansion, rewriting, combination, and suggestion of ideas. In: Proceedings of the 14th Conference on Creativity and Cognition, pp. 623–627 (2022)
14. Diedrich, J., Benedek, M., Jauk, E., Neubauer, A.C.: Are creative ideas novel and useful? Psychol. Aesthet. Creat. Arts **9**(1), 35 (2015)
15. Dow, S.P., Heddleston, K., Klemmer, S.R.: The efficacy of prototyping under time constraints. In: Proceedings of the Seventh ACM Conference on Creativity and Cognition, pp. 165–174 (2009)
16. Du, Y., Li, S., Torralba, A., Tenenbaum, J.B., Mordatch, I.: Improving factuality and reasoning in language models through multiagent debate. arXiv preprint arXiv:2305.14325 (2023)
17. Georgiev, G.V., Georgiev, D.D.: Enhancing user creativity: semantic measures for idea generation. Knowl.-Based Syst. **151**, 1–15 (2018). https://doi.org/10.1016/j.knosys.2018.03.016. https://www.sciencedirect.com/science/article/pii/S0950705118301394

18. Girotra, K., Terwiesch, C., Ulrich, K.T.: Idea generation and the quality of the best idea. Manag. Sci. **56**(4), 591–605 (2010)
19. Guilford, J.P.: Creative abilities in the arts. Psychol. Rev. **64**(2), 110 (1957)
20. Hackl, V., Müller, A.E., Granitzer, M., Sailer, M.: Is GPT-4 a reliable rater? evaluating consistency in gpt-4 text ratings. arXiv preprint arXiv:2308.02575 (2023)
21. Hao, N., et al.: Reflection enhances creativity: beneficial effects of idea evaluation on idea generation. Brain Cogn. **103**, 30–37 (2016)
22. Kern, F.B., Wu, C.T., Chao, Z.C.: Assessing novelty, feasibility, and value of creative ideas with an unsupervised approach using GPT-4 (2023)
23. Kim, D., Cerigo, D.B., Jeong, H., Youn, H.: Technological novelty profile and invention's future impact. EPJ Data Sci. **5**(1), 1–15 (2016)
24. Leeds, A.J., Kudrowitz, B., Kwon, J.: Mapping associations: exploring divergent thinking through mind mapping. Int. J. Des. Creat. Innov. **7**(1–2), 16–29 (2019)
25. Luo, J., Sarica, S., Wood, K.L.: Computer-aided design ideation using innogps. In: International Design Engineering Technical Conferences and Computers and Information in Engineering Conference, vol. 59186, p. V02AT03A011. American Society of Mechanical Engineers (2019)
26. Ma, K., Grandi, D., McComb, C., Goucher-Lambert, K.: Conceptual design generation using large language models. arXiv preprint arXiv:2306.01779 (2023)
27. Rafailov, R., Sharma, A., Mitchell, E., Ermon, S., Manning, C.D., Finn, C.: Direct preference optimization: your language model is secretly a reward model. arXiv preprint arXiv:2305.18290 (2023)
28. Reiter-Palmon, R., Forthmann, B., Barbot, B.: Scoring divergent thinking tests: a review and systematic framework. Psychol. Aesthet. Creat. Arts **13**(2), 144 (2019)
29. Runco, M.A., Acar, S.: Divergent thinking as an indicator of creative potential. Creat. Res. J. **24**(1), 66–75 (2012)
30. Setiyawan, D.: Improving students' speaking skills in generating idea through new concept of mind mapping technique. In: International Conference on Educational Research and Innovation (ICERI 2019), pp. 227–231. Atlantis Press (2020)
31. Shih, P.C., Nguyen, D.H., Hirano, S.H., Redmiles, D.F., Hayes, G.R.: GroupMind: supporting idea generation through a collaborative mind-mapping tool. In: Proceedings of the 2009 ACM International Conference on Supporting Group Work, pp. 139–148 (2009)
32. Sun, M., Wang, M., Wegerif, R., Peng, J.: How do students generate ideas together in scientific creativity tasks through computer-based mind mapping? Comput. Educ. **176**, 104359 (2022)
33. Tao, M., Xie, R.: Mind map based computer network knowledge graph visualization research and application. In: Jia, W., et al. (eds.) SETE 2021. LNCS, vol. 13089, pp. 3–12. Springer, Cham (2021). https://doi.org/10.1007/978-3-030-92836-0_1
34. Wahl, J., Hutter, K., Füller, J.: How ai-supported searches through other perspectives affect ideation outcomes. Int. J. Innov. Manag. **26**(09), 2240028 (2022)
35. Wang, H.C., Cosley, D., Fussell, S.R.: Idea expander: supporting group brainstorming with conversationally triggered visual thinking stimuli. In: Proceedings of the 2010 ACM Conference on Computer Supported Cooperative Work, pp. 103–106 (2010)
36. Wen, Y., Wang, Z., Sun, J.: Mindmap: knowledge graph prompting sparks graph of thoughts in large language models. arXiv preprint arXiv:2308.09729 (2023)
37. Xu, B., et al.: Expertprompting: instructing large language models to be distinguished experts. arXiv preprint arXiv:2305.14688 (2023)
38. Zampetakis, L.A., Tsironis, L., Moustakis, V.: Creativity development in engineering education: the case of mind mapping. J. Manag. Dev. **26**(4), 370–380 (2007)

Cooperative Multi-agent Approach for Automated Computer Game Testing

Samira Shirzadeh-hajimahmood[1], I. S. W. B. Prasteya[1(✉)],
Mehdi Dastani[1], and Frank Dignum[2]

[1] Utrecht University, Utrecht, The Netherlands
{S.shirzadehhajimahmood,s.w.b.prasetya,M.M.Dastani}@uu.nl
[2] Umeå University, Umeå, Sweden
frank.dignum@umu.se

Abstract. Automated testing of computer games is a challenging problem, especially when lengthy scenarios have to be tested. Automating such a scenario boils down to finding the right sequence of interactions given an abstract description of the scenario. Recent works have shown that an agent-based approach works well for the purpose, e.g. due to agents' reactivity, hence enabling a test agent to immediately react to game events and changing state. Many games nowadays are multi-player. This opens up an interesting possibility to deploy multiple cooperative test agents to test such a game, for example to speed up the execution of multiple testing tasks. This paper offers a cooperative multi-agent testing approach and a study of its performance based on a case study on a 3D game called Lab Recruits.

Keywords: multi-agent testing · agent-based game testing · automated game testing

1 Introduction

Modern computer games are often complex, with a huge, fine grained interaction space, and many interacting game objects that influence the way a game behaves.

A common method for testing a game, to make sure that it behaves as the developers expect, is to use human players to play a computer game through various scenarios and report bugs [10,13]. This technique is known as *play testing*. In addition to being costly, such a manual process is also unreliable, e.g. due to human fatigue. The tests also need to be repeated when some modifications are applied to the game. The time and expense of having human testers repeat tests multiple times can be reduced by employing automated testing.

Agent-based approaches are among the recent methods studied towards achieving game testing automation [1,2,16,19]. Such an approach uses of a software agent that interacts with the game under test by taking the role of a player. The agent verifies the system by observing its state after the interactions, checking them if they satisfy some specifications. In particular intelligent agents have

D. Briola et al. (Eds.): EMAS 2024, LNAI 15152, pp. 23–41, 2025.
https://doi.org/10.1007/978-3-031-71152-7_2

properties such as reactivity and autonomy [4]. Under the hood such an agent runs in continuous cycles of deliberation, which makes it capable of responding immediately to changes in the environment (reactive), making them suitable to deal with the high interactivity of computer games. Autonomy means that agents can make decisions based on their internal state and the information available to them, allowing the agents to perform actions independently in an environment over which they have control and observability.

Many games are multi player. This opens up an interesting possibility of deploying multiple test agents to speed up testing, in particular when testing long scenarios that may take minutes or tens of minutes for each run. The overall duration of running a whole test suite can be quite significant, and therefore reducing would help in improving developers' productivity. However, a multi-agent setup is more complex [11]. A major challenge is cooperation. By cooperating, agents can improve the overall performance towards reaching common goals. However, coordination may be needed, or else the agents will get in each other way and their performance will suffer instead. Synchronizing the agent's information about their environmental perceptions can help, as each agent would then have the most recent information that other agents have, thus allowing it to make better decisions. Such synchronization does have its computation overhead though, and it is not always obvious to decide what information needs to be synchronized.

Compared to single-agent, the use of multi-agent for testing games is not a well explored area yet. One work we can mention is that of Schatten et al. [18] that presented a framework with which tests can be developed in a model-driven way. The framework implements Belief-Desire-Intention (BDI) agents and allows organizational dynamics to be modelled. However, the work does not include a study on the subject. There are works such as [7,22] that use multiple agents. The agents are trained with reinforcement learning to perform testing objectives, e.g. to interact and explore the game world as much as possible. These are individual agents that run in parallel to train a *common* model, or a population of common models. Arguably this is a form of multi-agent cooperation, but not in the sense that the agents directly cooperate with each other.

This paper aims to contribute an investigation into the subject of multi-agent game testing. A cooperative multi-agent testing approach will first be presented. At the moment, the approach is aimed at games with world exploration and puzzle elements. Next, the paper presents a study based on a 3D game called Lab Recruits to investigate whether, and how much, the use of cooperative agents can actually speed up testing.

The paper is structured as follows. Section 2 discusses the general idea of using cooperating agents for testing a game and some of the key issues of such a setup. Section 3 introduces the concept of testing task in game testing and some typical challenges of automating such tasks. Then, Sect. 4 presents our multi-agent testing algorithm. Section 5 presents a set of experiments to study the performance the multi-agent setup. Section 6 discusses some related work, and finally Sect. 7 concludes and mentions some future work.

2   Multi Agent Setup

Consider a simple game level in Fig. 1-left, containing three yellow treasure boxes (T_k). Picking up the boxes awards the player some points, which are necessary to complete the game. Imagine that the tester wants to verify that these boxes are indeed reachable from the game initial state and that their logic is correct. So, the tester has *multiple* 'testing tasks' that need to be done: one task for every T_k. For convenience, let's use T_k to also denote the task. In a single test-agent setup, a single agent will do all testing tasks, one at a time. For T_k the test agent will first need to find corresponding box, and hence verifying its reachability, and then verify whether the points rise after picking it up is correct.

In a multi agent setup, we have multiple test agents that work on a set $\mathcal{T}$ of testing tasks. We will focus on the setup where the agents target the same instance of the game under test (GUT), exploiting its multi player capability[1]. The agents have to figure out how to divide the work. This is less trivial than it sounds. The agents can choose to do different tasks in parallel. For example, agent Blue in Fig. 1-left can take T_1 and agent Green can take T_3. This division of tasks is ideal because T_1 is closest to agent Blue, and T_3 is closest to agent Green. However, if the area is large and the agents do not have full visibility on the world, it is not possible to know upfront which division of tasks is the best. Alternatively, we can have multiple agents working in parallel on the same task. For example, suppose agent Blue decides to do T_3. Without full visibility, it does not know where T_3 is, and may end up searching the entire game world before it finally finds T_3. Having agent Green to also work on T_3 would speed up the task, as it happens to be close to it.

In our study we will focus on autonomous agents that dynamically chose the task they want to do, as opposed to having a central process that allocate the tasks. By 'dynamic' we mean that while an agent is exploring the game it on the fly decides on taking or ignoring a task.

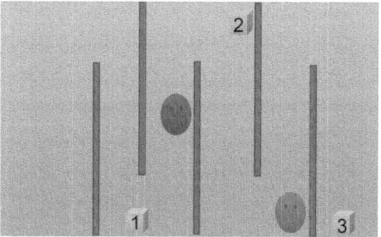 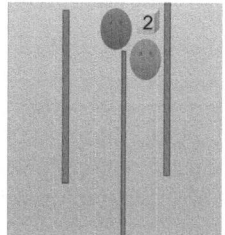

Fig. 1. Two simple levels of a hypothetical game.

Cooperation. We will employ information synchronization and coordination as the form of cooperation in our setup. Sharing and synchronising the agents' observation may save the effort that each agent would otherwise need for exploration and data collection. E.g. in the previous example where agent Blue targets

---

[1] As opposed to performing parallel testing against multiple instances of the GUT.

T_3, if another agent shares the location of T_3, agent Blue might be able to find a path to it faster. In the study in Sect. 4 we will look at several options in the degree of information sharing. For example, agents may only share partial knowledge about the game. Such characteristics would have an impact on how successful the testing task is executed.

Having multiple agents running simultaneously may require some coordination. For example, if two agents run into one another in a narrow corridor e.g. as in Fig. 1-right they will get stuck. Generally, executing a task may require resources critical to the task, which should not be shared, or else the task may be disrupted or even cannot be completed. The narrow corridor in Fig. 1-right is such a resource. In a game there are often objects that act as critical resources towards certain testing tasks, for example keys, switches, or even healing items. Access to such resources needs to be coordinated, e.g. through locking.

On top of the aforementioned challenges, the agents also have to deal with the game logic itself, which can be a challenge of its own. We will discuss more on this in the next section. And later, in Sect. 4, we will discuss our multi-agent algorithm. It features the aforementioned dynamic task selection, information sharing, and locking of key resources.

3   Problem Setup

In this section, we describe a general game setup and outline the challenges of this setup. We abstractly treat a game under test as a structure $G = (A, O)$ where A is a set of players/agents and O is a set of game objects that have physical locations in the game. We will use some or all agents to test the game, so in our setup they are test agents. Game objects have their own state. Some objects are interactable. Some may be hazardous. Objects such as doors are called *blockers*; these can block the agent's access to an area. Dealing with blockers is important for testing tasks that aim to verify the reachability of a state.

Interacting with an object o may change the state of other objects. To provide challenges for players, game designers often make blockers' logic non-trivial. For example, it may require an interaction with another object, called an *enabler*, to unblock a blocker. The location of the enabler can be far, and not easy to find. Or it can be placed in an area that is guarded by another blocker, that in turn requires its own enabler to be found and activated, and so on. Across different games there are different types of enablers. E.g. a toggling switch toggles the state of associated blockers (from blocking to unblocking, and the other way around). A one-off switch can only be used once. A key must be picked up, and brought to a blocker to be used, and so on. In this paper, we will restrict ourselves to toggling switches.

Each agent $a \in A$ is assumed to only be able to *observe* objects and parts of the game/environment that it *physically can see*. Also, the agent does not know upfront how to how to solve complex tasks, such as unblocking a blocker. Examples of primitive actions available to an agent are *interacting* with an object (if the agent is close enough to it) and *moving* in any direction for a small distance. In our setup we will assume that a high level navigation action is also available to the agent, to auto-navigate to a specified location. This can be achieved e.g. by leveraging a game testing framework like iv4XR [15] that comes with a path planning module.

The agent can take one or more testing tasks to do. Abstractly, such a task is be formulated as follows:

$$TestingTask = (o, \psi, S) \tag{1}$$

where ψ is a predicate to hold on an object o and S is a stop condition to terminate the test.

We will focus on tasks whose objective is to verify whether the state of some game object o, characterized by the predicate ψ, is *reachable*. 'Reachable' means that there exists a sequence of agent's actions, starting from the game initial state, that leads to a state where ψ is true. This is simple but still represents many useful testing tasks. For example, if o is a blocker, ψ can specify that o is open and visible to the agent. Verifying that ψ is reachable (thus that o can be unblocked, by activating some game logic) implies that the area that o guards is thus reachable for the player, which is important if the area is critical towards the game's story line.

We treat a testing task as a goal that a test agent wants to automatically achieve/solve (and thus providing test automation). To do this, the agent needs to *search* for a sequence of interactions that reach a state satisfying ψ (thus confirming its reachability), while respecting the game rules. Finding such a sequence is usually not trivial. Different heuristics are defined for this, which we will explain later. The parameter S in a testing task is used to terminate the task, e.g. based on time budget, after which the goal ψ is judged as unreachable.

4   Multi Agent Testing Algorithm

We propose a cooperative multi-agent approach to solve the given set of testing tasks automatically. The details are provided in this section. The approach has two main algorithms. Algorithm 1 takes a set $\mathcal{T}$ of testing tasks that the developers have specified and need to be carried out. The algorithm introduces some variables to keep track of the status of the tasks, e.g. which ones are completed, then runs N agents. It also deals with information sharing. Algorithm 2 called SOLVER defines how each agent chooses testing tasks and how it proceeds to complete a chosen task.

Algorithm 1. *It gets a set of tasks $\mathcal{T}$ and run N test agents.*

1: **procedure** COOPERATIVEAGENTS($\mathcal{T}$)
2:      $toDo = \emptyset$
3:      $done = \emptyset$
4:      $agent_1$.SOLVER($\mathbf{H}_1$) $\parallel$ ... $\parallel$ $agent_N$.SOLVER($\mathbf{H}_N$)
5:          $\parallel$ SYNC()
6:          $\parallel$ $done{=}\mathcal{T} \vee budget \leq 0 \ \rightarrow$ **terminate**   ▷ terminate the whole procedure

---

The agents run in principle in parallel, each will repeatedly select a task from $\mathcal{T}$ and try to complete it. Certain coordination will be needed; we go into more detail about that later. The notation $P \parallel Q$ in Algorithm 1 denotes a parallel execution of processes P and Q. A process is a program that sequentially executes primitive actions. For an agent a, the process a.SOLVER runs the algorithm SOLVER for the agent a. The process SYNC is responsible for regular sharing and synchronization of agents' observations with each other.

The agents attempt to complete as many tasks from $\mathcal{T}$ as possible according to their task selection policy, as long as the budget that was given is not used up. Variables *toDo* and *done* are empty at the beginning and will be updated during the test execution. When an agent discovers an object o which is targeted by a testing task $T \in \mathcal{T}/done$, this T is added to the set *toDo* to keep track of uncompleted tasks whose location of their target objects are known. When T is completed, it is moved from *toDo* to the set *done*. This is done in Algorithm 2 SOLVER.

In SOLVER, the agent that runs it continues attempting to solve tasks until there is no task left and there is no unexplored area left. To choose a task from the *toDo* the agent uses an assigned selection heuristic *selectH*. E.g. the heuristic might favor high-valued tasks. We will go for a scheme where each task is worked on by at most one agent. This is enforced by removing the selected task from *toDo*.

Suppose $T = (o, \psi, S)$ is the selected task. To check if ψ already holds the agent needs to be close enough to the object o to be able to observe its state. To do this the agent invokes NAVIGATETO(o) to steer itself from its current position to the location of o. The travel to o can be done by implementing a graph-based path-finding algorithm such as A* [8,12].

Algorithm 2. *For selecting and executing tasks, parameterized by two heuristics.*

1: **procedure** SOLVER(*selectH*, *findH*)
2:      **while** *budget* > 0 **do**
3:          **if** *toDo* $\neq \emptyset$ **then**
4:              $T \leftarrow selectH(toDo)$ ▷ use the task-selection heuristic
5:              **if** $T \neq null$ **then**
6:                  $(o, \psi, S) \leftarrow T$
7:                  $toDo \leftarrow toDo/\{T\}$
8:                  NAVIGATETO(o)
9:                  **if** $\neg\psi$ **then** DYNAMICGOAL($o, \psi, S, findH$)
10:                  **if** ψ **then** *done* $\leftarrow$ *done* $\cup \{T\}$
11:                  **else** *toDo* $\leftarrow$ *toDo* $\cup \{T\}$
12:          **else**
13:              **if** there is terrain unexplored **then** FINDTASK( )
14:              **else return**

When the agent reaches o, and its state satisfies ψ the testing task T is completed with a positive result (pass). That is, it is confirmed that the state ψ is reachable. If the state of o at that moment does not satisfy ψ the agent needs to do something to change the state of o. A quite common logic in games is that toggling the state of an object q requires another object i to be interacted (so-called 'enabler' in Sect. 3). We do not assume that the agent has pre-knowledge of which object is the enabler (or enablers, if there are more than one) of a particular target o. So, it invokes the algorithm DYNAMICGOAL to search for such an enabler.

dynamicGoal(o,ψ,S, $findH$). This procedure can be thought of as deploying a goal to change o to a state satisfying ψ. The procedure first calculates a set Δ of objects that have been seen by the agent and have not been 'tried' before (line 3). These are candidate objects, whose interaction might change the state of the target o. An object $i \in \Delta$ is selected based on the $findH$ heuristic. For example, the heuristic might favor objects of a certain type, or it might favor closer i. When i is selected, it is marked to avoid choosing it again. If $findH$ cannot come up with an i, e.g. because Δ is empty, the agent explores the game, searching for a more objects. If we have an i, the agent navigates to it. Once i is reached, an appropriate action (such as picking up or interacting) is performed on i. In order to determine whether o has changed and ψ is met, the agent navigates back to o. Some coordination is also needed during these steps. The object i is critical towards checking ψ. That is, other agents should refrain from messing with i. To enforce this, we employ locking on i, which is released again after the checking of ψ. If ψ is established, DYNAMICGOAL() is done. Else, the process of calculating Δ and selecting (another) i is repeated. This goes on either until ψ is verified, or the stop condition S becomes true (and then the verification verdict would be a 'fail').

To give a more precise example of when to deploy a *dynamicGoal*, consider the following testing task:

Example 1. Consider the door d_1 in the game in Fig. 2. $T_1 = (d_1, d_1.open = true, S)$ where S is some stop condition.

Suppose an agent shown in Fig. 2 takes the task T_1. Since d_1 is closed at that moment, a dynamic goal to open d_1 is added (a call to DYNAMICGOAL). This would then try buttons b_1 and b_2 (see Fig. 2) to make d_1 open. It will not try a button twice, as it marks buttons it has touched.

Back in SOLVER, the agent uses Algorithm 4 FINDTASK when the *toDo* set is empty (there is no open task, whose location of its target object is known). The agent explores the game world to learn the game's spatial layout, finding game objects as it goes. A graph-based exploration algorithm such as [17] can be used. It stops upon finding some new target objects (objects targeted by tasks), or if there is no terrain left to explore. The overall exploration heuristics may affect the overall task-solving performance. A few examples are mentioned below:

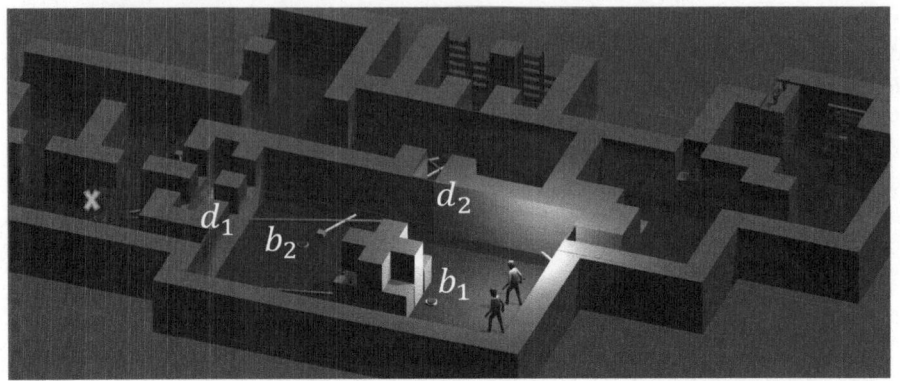

Fig. 2. Screenshot of the game Lab Recruit.

Algorithm 3. *For solving a single task, parameterized by one heuristic.*

1: **procedure** DYNAMICGOAL($o, \psi, S, findH$)
2:     **while** $\neg\psi \wedge \neg S$ **do**
3:         $\Delta \leftarrow \{i \mid i \in seenObj \wedge \neg mark_o(i) \wedge \neg locked(i)\}$
4:         choose $i \in \Delta$, based on $findH$ ▷ use the object-selection heuristic
5:         **if** $i = null$ **then**
6:             **if** there is terrain unexplored **then**
7:                 EXPLORE( )   ▷ explore world to find new objects
8:             **else**
9:                 **return**
10:        **else**
11:            $mark_o(i) \leftarrow true$ ▷ mark i as tried for o
12:            LOCK(i)
13:            $navigateTo(i)$
14:            $applyAction(i)$ ▷ such as interact
15:            $navigateTo(o)$
16:            UNLOCK(i)

- *Gradually*: the agent explores the world only until it sees new target objects. Algorithm 4 does this.
- *Aggressive*: as Algorithm 4, but the agent does not stop until there is nothing left to be explored.
- *Limited budget*: as Algorithm 4, but the algorithm is given a certain budget, and stops when the budget runs out.

Synchronization Level. To later investigate the impact of information sharing and synchronization between the agents, we consider two levels of sharing:

- *Basic*: the agents share seen tasks and solved tasks. Algorithm 1 already does this, by maintaining common *toDo* and *done* sets. Additionally, the agents also share the *location* of tasks' target objects.

Algorithm 4. *For finding new tasks.*

1: **procedure** FINDTASK( )
2:     **while** there is terrain unexplored **do**
3:         BASICEXPLORE( )
4:         $V \leftarrow$ newly observed objects
5:         $W \leftarrow \{(o, \psi, S) \mid o \in V \wedge (o, \psi, S) \in T/(toDo \cup done)\}$
6:         **if** $W \neq \emptyset$ **then**
7:             $toDo \leftarrow toDo \cup W$
8:             **return**

– *Extended*: this extends the basic sharing above by having the agents to also share information about explored areas to each other, e.g. information about discovered navigation mesh and object states. As common in a multi-agent setup, each agent has its own state. So, sharing information involves sending the information from one agent to another, and synchronizing the sent information into the receiving agent's own belief. This incurs some computation overhead.

5   Experiments

This section discusses a series of experiments aimed to investigate the following research questions:

– **RQ1:** *does multi-agent speed up testing?*
– **RQ2:** *how well can multi-agent deal with complex logic?*

We implement the agents using iv4XR[2], a Java multi-agent programming framework with a particular focus on game testing [15]. The purpose of an iv4XR agent is to control an in-game entity; for instance to control a player character of a game. As such, the agent can interact with game and control it just like a human player can. The framework is inspired by the popular Belief-Desire-Intention concept of agency [9], where an agent has *belief*, representing information the agent has about its current environment. Iv4XR provides automated world navigation and exploration algorithms [17], and test agents can be equipped with them. Having such a feature enables us to define testing tasks at a more functional level, allowing us to abstract away details related to, for example, physical 3D navigation. In our multi-agent approach, each agent simulates a player and responds dynamically to the game under test.

For the experiments, a multi-player 3D game called Lab Recruit (LR) is used[3]. Figure 2 shows an example screenshot of the game. LR allows new game *levels*[4] to be defined using plain text files. This allows us to generate a range of

---

[2] https://github.com/iv4xr-project/aplib.
[3] https://github.com/iv4xr-project/labrecruits.
[4] In gaming, a 'level' refers to a world or a maze, playable within the same game. To extend the play-value of a game, developers often provide a set of levels.

various levels for our experiments. The playing goal of an LR level can simply be to explore it, or to reach a certain end-room. There are two types of game objects in LR that are of particular interest for the experiments: doors and buttons. A door guards the access to the rooms it connects. The state of a door can be altered (e.g. from closed to open) by interacting with a button that is connected to it. The players do not know upfront which buttons are connected to which doors. Furthermore, the players' have limited view range. Throughout the game, players can be thought to gain points by going through rooms (e.g. due to certain items in the rooms). Some rooms give much more points, and are thus important for the game play. Verifying that all doors in a level can be opened and reachable would prove the level's basic correctness. If time is limited, verifying the doors guarding high valued rooms can be considered as more important.

Several factors affect the performance a multi-agent setup, such as the size of the game levels and the task distribution among agents. To investigate them different LR levels are created. They are all variations of a level we will call *Basic-Level*. This is a level with a $10m \times 10m$ main hall with ten doors (blockers) guarding access to side rooms. There is a button in front of each door that opens the door. Six of the doors have in-game points of one, and four have in-game points of ten (they are guarding high-value rooms). The higher point doors are d_2, d_3, d_6, and d_9.

Testing Tasks. In the experiments, we consider a set of testing tasks, one T_d for each door d in the target level, to verify that a state where the door d is open is reachable. *Basic-Level* has thus ten testing tasks.

Heuristics Setting . Recall that each agent runs the algorithm SOLVER. It is parameterized by two heuristics: *selectH* and *findH*. For the task selection heuristic (*selectH*), three heuristics are taken into consideration: one that chooses tasks randomly, one that targets tasks whose value is higher than a given threshold, and one that targets tasks with values below a threshold. Agents that use them are referred to as A_R, A_H and A_L respectively. The *findH* heuristic (to choose a candidate enabler to try) is set to choose a button that is closest to the agent's position. The heuristic for FINDTASK is set to be the same as what is already in its algorithm, namely to explore gradually.

Example. Take a look at the level depicted in Fig. 2. Suppose the agents initially observe nothing because of their limited visibility range. They then begin to gradually explore the level. Imagine that they see d_1 and d_2. Since these are targets of testing tasks, the corresponding tasks T_{d1} and T_{d2} are added to the *toDo* set. Both are worth one point. Since the testing task is not empty, the agents first look through the *toDo* to see if any tasks are available before choosing one. Suppose one of the agents is A_L. The two tasks in *toDo* are of low value, so they are targets for A_L. Imagine that T_{d1} is chosen. The agent A_L then navigates to d_1. As it is closed, A_L invokes DYNAMICGOAL to open it. Suppose at that point A_L has seen the button b_1, and it also happens to be located nearest to A_L. By the heuristic *findH*, the agent then chooses b_1, to be tried (interacted) in order flip the state of d_1 to open. If this happens and confirmed (by travelling to d_1 to confirm its state), task T_{d1} is completed and the agent can proceed to the next testing task.

All experiments were run on a Windows machine equipped with an Intel(R) i7-8565U (4 cores) processor at 2.8 GHz and 32 GB RAM. Every run in the experiment is repeated three times, and the result is the average of the runs.

5.1   RQ1: Does Multi-agent Speed Up Testing?

To answer the RQ, we consider a number of factors that affect performance:

- Information synchronization. The two synchronization levels, basic and extended, mentioned in Sect. 4 will be considered.
- Different team compositions, consisting of agents with different task selection heuristics (*selectH*), will be considered.
- View distance: agents' limited visibility complicates exploration and task finding. We would like to investigate how the performance is affected if a larger view distance is allowed.

Effect of Information Synchronization. We run our multi-agent setup on ten levels, variations of *Basic-Level* with increasing size. For each level, we deployed a team of two agents, namely $\{A_H, A_L\}$. Two information synchronization levels are tried: basic and advanced. The agents' visibility range is set to six.

Figure 3 shows the results. The multi-agent setup with extended synchronization outperforms the single-agent setup, in particular in bigger levels, despite the overhead of having to synchronize information. E.g. it is nearly 35% faster than a single agent on the 100×100 level. When an agent chooses a task whose target object o it has never seen before, the shared navigation information from the other agent may help it to find o, saving time that is otherwise needed for exploring the world in order to find it. In contrast, basic synchronization does share the locations of target objects, but not the path to them. So in this case the agent still has to search the level to actually get to o. Using only basic synchronization, the multi agent setup is still faster than a single agent, but the results clearly show that using extended synchronization, despite its overhead, pays off.

Figure 4 shows the points collected after a specific time on the 100×100 level. Recall that opening a door gives points, so the collected total points correlate with the number of tasks completed. A steeper increases in the graph corresponds to the completion of the verification of a high-valued door, which is more important. When a total of 46 points is reached, all tasks are completed. Multi-agent with extended synchronization can complete all the tasks in five minutes, while a single agent can only complete two important tasks.

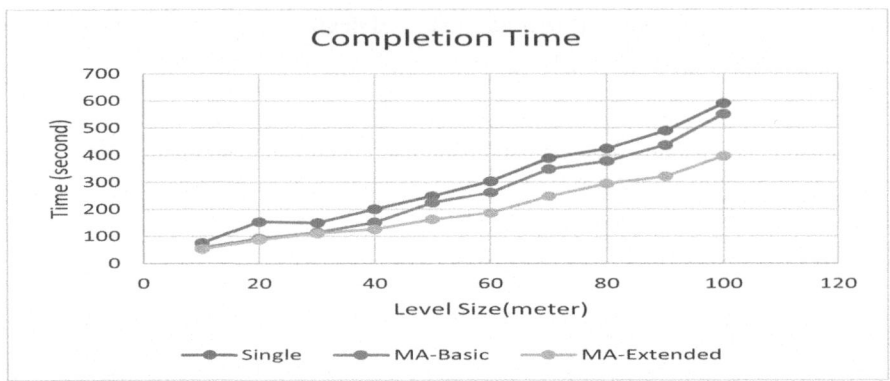

Fig. 3. The time needed to complete/solve all the given testing tasks. The *x-axis is the level size, e.g.* 20×20. The *y-axis is time in second. The graph* Single (orange) shows the completion time when we just use one agent. The graphs *MA-Basic* (gray) and MA-Extended (yellow) show the completion time when we use two agents, using the basic and respectively extended information synchronization. (Color figure online)

Different Team Composition. In this experiment, we run different teams of agents on a 100×100 level. A team consists of agents with different task selection heuristics. In addition to the aforementioned A_H, A_L, and A_R agents we add A_{EX} and A_E. Agent A_{EX} does not select any tast. It just explores the world to discover tasks' target objects to help other agents by sharing information. Agent A_E is an eager agent that takes a task as soon as it sees its target object.

Figure 5-left shows the results for different teams of three agents. The results show that including a dedicated exploration agent in a team (team (A_{EX}, A_L, A_H)) does not really improve the performance. This is because the agents still need to do the tasks. On the other hand, the performance is *not* significantly worse either, despite having one less worker agent, which shows that the shared information from A_{EX} does help.

We also conducted an experiment to examine the impact of team size. Figure 5-right shows the performance of teams consisting of one up to five eager agents. Only eager agents are used because in the previous experiment they have the best performance. The outcome indicates that performance gets better as the number of agents increases. When there are five agents instead of only one, the testing time is reduced by nearly one-third and by more than half when there are two agents. The performance of five agents is not much different from four agents, however. A possible reason is because we have only have four CPU cores in our experiment setup.

View Distance. To investigate the impact of view distance we run a setup with two agents on a 100×100 level, with varying view distance. Figure 6 shows the results. It shows that when the view distance increases, test performance improves. This is as expected, as by increasing the view distance, the agents can

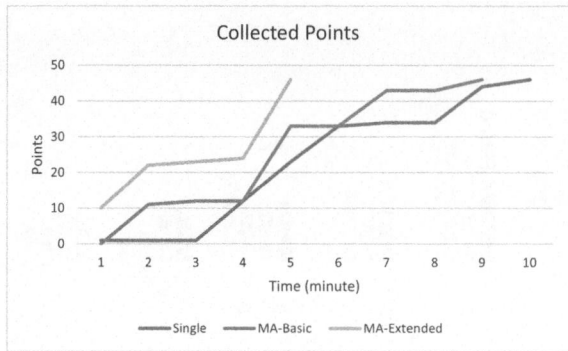

Fig. 4. Total points collected over time on a level with size 100×100. An agent gets some points when completing a testing task. More critical tasks give more points. The current total of collected points correlates with the number of done tasks at that moment.

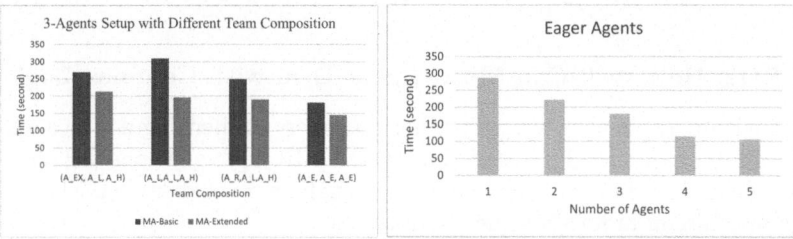

Fig. 5. Setups with three agents with different task selection heuristics on a 100×100 level. In addition to A_R, A_L and A_H, we have A_{EX} and A_E; these are agents with exploration and eager heuristics, respectively. In the graph on the right, only eager agents are used, but with one up to five of them.

see more objects/tasks and can choose a task based on how far it is from its position. Multi-agent setups consistently outperforms the single-agent setup, which is also expected. However, when the view distance increases, the performance of multi-agent setups using various strategies is nearly equal. Also, at some point further increase of the view distance does not significantly alter performance. The reason is that, even though the locations are known, the agent still needs to navigate to each task to solve it, and this costs time.

It should be noted that enlarging the view distance may not be an option provided by the game under test, e.g. to keep the amount of data that the game needs to send over to the agents light weight.

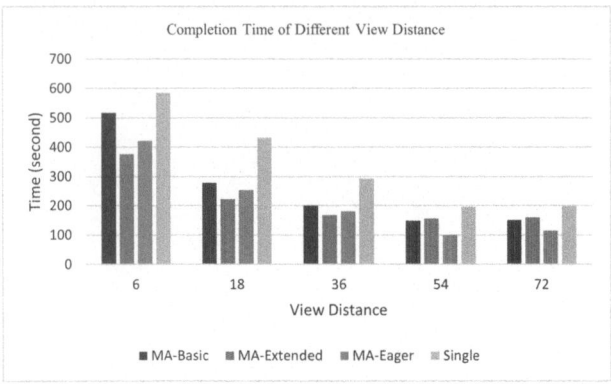

Fig. 6. The completion time of different setups under different view distance on a 100×100 level. MA-Basic and MA-Extended use two agents A_H and A_L with basic and extended synchronization, respectively. MA-Eager uses two eager agents with advanced synchronization.

5.2   RQ2: How Well Can Multi-Agent Deal with Complex Logic?

Game logic might make solving a testing task more challenging as the agents do not have full pre-knowledge about the logic. For RQ2 we will consider a number of door-logics, listed below, which are increasingly more challenging. These logics are quite common in for example RPG games.

– *Distant-connection logic.* A door has this logic if its enabler is located far from it. No door in *Basic-Level* has far enabler. So in the experiments later, we will create variations of the level.
– *Chained-connection logic.* A door d has this logic if its enabler is 'hidden' in another room, guarded by its own door. So, to open d multiple enablers have to be interacted, and in a specific order. It gets more complicated if the chaining is deeper than one (deeper chains are not included in our experiments).

Distant-Connection Logic. To investigate how well a multi-agent setup can deal with the distant-connection logic, a variation of a 30×30 *basic-level* is used. Some of the doors are changed to have a distant connection logic, by placing its corresponding button in a randomly far location. We created five different instances of *basic-level* with different numbers of such doors, starting from two to ten. We compare a single agent with a team of two agents $\{T_H, T_L\}$, using either basic or extended synchronization.

Table 1 shows the result. It shows that when the number of distant enablers increases, the time needed to finish the task increases, too. Even with extended synchronization, it becomes harder for agents to solve all the tasks.

Multi-agents with advanced synchronization can perform better than the other two other setups, except when all doors in the level have the distance connection logic, where the single agent setup is unexpectedly superior. The likely cause is accidental tasks solving. This happens when an agent unintentionally completes a task that is not intended for it. This occurs when the agent interacts with i' that is linked to d' while searching for an enabler to open a door d. The task $T_{d'}$ is then declared as completed, though T_d remains uncompleted. If the door is open when the agent sees it, it will be considered completed and removed from the testing tasks.

Table 1. The completion time (second) on a setup with doors with distant connection logic.

#DC	Single	MA-Basic	MA-Extended
2	210	159	117
4	265	209	195
6	315	289	215
8	352	333	232
10	180	352	264

Chained-Connection Logic. Figure 2 shows an example of a level with a 'hidden' button, marked by X. This means that to open d_2, d_1 must first be opened. If the agents take the tasks in such a way that d_2 is to be opened by agent A and d_2 by agent B, this presents a challenge. Until B opens d_1, d_2 cannot be opened. So, A has to wait, and we lose parallelism. Note that the doors' logic is not known to the agents upfront, so it also not possible for the agents to know upfront what an ideal task distribution is. Three distinct levels are created, each with a unique arrangement of one, two, and three hidden buttons. Our comparison of the time required to complete all tasks is shown in Table 2.

The multi-agent setup with extended information synchronization outperforms the single-agent setup. Increasing the number of hidden buttons increases the overall testing time. Having three chained-connection doubles the testing performance. As previously mentioned, one of the causes is the choices the agents make when selecting the tasks to do. The choices taken may force an agent to wait for another agent to access to certain areas, and hence the overall task solving becomes longer. Secondly, by attempting random buttons that are actually not connected to the door that guards a target room, the agent may block access to another area.

Table 2. The completion time (second) on a setup with different numbers of chained connections in a basic level with a size of 30.

#HB	Single	MA-Eager	MA-Extended
0	149	128	111
1	214	145	140
2	307	254	191
3	337	308	241

6   Related Work

Automated game testing is a challenging problem. The interaction space of a game is often very large and it is challenging for an algorithm to steer a game under test to get to a particular state that needs to be tested. Much of recent work on automated game testing has been focused on the use of AI [21]. For example, the use of Monte Carlo Search Tree (MTCS) for generating play tests was studied in [2,3]. The use of reinforcement learning was studied in e.g. [6,14,22]. These approaches require little human steering, though the training time could be excessive. Model-based games testing was studied in [5,10]. These approaches use a behavior model e.g. in the form of an Extended Finite State Machine (EFSM), from which test cases are generated. Test generation is fast, but on the other hand an EFSM model is needed. The model needs to be refined enough to make sure that the generated test cases are actually executable. Crafting such a model is costly.

Most of the works mentioned above [2,3,5,6,14,22] are arguably agent-based in a broad sense that they use a test agent to control the player character of the game under test. In our previous work, we studied the use of BDI agents [16,20]. E.g. these agents memorize the states of seen game objects, believing that they remain unchanged until proven otherwise. The agents also use path planning to navigate the world, based on navigation information they have in their belief. This eliminates the need for expensive training as in e.g. reinforcement leaning, though on the other hand, additional implementation effort may be needed to enable a navigation graph to be constructed automatically during the tests.

The work in [5] combines model-based testing, search-based testing (SBT), and agent-based testing. An SBT algorithm is used to generate test-cases from an EFSM model. The model in [5] can remain quite abstract. The approach exploits a BDI agent as a smart executor of test sequences generated from such an abstract model. The work in [6] combines reinforcement learning and BDI agents. The BDI layer is used to provide an abstract concept of actions (e.g. to auto-navigate to a given target object), so that the reinforcement learning part only needs to deal with such abstract actions.

Most of the approaches mentioned above are single agent. The works in [7,22] use multiple agents, though these are individual agents that run in parallel to train a *common* model, or a population of common models. Arguably this is a form of multi-agent cooperation, but not in the sense that the agents directly cooperate with each other. The latter, so the use of cooperating agents for game testing, has not been much studied.

7 Conclusion and Future Work

We presented a cooperative multi-agent testing approach, targeting mainly puzzle-based and world-exploration games and evaluated the approach using a case study of a 3D game called Lab Recruits. Basic and extended information synchronisation were considered, as different levels of cooperation. In the latter, agents share information about explored areas to each other in addition to sharing the location of testing tasks' target objects which is shared at the basic level. For the purpose of evaluation in the case study, we implemented the approach on top of an agent programming framework called iv4XR. The framework's main use case is for automating game testing. Agent concepts such as goals and tactics are exploited to provide an abstract way to program a play test. The implementation is in principle reusable. It can be used to do multi-agent testing for other games that implement an interface to iv4XR. Implementing the interface does require effort, e.g. to provide a library of basic game-specific tactics and functions for constructing a navigation graph from a game world. However, this is a one-off investment, after which automated game testing would become possible via iv4XR, including multi agent testing using our approach.

In the case study we evaluated the differences in test performance between a single-agent and multi-agent setups. During the experiment, the multi-agent setup with extended information sharing consistently performs better than single agent and multi-agent with just basic sharing. Adding more agents was demonstrated to improve performance. Also, the multi-agent setup is shown to be able to handle complex game logic, while still being superior to a single agent. Whether the results would generalize to other games would need further study; this is future work.

Future Work. The study was done with one case study. For future work, we would like to investigate more case studies, e.g. more games, considering more variations in the layout of the game world, and considering different cost models (e.g. how tasks with different values are actually distributed over the game worlds). Also, currently information synchronization is done by greedily pushing the information to share. We can consider a more lazy pull-based mechanism. It is more complex, but may give further performance improvement. This is future work.

In our study we focused on the use of a multi-agent approach for speeding up automated functional play testing, e.g. to verify the reachability of a family of game states. Another interesting application is to use such a setup to verify the multi-player quality of a game, e.g. whether the game allows natural cooperation, or natural competition, between players to achieve key objectives in the game. This would be very useful, as after all the main motivation for adding a multi player mode to a game is to let players explore cooperation and competition among themselves. A study in this direction is future work as well.

We mentioned that our multi-agent testing approach is reusable to target other games that implement an interface to iv4XR. We also mentioned that implementing this interface currently requires substantial effort. We are currently working on porting the core of iv4XR to C# along with a tight integration with the popular game engine Unity. This integration would significantly reduce the amount of effort to build the interface, which in turn would make our multi-agent approach would become more accessible to Unity game developers.

References

1. Albaghajati, A.M., Ahmed, M.A.K.: Video game automated testing approaches: an assessment framework. IEEE Trans. Games **15**, 81–94 (2020)
2. Ariyurek, S., Betin-Can, A., Surer, E.: Automated video game testing using synthetic and human-like agents. IEEE Trans. Games **13**, 50–67 (2019)
3. Ariyurek, S., Betin-Can, A., Surer, E.: Enhancing the monte carlo tree search algorithm for video game testing. In: 2020 IEEE Conference on Games (CoG). IEEE (2020)
4. Ch. Meyer, J.J.: Agent technology. In: Wiley Encyclopedia of Computer Science and Engineering, pp. 1–8 (2007)
5. Ferdous, R., Kifetew, F., Prandi, D., Prasetya, I.S.W.B., Shirzadehhajimahmood, S., Susi, A.: Search-based automated play testing of computer games: a model-based approach. In: O'Reilly, U.-M., Devroey, X. (eds.) SSBSE 2021. LNCS, vol. 12914, pp. 56–71. Springer, Cham (2021). https://doi.org/10.1007/978-3-030-88106-1_5
6. Ferdous, R., Kifetew, F., Prandi, D., Susi, A.: Towards agent-based testing of 3D games using reinforcement learning. In: 37th IEEE/ACM International Conference on Automated Software Engineering (2022)
7. Gordillo, C., Bergdahl, J., Tollmar, K., Gisslén, L.: Improving playtesting coverage via curiosity driven reinforcement learning agents. In: 2021 IEEE Conference on Games (CoG), pp. 1–8. IEEE (2021)
8. Hart, P.E., Nilsson, N.J., Raphael, B.: A formal basis for the heuristic determination of minimum cost paths. IEEE Trans. Syst. Sci. Cybern. **4**(2), 100–107 (1968)
9. Herzig, A., Lorini, E., Perrussel, L., Xiao, Z.: Bdi logics for bdi architectures: old problems, new perspectives. KI-Künstliche Intelligenz **31**(1), 73–83 (2017)
10. Iftikhar, S., Iqbal, M.Z., Khan, M.U., Mahmood, W.: An automated model based testing approach for platform games. In: 2015 ACM/IEEE 18th International Conference on Model Driven Engineering Languages and Systems (MODELS), pp. 426–435. IEEE (2015)
11. Liu, Y., Li, Z., Jiang, Z., He, Y.: Prospects for multi-agent collaboration and gaming: challenge, technology, and application. Front. Inf. Technol. Electron. Eng. **23**(7), 1002–1009 (2022)
12. Millington, I., Funge, J.: Artificial Intelligence for Games, 3rd edn. CRC Press, Boca Raton (2019)
13. Ostrowski, M., Aroudj, S.: Automated regression testing within video game development. GSTF J. Comput. **3**(2) (2013)

14. Pfau, J., Smeddinck, J.D., Malaka, R.: Automated game testing with icarus: intelligent completion of adventure riddles via unsupervised solving. In: Extended Abstracts Publication of the Annual Symposium on Computer-Human Interaction in Play, pp. 153–164 (2017)
15. Prasetya, I.S.W.B., Dastani, M., Prada, R., Vos, T.E.J., Dignum, F., Kifetew, F.: Aplib: tactical agents for testing computer games. In: Baroglio, C., Hubner, J.F., Winikoff, M. (eds.) EMAS 2020. LNCS (LNAI), vol. 12589, pp. 21–41. Springer, Cham (2020). https://doi.org/10.1007/978-3-030-66534-0_2
16. Prasetya, I., et al.: An agent-based approach to automated game testing: an experience report. In: 13th International Workshop on Automating Test Case Design, Selection and Evaluation (2022)
17. Prasetya, I., et al.: Navigation and exploration in 3d-game automated play testing. In: Proceedings of the 11th ACM SIGSOFT International Workshop on Automating TEST Case Design, Selection, and Evaluation, pp. 3–9 (2020)
18. Schatten, M., Đurić, B.O., Tomičič, I., Ivkovič, N.: Automated MMORPG testing – an agent-based approach. In: Demazeau, Y., Davidsson, P., Bajo, J., Vale, Z. (eds.) PAAMS 2017. LNCS (LNAI), vol. 10349, pp. 359–363. Springer, Cham (2017). https://doi.org/10.1007/978-3-319-59930-4_38
19. Shirzadehhajimahmood, S., Prasetya, I., Dignum, F., Dastani, M.: An online agent-based search approach in automated computer game testing with model construction. In: 13th International Workshop on Automating Test Case Design, Selection and Evaluation (2022)
20. Shirzadehhajimahmood, S., Prasetya, I., Dignum, F., Dastani, M., Keller, G.: Using an agent-based approach for robust automated testing of computer games. In: Proceedings of the 12th International Workshop on Automating TEST Case Design, Selection, and Evaluation, pp. 1–8 (2021)
21. Zarembo, I.: Analysis of artificial intelligence applications for automated testing of video games. In: Proceedings of the 12th International Scientific and Practical Conference, volume II, vol. 170, p. 174 (2019)
22. Zheng, Y., et al.: Wuji: automatic online combat game testing using evolutionary deep reinforcement learning. In: 2019 34th IEEE/ACM International Conference on Automated Software Engineering (ASE), pp. 772–784. IEEE (2019)

On the External Concurrency of Current BDI Frameworks for MAS

Martina Baiardi⬛, Samuele Burattini$^{(\boxtimes)}$⬛, Giovanni Ciatto⬛,
Danilo Pianini⬛, Alessandro Ricci⬛, and Andrea Omicini⬛

Department of Computer Science and Engineering (DISI), Alma Mater
Studiorum–Univerisitá di Bologna, Via dell'Universitá 50, 47522 Cesena, FC, Italy
{m.baiardi,samuele.burattini,giovanni.ciatto,danilo.pianini,
a.ricci,andrea.omicini}@unibo.it
https://www.unibo.it/sitoweb/

Abstract. The execution of Belief-Desire-Intention (BDI) agents in a
Multi-Agent System (MAS) can be practically implemented on top of
low-level concurrency mechanisms that impact on efficiency, determinism, and reproducibility. We argue that developers should specify the
MAS behaviour independently of the execution model, and choose or
configure the concurrency model later on, according to the specific needs
of their target domain, leaving the MAS specification unaffected. We
identify patterns for mapping the agent execution over the underlying
concurrency abstractions, and investigate which concurrency models are
supported by some of the most commonly used BDI platforms. Although
most frameworks support multiple concurrency models, we find that they
mostly hide them under the hood, making them opaque to the developer,
and actually limiting the possibility of fine-tuning the MAS.

Keywords: Agent-Oriented Programming · Concurrency · BDI
Agents · Threading · Parallelism

1 Introduction

The Agent-Oriented Programming (AOP) paradigm was introduced almost
thirty years ago [39] as a way to model software in terms of autonomous computational entities capable of carrying on several courses of action *simultaneously*—
there including, interacting with their environment and among each other. Since
its conception, AOP has been strictly linked with the *strong* notion of agency [44],
where agents are assumed to be aware of their own goals and able to reason about
if, when, and how to pursue them—not necessarily in a predefined order. Along
this line, AOP frameworks evolved to embrace the Belief-Desire-Intention (BDI)
model [10], where agents are modelled and implemented by means of abstractions
mimicking typically human-level notions. By construction, BDI agents are able
to carry on multiple intentions at any given time [34], and many research and

D. Briola et al. (Eds.): EMAS 2024, LNAI 15152, pp. 42–63, 2025.
https://doi.org/10.1007/978-3-031-71152-7_3

software-development efforts have been devoted to the definition of BDI architectures and programming languages giving precise semantics to the *concurrent*
execution of such intentions [9].

As computational entities, agents are autonomous as they encapsulate their
own *control flow* [30]. Control-flow encapsulation is commonly referred to as
computational autonomy [31], and it is considered a necessary – yet not sufficient
– pre-requisite for autonomy in software agents.

On mainstream programming platforms – such as the Java Virtual Machine
(JVM) [12], used for the implementation of many BDI frameworks –, computational autonomy can be achieved by mapping each agent onto a control-flow-
related primitive: a thread, a process, or an event loop. This, in turn, enables and
constraints the ways by which multiple agents may be *concurrently* executed. In
this paper we refer to the mapping between BDI abstractions and the underlying
concurrency primitive as the *concurrency model* of the framework.

The selection of an appropriate concurrency model deeply impacts several
aspects of the agent programming framework: efficiency, determinism, and reproducibility. In particular, the concurrency model determines whether, and to what
extent *(i)* multiple agents can run in parallel, and *(ii)* one agent can carry on parallel activities. Parallelism, in turn, affects the efficiency of MAS execution (particularly on hardware supporting true parallel execution) and the determinism
of the overall MAS dynamics. In fact, parallelism introduces non-deterministic
interleaving of the agent's actions, undermining predictability and reproducibility, which may be a strict requirement in some applications, such as multi-agent
based simulation [5]. Finely capturing and controlling concurrency is crucial in
modern software engineering, even beyond MASs: consider, for instance, trends
such as event-driven [15] and reactive [4] programming.

Unfortunately, dealing with concurrency is commonly acknowledged as error-
prone and challenging. Thus, mainstream programming languages and platforms
are featuring more and more constructs helping developers to leverage concurrency through better abstractions (e.g., Javascript's async/await [28], Akka's
reactive streams [16], and Kotlin's coroutines [20]), hiding part of the subtle
intricacies under the hood. AOP tools and frameworks are no exception to this
trend: they come with one or more concurrency models, often (in compliance
with the information hiding principle) hidden under the hood to let program-
mers focus on the agents' behaviour.

In this work we argue that, although the separation of concurrency models
and MAS specifications is paramount, removing control from developers' hand is
not the best solution: they should be aware of available possibilities and related
trade-offs, and select (and, possibly, swap) them depending on the specific needs
of their application and execution environment. This is particularly true for BDI
agent technologies, where the semantics of intention scheduling may be realised
in many different ways.

Contribution. In this work, we introduce the notions of *internal* and *external* concurrency, capturing, respectively, the concurrency among agents' activities and the concurrency induced by the selection of the mapping of multiple

agents onto the underlying concurrency abstractions. These two abstractions influence each other: enforcing one restricts the range of possibilities of the other, impacting performance, determinism, and reproducibility. Despite that, the previous literature focuses on internal concurrency, leaving the external one as an implicit consequence of the choices made to support internal behaviour. Thus, in this paper we provide a taxonomy of concurrency models that may be adopted by BDI frameworks, and we classify several notable BDI agent technologies accordingly. Finally, we draw practical engineering recommendations for the development of BDI agent technologies, suggesting to take into account the control of *external* concurrency at design time.

Structure. The remainder of this paper is structured as follows. In Sect. 2 we define internal and external concurrency in BDI agents, and discuss how they have been considered in related works in the AOP community. We analyse concurrency models commonly adopted in modern software development, then (Sect. 3) we discuss how agents (and their internal components) can be mapped onto them, evaluating the pros and cons. In Sect. 4 we evaluate several BDI technologies from the AOP community from a concurrency-related perspective, eliciting the available concurrency models and their degree of configurability. Finally, in Sect. 5 we elaborate on the importance of configurable concurrency models well-separated from the agent's behaviour specification.

2   Background

In this section we first recall basic notions to frame the concepts of *internal* and *external* concurrency, then look at the existing work specifically addressing concurrency in the context of BDI AOP, thus framing our contribution with respect to the state of the art. Then we discuss the lower-level concurrency abstractions required to understand the remainder of the paper.

2.1   Internal Vs External Concurrency

A multi-BDI-agent system can be modelled in Calculus of Communicating Systems (CCS) [29] as a set of agents running in parallel. Each agent is essentially an infinite loop where, at each iteration step, the three main stages of the agent's control loop are executed—sensing, deliberating, and acting. More formally:

$$
\begin{aligned}
Mas &::= Agent_1 \parallel \ldots \parallel Agent_N \\
Agent &::= \texttt{sense} \cdot \texttt{deliberate} \cdot \texttt{act} \cdot Agent
\end{aligned}
\tag{1}
$$

where *(i)* operation sense handles new percepts and incoming messages, generating belief update events accordingly, *(ii)* operation deliberate chooses how to handle those events and picks the next action to be executed and *(iii)* operation act executes the selected action—e.g. sending a message, affecting the environment, or changing the agent's internal state.

This simple modelling focuses on the control loop of agents, while hiding another key aspect of MAS: interaction among agents —i.e. how each agent's actions may influence other agents. Interaction may consist of either communication (e.g. direct message passing) or stigmergy (e.g. indirectly altering the environment to affect other agents). In both cases, interaction implies one agent acting and another agent perceiving the effects of that action, so, as far as concurrency and control-loops are concerned, the modelling above is sufficient.

Internal Concurrency is the way in which those operations are modelled, there including whether they are further decomposable or not, their degree of concurrency, and their interleaving. For instance, in [45], two major patterns are identified: the *synchronous* one, where *all* percepts and messages are *sequentially* handled in the sensing stage, and *only one* action is selected by the deliberation stage and executed by the action stage:

$$
\begin{aligned}
Agent &:: = Sense \cdot Deliberate \cdot Act \cdot Agent \\
Sense &:: = \mathtt{sense}_1 \cdot \ldots \cdot \mathtt{sense}_M \\
Deliberate &:: = \mathtt{deliberate} \\
Act &:: = \mathtt{act}
\end{aligned}
\tag{2}
$$

and the *asynchronous* one, where *multiple* percepts and messages are *concurrently* handled in the sensing stage, and deliberation and action stages are executed concurrently as well:

$$
\begin{aligned}
Agent &:: = Sense \parallel Deliberate \parallel Act \\
Sense &:: = (\mathtt{sense}_1 \parallel \ldots \parallel \mathtt{sense}_M) \cdot Sense \\
Deliberate &:: = (\mathtt{deliberate}_1 \parallel \ldots \parallel \mathtt{deliberate}_L) \cdot Deliberate \\
Act &:: = (\mathtt{act}_1 \parallel \ldots \parallel \mathtt{act}_K) \cdot Act
\end{aligned}
\tag{3}
$$

Other patterns may be defined in this framework; e.g., the single step of the control-loop can be modelled as a fork/join, where all percepts are handled concurrently, then all deliberations are handled concurrently, and then all actions are executed concurrently. Yet, the key point is that all models focus on the execution of the agent's control loop, and, by extension, on the interleaving of the agent's intentions. For instance, a system modelled as in Eq. 2 would only support *simulated* parallelism —e.g., a very common implementation is: each cycle of the control-loop executes a single action from a single intention. Conversely, a system modelled as in Eq. 3 would support *true* parallelism —so, in principle, two or more action could be executed in the same moment.

External Concurrency, conversely, is what we focus on in this paper—i.e., the way the control loops of multiple agents are mapped onto the underlying concurrency abstractions (Sect. 2.3). In other words, we are interested in understanding how Eq. 1 can be – and commonly is – implemented in practice. Arguably, understanding and explicitly modelling external concurrency is crucial, as the external concurrency model constrains and supports the admissible internal concurrency models: the relationship between the two is bi-directional. Also, we argue that the external concurrency model has the most impact on the overall system properties. For instance, even a massively-parallel agent internal concurrency model would not lead to any speedup compared to a sequential execution if the external concurrency model enforces execution in a single control flow. At the same time, even if agents are internally sequential and predictable, an external model mapping them on multiple threads may lead to unpredictable interleaving of actions, thus affecting predictability of the whole MAS.

We further elaborate on this in Sect. 3, where we present different models of external concurrency that are at the core of this contribution.

2.2   Related Work

The existing literature on concurrency in BDI systems mainly focuses on *internal* concurrency. For instance, a recent survey [41] provides an overview of BDI architectures, including considerations on how different platforms deal with the interleaving of agents' intentions. Moreover, the discussion about concurrency in BDI systems typically concerns the *interleaving* of sequentially-executed intentions, rarely about their *parallel* execution—also known as *true concurrency* [40]. Interaction among agents that need to share mutable data has also received attention. In particular, the shared data has been modelled with the abstraction of *artifact* [37], capturing *safety* and *synchronisation*; adopting specialised abstractions can in turn impact internal concurrency [36]. Finally, the impact of concurrency on performance has been investigated in [45], focussing on the effects that different concurrency configurations mapping the agent control loop can have on both individual agents and the whole MAS.

2.3   Underlying Concurrency Mechanisms

The structured programming theorem [8] states that any computable function can be expressed in terms of selection (executing one of two subprograms depending on a condition), iteration (repeatedly executing a subprogram until a condition is met), and *sequence* (executing a subprogram after another). The latter is the foundation of the so-called *control flow* of a program, and it is rooted in the assumption that instructions are *totally* ordered. In concurrent programs, instead, the execution of instructions is rather *partially* ordered [26]: although subprograms are executed in a given order, instructions of different subprograms may interleave, producing a different total ordering. Concurrent execution can be especially beneficial (and difficult to govern [6]) when the underlying architecture supports multiple control flows (multiple processors, cores, or portions of the execution pipeline).

The realisation of concurrent programs boils down to minimising the amount of ordering constraints imposed on the execution of instructions while guaranteeing correctness, and can be performed through formal or practical tools. Formalism dedicated to concurrent programming include process algebras [24], CCS [29], Petri nets [35], and actors [1]. From a practical perspective, some of them are captured by programming languages, with either a dedicated syntax or libraries, sometimes adopting a custom naming convention, ultimately preserving the underlying semantics. In the following, we introduce the most common concurrency abstractions available in most modern programming languages.

Threads. Threads are a facility provided by Operating Systems OSs to execute sequential programs that share memory; they are considered the basic unit of concurrency [18]. Although the code executed by each thread is sequential, multiple threads run concurrently (scheduled by the OS onto multiple logical cores and/or in a time-sharing fashion), thus the execution of multiple threads may interleave arbitrarily. Since they share memory, threads may easily interact with each other by reading/writing the same memory locations, causing race conditions and other concurrency-related issues. Thus, multi-threaded programs commonly require synchronisation, typically achieved by means of arguably low-level primitives such as *locks, semaphores,* and *monitors,* enforcing partial ordering among instructions of different threads. Other concurrency abstractions are constructed by coordinating threads by means of these and similar mechanisms.

Processes. Processes are similar to threads, but (normally, in modern OSs) they do not share memory; rather, inter-process communication occurs through OS mediation via mechanisms such as *pipes, sockets,* or the *file system.* Internally, processes can spawn multiple threads: thus, from a concurrency perspective, they can be intended as containers of threads sharing the process' memory space.

Event Loops. In event-driven programming [15], event loops are abstractions to express concurrent programs while hiding the intricacies of low-level thread synchronisation. An event loop is a single thread executing multiple tasks (subprograms) sequentially from different sources (users, the OS, or other parts of the program). Tasks can be scheduled by registering the corresponding subprogram on the event loop; internally, this operation appends the subprogram to a First-In-First-Out (FIFO) queue internal to the event loop. The event loop's thread executes the tasks in the queue in order, waiting if the queue is empty: any task scheduled on the event loop is *eventually* executed. The perception of parallelism of an event loop come from the fact that new tasks can be scheduled with no need to wait for any previous one to be completed. On the other hand, the sequential nature of event loops becomes evident in case of long-running tasks (e.g., I/O operations), that may lead subsequent ones to starvation. To mitigate this issue, event-loops are commonly coupled with non-blocking I/O [11], where blocking read/write primitives are replaced with asynchronous events.

Notably, event loops are the backbone of many interesting features that are popping up in modern programming languages – there including JavaScript, Python, C#, etc. –, such as `Promises`, asynchronous functions, and `await` operators (cf. [28]). In these languages, the event loop is hidden under the hood, and developers are not required to interact with it directly, but rather by means of the aforementioned features. As far as this paper is concerned, we stick to the low-level abstraction of the event loop, as our goal is to make concurrency controllable for AOP developers —rather than hiding it via syntactic sugar.

Executors. Borrowing from the Java's nomenclature,[1] executors generalise event loops by supporting multiple threads. From the user viewpoint, executors are essentially event loops with a configurable number of threads. They support tasks to be enqueued in the same way as event loops do, yet consumption of tasks from the queue is transparently performed by multiple threads (thus, potentially, in parallel). Executors may be further categorised depending on whether their backing thread count can change at runtime. Fixed-sized executors are created with a specific count number of threads N, which imposes an upper bound on the maximum degree of parallelism, as at most N tasks may be executed in parallel at any given moment. Conversely, variable-sized executors may *dynamically* change the number of threads in response to the runtime conditions. A typical case where variable-sized executors are preferable is in the presence of multiple long-running blocking tasks. For instance, assume N such tasks to be selected for parallel execution: the fixed-sized executor would be blocked, starving the other tasks and leaving resources unused; the variable-sized executor, instead, could spawn new threads to execute the other tasks, and let them terminate once no blocking tasks are being run.

Concurrency Abstractions in Practice. Although all the aforementioned concurrency abstractions are equivalent in terms of expressiveness, there are relevant practical implications associated with any choice.

Consider, for instance, the CCS system $a \cdot b \cdot c \parallel x \cdot y \cdot z$, modelling two parallel suprograms performing a sequence of atomic tasks. Such a system, as specified, allows tasks to interleave arbitrarily, as far as their order within the subprogram is respected (for instance, b can never happen before a, but a, x, y, z, b, c is a perfectly valid execution). When subprograms are executed by independent threads, this semantics is respected. When using an event loop, instead, some combinations become impossible, as the execution of the next task is scheduled after the previous one's completion; consequently, if both a and x are enqueued, only two round-robin inter-leavings are possible, depending on which one is on the top of the queue: a, x, b, y, c, z or x, a, y, b, z, c. So, we say that implementing the concurrent system on an event loop reduces the non-determinism as well as developers' degrees of control. With an executor, all possible interleavings are still possible, but the degree of parallelism can be selected.

Generalising on this observation, we may state that the choice of concurrency abstraction has an impact on the determinism and controllability of the concurrent system.

About BDI Technologies. Since the introduction of the Belief-Desire-Intention framework [10], the community produced many technologies for pro-

---

[1] https://archive.is/zF1FL.

gramming BDI agents, most of which are based on (or inspired by) the AgentSpeak(L) semantics [34]. In the remainder of this paper, we compare several major BDI technologies from a concurrency perspective. We focus on those technologies that appear to have some running software implementation that is actively maintained and used by the community. Hence, we build upon the recent work by Calegari *et al.* [12], which surveys the state-of-the-art of logic-based agent-oriented technologies, and we select the ones aimed to support general-purpose BDI agents programming, via *open-source* software implementations. Because of this criterion, we include in our analysis the following technologies: Astra [14], GOAL [22], Jadex [33], JaKtA [2], Jason [9], PHIDIAS [19], and SPADE-BDI [32]. Of these, Astra, Jadex, JaKtA, and Jason are based on the JVM platform, PHIDIAS and SPADE-BDI are based on Python, and GOAL is based on both the JVM and SWI-Prolog [42] —details about the underlying software plaftorm are relevant to understand the empirical analysis described in Sect. 4.1.

We remark that this selection is not meant to be exhaustive. In particular, many well-known AOP technologies are not included in our analysis (precisely because they are not BDI), namely: JADE [7], SPADE [32], SARL [38], or Kiko [13]. Similarly, we exclude BDI technologies that are closed source – e.g., JACK [43] –, or not actively maintained (at the time when the survey by Calegari *et al.* [12] was conducted) —e.g., AFAPL[2], 2APL [17], or 3APL [23].

3   A Taxonomy of Concurrency Patterns for MAS Execution

In this section we identify the most relevant *external* concurrency models for MASs—namely, how the atomic parts of the agent' control loop get mapped onto the underlying abstractions described in Sect. 2.3. Different *internal* concurrency models dictate different levels of granularity of the atomic components of the control loop, thus influencing the *external* concurrency model. Consequently, we focus on the mapping of the largest possible autonomous unit in AOP, the entire agent, discussing the potential external concurrency models for a MAS.

One-Agent-One-Thread (1A1T). Each agent is mapped onto a single thread, which executes its whole control loop. Hence, the MAS consist of several threads managed by the OS scheduler, and the interleaving among different agents' operations is unpredictable. The controllability of the MAS execution is abysmal, as control is delegated to the OS; for the same reason, determinism is minimal. Additionally, with 1A1T the active thread count of the MAS is unbound, and when such count largely exceeds the logical processors performance degrades [27].

All-Agents-One-Thread (AA1T). The whole MAS is executed on a single thread which internally schedules all agents' execution in a custom way, following some (usually cooperative) scheduling policy—e.g., round-robin. Most commonly, the

---

[2] https://archive.ph/Hozbl.

internal scheduling policy alternates agents at the control loop step or stage level. By omitting the former case for the sake of conciseness, the latter can be formalised as follows (provided that the scheduling policy is round-robin):

$$
\begin{aligned}
Mas &::= Sense \cdot Deliberate \cdot Act \cdot Mas \\
Sense &::= \mathtt{sense}_1 \cdot \ldots \cdot \mathtt{sense}_N \\
Deliberate &::= \mathtt{deliberate}_1 \cdot \ldots \cdot \mathtt{deliberate}_N \\
Act &::= \mathtt{act}_1 \cdot \ldots \cdot \mathtt{act}_N
\end{aligned}
\tag{4}
$$

Using a single thread with custom internal scheduling policy renounces parallelism (hence, performance) in favour of controllability: thus, it is a good choice when determinism, reproducibility, and predictability are primary concerns—as in many simulated or time-critical scenarios. Notably, because of the cooperative nature of the scheduling, sensing, deliberation, and actuation operations should terminate as quickly as possible, to avoid blocking the whole MAS.

All-Agents-One-Event-Loop (AA1EL). The whole MAS is executed on a single event loop, which internally schedules all agents' execution with a FIFO queue of tasks, ensuring fairness by design if all new tasks in the event loop are inserted by other tasks of the event loop. At the conceptual level, this is equivalent to a fair AA1T; as such, controllability and performance are akin to AA1T. In practice, however, AA1EL requires explicitly modelling the agent's control loops activities as tasks on the event loop, thus, despite the conceptual equivalence, technical implementations of AA1T and AA1EL may be fairly different.

All-Agents-One-Executor (AA1E). Similarly to AA1EL, each atomic operation is mapped onto a task to be enqueued on a shared executor. This model enables the parallel execution of multiple agents, and, if the internal concurrency model supports it, the parallel execution of the same agent's activities. In case each agent enqueues at most one task at a time (a solution often used to enforce consistency), AA1E is conceptually equivalent to 1A1T. However, AA1E is preferable from a technological perspective, as the agent (and agent's actions) count is decoupled from the thread count, resulting in finer control on the degree of parallelism (by governing the amount of threads in the executor), as well as in a better exploitation of the underlying resources. Furthermore, the granularity of the interleaving may be tuned by choosing how to model events and tasks.

For instance, one may model the entire control loop step as a single task, hence making the interleaving more coarse-grained —formally:

$$
\begin{aligned}
Mas &::= Agent_1 \parallel \ldots \parallel Agent_n \\
Agent &::= Step \cdot Agent \\
Step &::= \mathtt{step}
\end{aligned}
$$

where $\mathtt{step}$ represents one single execution of all stages, from sensing to acting.

Two further specialisations of this model are possible, depending on whether the executor is fixed- or variable-size. In the former case, there is an upper bound on the amount of threads the MAS can leverage. Although helpful to limit the resource exploitation in constrained environments, it may introduce subtle interdependencies among agents. For instance, when there are M agents and $N < M$ threads, if N agents are performing blocking operations, then the other $M - N$ agents must wait. Of course, the fixed-sized executor with $N = 1$ is equivalent to AA1EL. If the executor is variable-sized, then the number of threads is adjusted dynamically, upon need—i.e., by trying to match the count of active threads and logical processors. AA1E is generally preferable over 1A1T, as the total thread count is controllable.

3.1 Concurrency at Different Levels of Granularity

Concurrency abstractions may be combined to form more complex ones. For instance, both processes and executors are composed by threads. Threads in a process may be part of the same executor, or multiple ones. In a distributed setting, a system may be composed by many processes spread across a several machines, losing shared memory and thus requiring serialisation to communicate. In orchestration frameworks, the same service may consist of multiple containers, distributed on different machines, each one running multiple processes.

In principle, when implementing a MAS, agents may be mapped onto any of these concurrency abstractions with different trade-offs between flexibility and controllability. For instance, when One-Agent-One-Process (1A1P) is adopted, the agent's internal control loop may be implemented with multiple threads, but communication among agents will require (de)serialisation, as agents will not share memory with each other. For BDI agents, threads may be used to model intentions, paying a price in terms of implementation complexity (as agent-specific synchronisation mechanisms would be required) to obtain an extremely fine-grained degree of control over the execution.

Combinations (and complexity) can scale arbitrarily, as in principle any AOP abstraction can be mapped on any lower-level concurrency abstraction —thus allowing uncommon combinations such as One-Agent-One-Container or One-Intent-One-Process. For the sake of simplicity, in this paper we focus on the cases listed in Sect. 3, which we show suffice to capture the behaviour of all the selected BDI technologies. However, we discuss the implications of more nuanced concurrency models briefly in Sect. 5.

4 Analysis of BDI Technologies and Concurrency Models

In this section, we inspect the external concurrency models supported by a selection of actively-maintained open source BDI programming frameworks. In particular, we focus on Astra [14], GOAL [22], Jadex [33], JaKtA [2], Jason [9], PHIDIAS [19], and SPADE-BDI [32]. We do not claim this selection to be exhaustive, so we leave a more complete analysis for future works.

4.1 Methodology

We performed our analysis in three steps:

Listing 1.1. ASL description for *pinger* agent.

```
!ping.

+!ping <-
    .revealCurrentThread("intention 1");
    .send(pong, tell, ball);
    !!showThread(2);
    .revealCurrentThread("intention 1").

+ball <-
    !!showThread(4);
    .revealCurrentThread("intention 3").

+!showThread(X) <- .revealCurrentThread("intention " + X).
```

Listing 1.2. ASL description for *ponger* agent.

```
+ball[source(X)] <-
    .revealCurrentThread("intention 5");
    .send(X, tell, ball);
    !!showThread(6);
    .revealCurrentThread("intention 5").

+!showThread(X) <- .revealCurrentThread("intention " + X).
```

1. *empirical evaluation* through a synthetic benchmark designed to reveal how many threads are involved in the execution of a MAS and how they interleave;
2. *documentation and source code inspection* to understand implementation details and customisability.
3. *direct contact* with the current maintainers, asking for confirmation of our findings and for further details, including a subjective evaluation of the feasibility of supporting additional external concurrency models.

Empirical Evaluation. We created a benchmark [3] to reveal how threads are leveraged in a BDI MAS. The benchmark consists of a simple MAS, composed by two agents enacting one round of a ping–pong protocol: the pinger agent initiates the protocol by sending a message to the ponger agent, which replies by sending a message back to the pinger. To reveal how threads are used, we make agents execute a custom action – revealCurrentThread – before and after each message sending and reception. As a reference, we show our Jason implementation for pinger (Listing 1.1) and ponger (Listing 1.2). To maximise the likelihood of intercepting all threads, when supported we force agents to pursue different intentions simultaneously (in the reference specification, this is done through the Jason operator !!). We then analyse the trace obtained by multiple executions of the benchmark, and we use it to understand how many threads the agent is using to execute its intentions and in which order intentions (of different agents) are executed and interleaved. By repeating this analysis we empirically infer which concurrency model is used to execute agents.

Listing 1.3. An example of execution on which each agent executes its steps on its thread.

```
[pinger]  Intention 1 is executed on thread: pinger
[pinger]  Intention 1 is executed on thread: pinger
[ponger]  Intention 5 is executed on thread: ponger
[pinger]  Intention 2 is executed on thread: pinger
[ponger]  Intention 5 is executed on thread: ponger
[pinger]  Intention 3 is executed on thread: pinger
[ponger]  Intention 6 is executed on thread: ponger
[pinger]  Intention 4 is executed on thread: pinger
```

One possible trace log is reported in Listing 1.3, showing the benchmark output when executed in Jason —as implemented in Listing 1.1 and Listing 1.2.

There, logs suggest that Jason may implement 1A1T concurrency model, as each agent is always logged by the same thread, the same thread is never used by two different agents, and the thread identifier is associated to the name assigned to the agent in the MAS specification. Accordingly, for each BDI technology, we re-implement the benchmark in the most idiomatic way possible, and we run it.

We were not able to reproduce our benchmark on Jadex, SPADE-BDI, and GOAL. We then did not infer the concurrency model used in these technologies and moved to the following step of our evaluation.

Documentation and Source Code Inspection. In general, the empirical evaluation can let *some* external concurrency model emerge, but it cannot be exhaustive: as discussed in Sect. 2.3, some abstraction may not show all their possible behaviours even after repeated executions, and some may produce the same outputs. Also, the empirical evaluation of some platforms is more difficult to implement and less revealing. For instance, the JVM thread inspection primitives (with which Jason can interact) are more expressive than SWI-Prolog ones (with which GOAL interacts). We thus inspected the source code and the official documentation of the surveyed frameworks to learn as much as possible.

In detail, while inspecting the source code of JVM-based BDI technologies, we look for usages of (Java) standard-library classes such as `Thread`, `Executor`, `ExecutorService`, `ForkJoinPool`, as well as usages of parallel streams. Similarly, for Python-based technologies, we look for usages of (Python) standard-library types such as `Thread`, `AbstractEventLoop` (or subclasses), `Task`, as well as usages of coroutines.

After inferring the concurrency model of each BDI technology, we assess if and to what extent the concurrency model can be *customised* by the users of that technology, by looking for ad-hoc syntax or Application Programming Interface (API) letting MAS specifications customise the concurrecy model.

Direct Contact. Once the results from the previous steps were gathered, we contacted maintainers of each framework so as to confirm our assessment and gain additional insights. This operation was useful to get past what is available

Table 1. Summary of BDI technologies and their concurrency models. The symbols ✓, ~, and × indicate, respectively, that the concurrency model is supported, that it could be supported with a custom implementation, and that it is not supported.

Model → Tech. ↓	1A1T	AA1T	AA1EL	AA1E fixed	AA1E variable	1A1P
Astra	~	~	✓	✓	✓	~
GOAL	✓	×	×	×	×	×
Jadex	~	✓	~	~	✓	✓
JaKtA	✓	✓	✓	✓	✓	~
Jason	✓	~	✓	✓	~	✓
PHIDIAS	✓	×	×	×	×	✓
SPADE-BDI	×	×	✓	×	×	✓

out-of-the-box, and what could be achieved with reasonably limited extensions. We described the developers the taxonomy of Sect. 3 and reported our results. We asked them to evaluate on our findings, adding comments about whether the non-supported external concurrency models were available out of the box (thus, missed by the analysis), could be supported with reasonable effort, or required extensive rewriting of the codebase: a template of the email sent to all maintainers can be found in Appendix A. We received answers from all developers except for Jason and SPADE-BDI; all answers confirmed our initial results.

4.2 Results

Table 1 summarises the results of our analysis. When evaluating 1A1P, we also require agents to be capable of inter-process communication, e.g., by means of protocols such as TCP/IP. In the rest of this section, we detail how the analysis is performed for each technology, summarising the most prominent findings.

Astra. Astra [14] is a BDI agent technology written in Java designed with a C-family syntax. Astra provides fine-grained control over the execution of the MAS entities, our benchmark indeed revealed that any iteration step of the control loop of the same agent may run on a different thread, suggesting a AA1E model. Source code inspection confirmed the analysis and revealed that the executor is *variable-sized*. Since Java executors can be used as event loops, AA1EL is supported, too.   Among the available implementations which are present in the Astra codebase, the `BasicSchedulerStrategy` (see Listing 1.4) is the one that supports the fixed-size AA1E concurrency model.

Astra also supports custom implementations of the concurrency model, which users may provide by implementing `SchedulerStrategy` interface. Thus, 1A1T and AA1T could be implemented quite easily. The maintainers of Astra confirmed our previous assertions, thus describing to us that there is also the possibility to implement the 1A1P concurrency model by the means of a custom

Listing 1.4. Snippet of Astra's code base (https://gitlab.com/astra-language/astra-core) showing how the All-Agents-One-Executor model is implemented.

```
// astra-interpreter/src/main/java/astra/execution/BasicSchedulerStrategy.
    java
import java.util.concurrent.ExecutorService;
import java.util.concurrent.Executors;
// ...
public class BasicSchedulerStrategy implements SchedulerStrategy {
  private ExecutorService executor =
    Executors.newFixedThreadPool(2);
  // ...
  public void setThreadPoolSize(int size) { /*...*/ }
  public void schedule(final Agent agent) {
    executor.submit(() -> {
      // ...
      agent.execute(); // run one step of the agent's control loop
      // ...
      schedule(agent); // schedules the next step
    });
  }
}
```

distributed messaging infrastructure implementation for Astra `Messaging` class, that currently is not provided.

GOAL. GOAL [22] is a Java BDI library distributed as an Eclipse IDE plugin that integrates with SWI Prolog through Java Native Interface (JNI) [25], that does not expose Java primitives. Due to its peculiar integration with SWI Prolog [42], GOAL is bound to the 1A1T model, and it does not support customisations without major changes to the code base. However, the library comes with an option for emulating AA1T; although internally agents are still executed on different threads, these are executed sequentially. The maintainers of GOAL also confirmed that, due to this strict integration with SWI Prolog, other concurrency models cannot be custom-built, even with major code changes.

Jadex. Jadex [33] is a BDI Java library. We analysed the latest version of the library, namely Jadex V, which improved modularisation and simplified agents' concurrency management through (Jadex V's terminology) `ExecutionFeatures`. Jadex V natively supports variable-sized AA1E as default behaviour, 1A1P and AA1T. Further customisation options could be implemented with custom `ExecutionFeatures` modules.

JaKtA. JaKtA [2] is a Kotlin-based Domain-Specific Language (DSL)[3] for BDI MAS running on the JVM. It exposes the concurrency model as a first-class abstraction in the DSL (see Listing 1.5) supporting custom models through the implementation of the `ExecutionStrategy` interface. By default, JaKtA uses AA1T to support reproducibility while debugging or simulating; but 1A1T,

---

[3] https://archive.is/El3fE.

Listing 1.5. Example of MAS configuration with execution strategy customisation in JaKtA.

```
mas {
    environment { /* external actions' definitions here */}
    agent("pinger") { /* pinger specification here */ }
    agent("ponger") { /* ponger specification here */ }
    executionStrategy { oneThreadPerAgent() } // first-class support
}.start()
```

Listing 1.6. Snippet of PHIDIAS code base (https://github.com/corradosantoro/phidias) showing how agents are executed on threads.

```
# phidias/lib/phidias/Runtime.py
import threading
class Runtime:
    # ...
    @classmethod
    def run_agent(cls, a):
        e = cls.engines[a]
        t = threading.Thread(target=e.run)
        t.start()
```

AA1E, and AA1EL are also supported natively. 1A1P is not supported out of the box, but could be implemented through an extension.

Jason. Jason [9] is a well-known AgentSpeak(L)-compliant BDI agent technology implemented in Java. Jason defaults to a 1A1T model, yet the concurrency models are customisable by specifying a different *infrastructure*. Similarly to JaKtA, these can be configured at MAS specification time and customised; implementations available out of the box provide support for AA1T (Local/threaded infrastructure), fixed-sized AA1E and AA1EL (Local/pool infrastructure); and 1A1P (Jade infrastructure).

PHIDIAS. PHIDIAS [19] is a Python internal DSL defaulting to the 1A1T concurrency model. We reach this conclusion by code inspection: Python's threads are explicitly created behind the scenes of each agent —as shown in Listing 1.6, which is taken from PHIDIAS' codebase. Even using threads, the execution in most Python interpreters is not parallel because of the Global Interpreter Lock (GIL).[4]

Inter-agent communication is implemented through HTTP, suggesting that 1A1P is supported too. However, there is no way to customise the concurrency model. In other words, the 1A1T and 1A1P models are hard-coded. The maintainers of PHIDIAS validated our analysis, confirming that only an entire model redesign would enable other concurrency models.

---

[4] https://archive.is/5KBqn.

Listing 1.7. Agent execution in SPADE-BDI inherits SPADE's event loops, which in turns are a feature from Python standard library, as demonstrated by these code snippets from the SPADE-BDI (https://github.com/javipalanca/spade_bdi) and SPADE (https://github.com/javipalanca/spade) codebases.

```
# spade_bdi/bdi.py
from spade.agent import Agent
class BDIAgent(Agent):
    # ...

# spade/agent.py
from spade.container import Container
class Agent(object):
    def __init__(self, ...):
        # ...
        self.container = Container()
        # ...
        self.loop = self.container.loop
        # ...

# spade/container.py
class Container(object):
    def __init__(self):
        # ...
        self.loop = get_or_create_eventloop() # uses Python's asyncio API
        # ...

    def run(self, coro: Awaitable) -> None:
        self.loop.run_until_complete(coro)
```

SPADE-BDI. SPADE-BDI [32] is a Python library adding BDI agents on top of SPADE [21]. In turn, SPADE supports inter-agent communication by means of the XMPP protocol, and a notion of agent similar to JADE (cf. [7]). Agents in both SPADE-BDI and SPADE are implemented via Python's native event loops and coroutines, providing native support for AA1EL. In particular, the `BDIAgent` class extends SPADE's `Agent` one, which in turns models the agent's control loop as a coroutine. As shown in Listing 1.7 – taken from SPADE's codebase –, coroutines are executed on event loops via standard Python API. We infer that SPADE-BDI supports the AA1EL and possibly the 1A1P concurrency models – as agents may interact across different processes via XMPP –, whereas customisability is not an option—as far as documented API are concerned.

5 Conclusion, Recommendations, and Future Works

The external concurrency model is a key aspect to be taken into account when designing or using a (BDI) MAS technology. Generally speaking, the more options the better, as applications can be finely tailored to the specific requirements of the problem at hand.

Controllability. Reproducibility and controllability are key aspects of MAS engineering, especially during debug and simulation. When full control is required, AA1T and AA1EL are the best choices, as they enforce a single control flow.

Performance. Better Performance is generally achieved by exploiting parallelism. Although the 1A1T model seems attractive for its simplicity, AA1E is preferable, especially whenever the agent count largely exceeds the logical processors.

Design of BDI Technologies. We argue that designers of BDI technologies should provide means to customise the concurrency model with a dedicated and well-documented API. Doing so requires careful consideration of the concurrency model as early as possible. Building a BDI platform around assumptions on the desired concurrency model may simplify the implementation, but it is likely to backfire later on, limiting extensibility and applicability —for instance, by preventing the system to scale up and down depending on the available resources. If assumptions are to be made due to technical constraints, some choices are more flexible than others; for instance, AA1E can emulate 1A1T and AA1EL, while the opposite does not apply. The key to design BDI platforms capable to adapt to multiple concurrency models is the *complete separation between agents' control loop and their target concurrency abstraction.* Following this principle, it should be possible to write the MAS specification once, then run it unchanged on different concurrency models.

Impact on Internal Concurrency. We discuss how internal concurrency models impact external concurrency models by bounding the maximum *granularity* at which the agent's control loop can be parallelised. However, the influence is bidirectional: binding specific BDI abstractions to one or more control flow (such as 1A1T or AA1T) may hinder further attempts to control the degree of parallelism by exploiting finer-grained internal concurrency models (e.g., parallelise at the level of intentions).

Final Remarks. The external concurrency of BDI agents is a paramount aspect of practical MAS engineering. In this paper, we define clear terminology and taxonomy to support decision-making about concurrency in MAS, addressing both the construction of MAS and the (re)design of BDI technologies. We analyse the state of the art of several relevant BDI technologies, showing that there is heterogeneity in terms of supported concurrency models and their customisability. We advocate for further research efforts to provide BDI technology designers with clear guidelines and best practices regarding practical external concurrency models, favouring harmonisation and standardisation.

5.1   Current Limitations and Future Works

One limitation of our work is that we focus on relatively small set of well-established BDI technologies: this is a deliberate choice of ours. Our intent, in this work, is to give a concise, self-contained, and insightful overview of the technical issues arising from the external concurrency of MAS technologies. However, we acknowledge that this work is just the first step in this direction. Along this line, we plan to apply our inspection on a wider range of MAS technologies, possibly adopting exhaustiveness as a criterion.

In fact, it is worth mentioning that our inspection methodology could be applicable, in principle, to *any* AOP technology, regardless of whether it is BDI or not: *external* concurrency is a key aspect of AOP technologies in general, whereas *internal* concurrency – as it is defined in this paper – is specific for the BDI paradigm—and, specifically, to the notion of *intention*.

Accordingly, we plan to extend our analysis to other AOP technologies, possibly beyond the realm of BDI architectures. Along this line, we also plan to widen the definition of *internal* concurrency, to account for other behavioural abstractions, possibly adopted by other AOP architectures. This would be for instance the case of *behaviours* in JADE [7] or SPADE [32].

Another limitation of our work is that we do not really explore the relationship among concurrency models and agents' *interaction*. While it may be reasonable, for a first exploration of the topic, to consider agent's interaction as a by-product of agent's perceptions and actions – and therefore negligible in terms of concurrency –, we acknowledge that this is a simplification. In particular, this may be too simplistic when AOP technologies are applied to distributed systems (where message passing cannot be reduced to an atomic operation), or when the focus of the MAS technology of choice is interaction itself (e.g. communication protocols).

Accordingly, we plan to extend our analysis to the interaction dimension of MAS. There, we intend to study the interplay among concurrency models and interaction patterns. Along this line, including non-BDI technologies tailored on interaction (cf. Kiko [13]) would be paramount.

Acknowledgements. This work has been partially supported by: (*i*) "WOOD4.0 - Woodworking Machines for Industry 4.0", Emilia-Romagna CUP E69J22007520009; (*ii*) "FAIR–Future Artificial Intelligence Research", Spoke 8 "Pervasive AI" (PNRR, M4C2, Investimento 1.3, Partenariato Esteso PE00000013), funded by the EC under the NextGenerationEU programme; (*iii*) "ENGINES - ENGineering INtElligent Systems around intelligent agent technologies" project funded by the Italian MUR program "PRIN 2022" (G.A. 20229ZXBZM), and (*iv*) 2023 PhD scholarship (PNRR M4C2, Investimento 3.3 DM 352/2022), co-funded by the European Commission and AUSL della Romagna. Also, the authors would like to thank all the researchers and developers who answered our request for comments for their invaluable help.

A   Appendix: Framework Maintainers Interview

```
Dear <Maintainer>,
we are reaching out to you to ask information about <X>.

Our research group is conducting research on how MAS platforms deal with the underlying
    concurrency mechanisms.
We are surveying several technologies to understand how they map the agents' lifecycle on
    the underlying mechanisms:

  1. One-Agent-One-Thread: Each agent is mapped into a single thread.
  2. All-Agents-One-Thread: The whole MAS is executed on a single thread, following a
      scheduling policy (i.e. Round-Robin).
  3. All-Agents-One-Event-Loop: The MAS is executed over an event-loop.
```

4. All-Agents-One-Executor: Similar to case 3, but it uses threads to allocate agents,
   resulting in an effectively parallel execution. We distinguish two sub-cases:
   a. fixed-sized executors (static thread count)
   b. variable-sized (dynamically changing thread count).
5. One-Agent-One-Process: which, internally, could exploit all the above taxonomies to
   execute its control loop.

We inspected your code source and identified that <X> currently supports <list of supported>,
however, we were not able to infer if it can supports <list of not supported>
Would you agree with the previous assertion?

Would it be possible to write custom extensions to implement <list of not supported> with no
   changes to the current code base of <X>?
If not, what about implementing the missing mechanisms directly?
Would it be feasible, in your opinion?
And if so, would you consider it easy, moderate, hard, or very hard?

References

1. Agha, G.A.: Actors: A Model of Concurrent Computation in Distributed Systems. MIT Press Series in Artificial Intelligence. MIT Press, Cambridge (1986). https://doi.org/10.7551/mitpress/1086.001.0001
2. Baiardi, M., Burattini, S., Ciatto, G., Pianini, D.: JaKtA: BDI agent-oriented programming in pure Kotlin. In: Malvone, V., Murano, A. (eds.) EUMAS 2023, vol. 14282, pp. 49–65. Springer, Heidelberg (2023). https://doi.org/10.1007/978-3-031-43264-4_4
3. Baiardi, M., Ciatto, G.: BDI Languages Concurrency Model Survey Repository: v1.0.0 (2024) https://doi.org/10.5281/zenodo.10948573
4. Bainomugisha, E., Carreton, A.L., Cutsem, T.V., Mostinckx, S., Meuter, W.D.: A survey on reactive programming. ACM Comput. Surv. **45**(4), 52:1–52:34 (2013). https://doi.org/10.1145/2501654.2501666
5. Bandini, S., Manzoni, S., Vizzari, G.: Agent Based Modeling and Simulation, pp. 184–197. Springer, New York (2009). https://doi.org/10.1007/978-0-387-30440-3_12
6. Batty, M.: Compositional relaxed concurrency. Phil. Trans. Roy. Soc. A: Math. Phys. Eng. Sci. **375**(2104), 20150406 (2017). https://doi.org/10.1098/rsta.2015.0406
7. Bellifemine, F., Caire, G., Greenwood, D.: Developing Multi-Agent Systems with JADE. Wiley, Hoboken (2007). https://doi.org/10.1002/9780470058411
8. Böhm, C., Jacopini, G.: Flow diagrams, Turing machines and languages with only two formation rules. Commun. ACM **9**(5), 366–371 (1966). https://doi.org/10.1145/355592.365646
9. Bordini, R., Hübner, J., Wooldridge, M.: Programming Multi-Agent Systems in AgentSpeak Using Jason. Wiley Series in Agent Technologies. Wiley, Hoboken (2007). https://doi.org/10.1002/9780470061848
10. Bratman, M.E., Israel, D.J., Pollack, M.E.: Plans and resource-bounded practical reasoning. Comput. Intell. **4**, 349–355 (1988). https://doi.org/10.1111/J.1467-8640.1988.TB00284.X
11. Buettner, D., Kunkel, J., Ludwig, T.: Using non-blocking I/O operations in high performance computing to reduce execution times. In: Ropo, M., Westerholm, J., Dongarra, J. (eds.) EuroPVM/MPI 2009. LNCS, vol. 5759, pp. 134–142. Springer, Heidelberg (2009). https://doi.org/10.1007/978-3-642-03770-2_20

12. Calegari, R., Ciatto, G., Mascardi, V., Omicini, A.: Logic-based technologies for multi-agent systems: a systematic literature review. Auton. Agents Multi-Agent Syst. **35**(1), 1:1–1:67 (2021). https://doi.org/10.1007/s10458-020-09478-3
13. Christie, S.H., Singh, M.P., Chopra, A.K.: Kiko: programming agents to enact interaction models. In: Proceedings of the 2023 International Conference on Autonomous Agents and Multiagent Systems (AAMAS 2023), pp. 1154–1163. IFAAMAS, London (2023). https://www.ifaamas.org/Proceedings/aamas2023/pdfs/p1154.pdf
14. Collier, R.W., Russell, S., Lillis, D.: Reflecting on agent programming with AgentSpeak(L). In: Chen, Q., Torroni, P., Villata, S., Hsu, J., Omicini, A. (eds.) PRIMA 2015. LNCS (LNAI), vol. 9387, pp. 351–366. Springer, Cham (2015). https://doi.org/10.1007/978-3-319-25524-8_22
15. Dabek, F., Zeldovich, N., Kaashoek, F., Mazières, D., Morris, R.: Event-driven programming for robust software. In: Proceedings of the 10th Workshop on ACM SIGOPS European Workshop, EW 10, pp. 186–189. ACM, New York (2002). https://doi.org/10.1145/1133373.1133410
16. Dadel, P., Zielinski, K.: Evolution of reactive streams API for context-aware mobile applications. Comput. Inf. **35**(4), 852–869 (2016). http://www.cai.sk/ojs/index.php/cai/article/view/3379
17. Dastani, M.: 2apl: a practical agent programming language. Auton. Agents Multi Agent Syst. **16**(3), 214–248 (2008)
18. Dijkstra, E.W.: Solution of a problem in concurrent programming control. Commun. ACM **8**(9), 569 (1965). https://doi.org/10.1145/365559.365617
19. D'Urso, F., Longo, C.F., Santoro, C.: Programming intelligent IoT systems with a Python-based declarative tool. In: Proceedings of the 1st Workshop on Artificial Intelligence and Internet of Things co-located with the 18th International Conference of the Italian Association for Artificial Intelligence, 2019. CEUR Workshop Proceedings, vol. 2502, pp. 68–81. CEUR-WS.org (2019). https://ceur-ws.org/Vol-2502/paper5.pdf
20. Elizarov, R., Belyaev, M.A., Akhin, M., Usmanov, I.: Kotlin coroutines: design and implementation. In: Onward! 2021: Proceedings of the 2021 ACM SIGPLAN International Symposium on New Ideas, New Paradigms, and Reflections on Programming and Software, Virtual Event/Chicago, IL, USA, 20–22 October 2021, pp. 68–84. ACM (2021). https://doi.org/10.1145/3486607.3486751
21. Gregori, M.E., Cámara, J.P., Bada, G.A.: A jabber-based multi-agent system platform. In: 5th International Joint Conference on Autonomous Agents and Multiagent Systems (AAMAS 2006), Hakodate, Japan, 8–12 May 2006, pp. 1282–1284. ACM (2006). https://doi.org/10.1145/1160633.1160866
22. Hindriks, K.V.: Programming rational agents in GOAL. In: El Fallah Seghrouchni, A., Dix, J., Dastani, M., Bordini, R.H. (eds.) Multi-Agent Programming, pp. 119–157. Springer, Boston, MA (2009). https://doi.org/10.1007/978-0-387-89299-3_4
23. Hindriks, K.V., de Boer, F.S., van der Hoek, W., Meyer, J.C.: Agent programming in 3apl. Auton. Agents Multi Agent Syst. **2**(4), 357–401 (1999)
24. Hoare, C.A.R.: Communicating sequential processes. Commun. ACM **21**(8), 666–677 (1978). https://doi.org/10.1145/359576.359585
25. Husaini, S.F.: Using the Java native interface. XRDS: Crossroads ACM Maga. Students **4**(2), 18–23 (1997). https://doi.org/10.1145/332100.332105
26. Lamport, L.: Time, clocks, and the ordering of events in a distributed system. Commun. ACM **21**(7), 558–565 (1978). https://doi.org/10.1145/359545.359563
27. Ling, Y., Mullen, T., Lin, X.: Analysis of optimal thread pool size. ACM SIGOPS Oper. Syst. Rev. **34**(2), 42–55 (2000). https://doi.org/10.1145/346152.346320

28. Loring, M.C., Marron, M., Leijen, D.: Semantics of asynchronous JavaScript. In: Ancona, D. (ed.) Proceedings of the 13th ACM SIGPLAN International Symposium on on Dynamic Languages, Vancouver, BC, Canada, 23–27 October 2017, pp. 51–62. ACM (2017). https://doi.org/10.1145/3133841.3133846

29. Milner, R. (ed.): A Calculus of Communicating Systems. LNCS, vol. 92. Springer, Heidelberg (1980). https://doi.org/10.1007/3-540-10235-3

30. Odell, J.: Objects and agents compared. J. Object Technol. **1**(1), 41–53 (2002). https://doi.org/10.5381/JOT.2002.1.1.C4

31. Omicini, A., Ricci, A., Viroli, M.: Artifacts in the A&A meta-model for multi-agent systems. Auton. Agents Multi-Agent Syst. **17**(3), 432–456 (2008). https://doi.org/10.1007/s10458-008-9053-x

32. Palanca, J., Rincon, J.A., Carrascosa, C., Julián, V., Terrasa, A.: A flexible agent architecture in SPADE. In: PAAMS 2022, Proceedings. Lecture Notes in Computer Science, vol. 13616, pp. 320–331. Springer, Heidelberg (2022). https://doi.org/10.1007/978-3-031-18192-4_26

33. Pokahr, A., Braubach, L., Lamersdorf, W.: Jadex: a BDI reasoning engine. In: Bordini, R.H., Dastani, M., Dix, J., El Fallah Seghrouchni, A. (eds.) Multi-Agent Programming. MSASSO, vol. 15, pp. 149–174. Springer, Boston, MA (2005). https://doi.org/10.1007/0-387-26350-0_6

34. Rao, A.S.: AgentSpeak(L): BDI agents speak out in a logical computable language. In: Van de Velde, W., Perram, J.W. (eds.) MAAMAW 1996. LNCS, vol. 1038, pp. 42–55. Springer, Heidelberg (1996). https://doi.org/10.1007/BFb0031845

35. Reisig, W.: Petri Nets: An Introduction, EATCS Monographs on Theoretical Computer Science, vol. 4. Springer, Heidelberg (1985). https://doi.org/10.1007/978-3-642-69968-9

36. Ricci, A., Santi, A.: Concurrent object-oriented programming with agent-oriented abstractions: the ALOO approach. In: Proceedings of AGERE!@SPLASH 2013, pp. 127–138. ACM (2013). https://doi.org/10.1145/2541329.2541333

37. Ricci, A., Santi, A.: From actors and concurrent objects to agent-oriented programming in simpAL. In: Agha, G., et al. (eds.) Concurrent Objects and Beyond. LNCS, vol. 8665, pp. 408–445. Springer, Heidelberg (2014). https://doi.org/10.1007/978-3-662-44471-9_17

38. Rodriguez, S., Gaud, N., Galland, S.: SARL: a general-purpose agent-oriented programming language. In: The 2014 IEEE/WIC/ACM International Conference on Intelligent Agent Technology. IEEE, Warsaw (2014). https://doi.org/10.1109/WI-IAT.2014.156

39. Shoham, Y.: Agent-oriented programming. Artif. Intell. **60**(1), 51–92 (1993). https://doi.org/10.1016/0004-3702(93)90034-9

40. de Silva, L.: An operational semantics for true concurrency in BDI agent systems. In: EAAI 2020, pp. 7119–7126. AAAI Press (2020). https://doi.org/10.1609/AAAI.V34I05.6199

41. de Silva, L., Meneguzzi, F., Logan, B.: BDI agent architectures: a survey. In: Proceedings of the Twenty-Ninth International Joint Conference on Artificial Intelligence, IJCAI 2020, pp. 4914–4921. ijcai.org (2020). https://doi.org/10.24963/ijcai.2020/684

42. Wielemaker, J., Huang, Z., van der Meij, L.: SWI-Prolog and the web. Theory Pract. Log. Program. **8**(3), 363–392 (2008). https://doi.org/10.1017/S1471068407003237

43. Winikoff, M.: JACK^{TM} intelligent agents: an industrial strength platform. In: Bordini, R.H., Dastani, M., Dix, J., El Fallah Seghrouchni, A. (eds.) Multi-Agent Programming. MSASSO, vol. 15, pp. 175–193. Springer, Boston, MA (2005). https://doi.org/10.1007/0-387-26350-0_7
44. Wooldridge, M.J., Jennings, N.R.: Intelligent agents: theory and practice. Knowl. Eng. Rev. **10**(2), 115–152 (1995). https://doi.org/10.1017/S0269888900008122
45. Zatelli, M.R., Ricci, A., Hübner, J.F.: Evaluating different concurrency configurations for executing multi-agent systems. In: Baldoni, M., Baresi, L., Dastani, M. (eds.) EMAS 2015. LNCS (LNAI), vol. 9318, pp. 212–230. Springer, Cham (2015). https://doi.org/10.1007/978-3-319-26184-3_12

SADMA: Scalable Asynchronous Distributed Multi-agent Reinforcement Learning Training Framework

Sizhe Wang, Long Qian, Cairun Yi, Fan Wu, Qian Kou, Mingyang Li, Xingyug Chen, and Xuguang Lan$^{(\boxtimes)}$

National Key Laboratory of Human-Machine Hybrid Augmented Intelligence, National Engineering Research Center for Visual Information and Application, Institute of Artificial Intelligence and Robotics, Xi'an Jiaotong University, Shaanxi 710049, China
{wangsizhe,qianlongym,yicairun,wf_fixer,xjtukouqian, limingyang}@stu.xjtu.edu.cn, {chenxingyu_1990,xglan}@xjtu.edu.cn

Abstract. Multi-agent Reinforcement Learning (MARL) has shown significant success in solving large-scale complex decision-making problems in multi-agent systems (MAS) while facing the challenge of increasing computational cost and training time. MARL algorithms often require sufficient environment exploration to achieve good performance, especially for complex environments, where the interaction frequency and synchronous training scheme can severely limit the overall speed. Most existing RL training frameworks, which utilize distributed training for acceleration, focus on simple single-agent settings and are not scalable to extend to large-scale MARL scenarios. To address this problem, we introduce a **S**calable **A**synchronous **D**istributed **M**ulti-**A**gent RL training framework called **SADMA**, which modularizes the training process and executes the modules in an asynchronous and distributed manner for efficient training. Our framework is powerfully scalable and provides an efficient solution for distributed training of multi-agent reinforcement learning in large-scale complex environments. Code is available at https://github.com/sadmaenv/sadma.

Keywords: Multi-agent Reinforcement Learning · Distributed Training · Large Scale Multi-agent Training

1 Introduction

Multi-Agent Reinforcement Learning (MARL) has achieved remarkable success in many real-world decision-making problems that involve multi-agent systems [10,22] across various domains, such as multi-player strategy games [3,18], network routing [21], and autonomous driving [4]. However, due to the involvement of interactions and cooperation among multiple agents, MARL environments tend to be extremely complex. Existing algorithms often require a lot of

---

S. Wang and L.Qian—Equal contributions.

D. Briola et al. (Eds.): EMAS 2024, LNAI 15152, pp. 64–81, 2025.
https://doi.org/10.1007/978-3-031-71152-7_4

Table 1. Comparison of SADMA with other multi-agent reinforcement learning libraries.

Library	Parallel Env	Distributed Support	Distributed Backend	Flexible Resource Allocation	Asynchronous Training
PyMARL	✓	✗	–	–	✗
MARLlib	✓	✓	Ray	✗	✗
SADMA	✓	✓	ZeroMQ	✓	✓

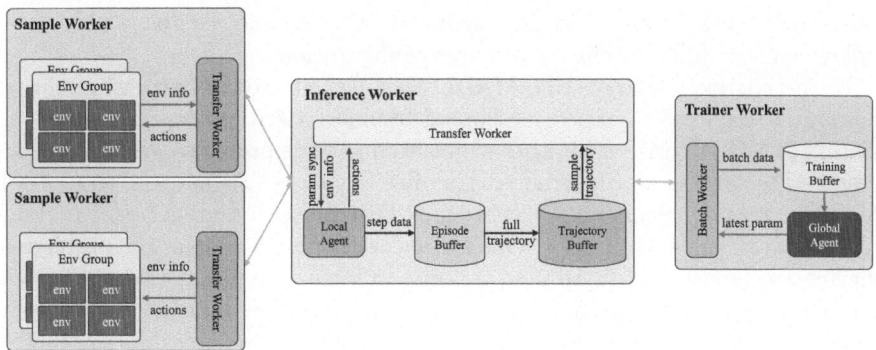

Fig. 1. Overall framework of SADMA. Our framework consists of five modules, each of which runs on a separate process and can be deployed anywhere in the cluster in a distributed manner with a unified data transfer interface. The sample worker is responsible for managing the execution of environmental entities, the inference worker generates actions based on the environment information, and the trainer worker updates network parameters using sampled data and sends the latest parameters to the inference worker.

interactions with the environment to learn effective strategies [24]. Furthermore, as the number of agents increases, the speed of interaction with environments may severely decrease due to the escalating complexity of inference within environments. This results in the need for extensive training time, particularly in intricate environments (Table 1).

In order to reduce training time, some researchers have suggested running multiple instances of the environment in parallel using multiprocessing techniques to improve the sample efficiency. Existing multi-agent reinforcement learning libraries such as PyMARL [17] and PyMARL2 [8] utilize python's multiprocess programming technique to realize environment parallelism. However, when confronted with large-scale complex multi-agent environments, environment instances may run very slowly and consume a lot of resources. Limited by the computational resources of a single machine, simple environment parallelism still cannot fulfill the demand. Although there are some relatively accessible open-source distributed RL algorithm libraries, such as RLlib [12], which utilize

Ray [15] as the distributed framework, their focus is on single-agent RL algo-rithms, with limited support for MARL algorithms. Recently, MARLlib [9] was introduced as an extension of RLlib to provide support for multi-agent reinforce-ment learning algorithms. However, MARLlib mainly focuses on the encapsu-lation and integration of algorithms and environments, and does not provide a diverse and flexible distributed training scheme for multi-agent reinforcement learning algorithms. In addition, MARLlib only implements a distributed sam-pling process, which is not able to utilize the distributed GPU resources to make full use of cluster computing resources to accelerate training. To the best of our knowledge, there is no open source unified framework for distributed training of multi-agent reinforcement learning algorithms that enables flexible and scalable deployment for different cluster resource configurations.

In the context of large-scale MARL training, effectively harnessing cluster computing resources to expedite training becomes a critical concern. However, existing MARL algorithm libraries suffer from various problems and limitations when facing large-scale distributed training demands. To address these chal-lenges, we propose **S**calable **A**synchronous **D**istributed **M**ulti-**A**gent RL train-ing framework called **SADMA**. Our framework hopes to address the problem of efficient acceleration of distributed training in large-scale multi-agent reinforce-ment learning training scenarios. Our framework leverages multiprocessing tech-niques and the lightweight asynchronous messaging library ZeroMQ (ZMQ) [7] to construct a flexible distributed training framework. We specifically analyse the causes of training time consumption in multi-agent reinforcement learning, and use efficient distributed parallel sampling and asynchronous training to fur-ther reduce the waiting time during the training process. To enable flexible distributed deployment and asynchronous training, we decouple and modularize the MARL training process. In addition, we design efficient and unified data transfer interfaces for cross-process and cross-machine communication, bringing flexibility and scalability to distributed deployments. Our framework adapts to different cluster configurations, allowing flexible deployment of modules in clus-ters to fully utilize computing resources. Furthermore, our framework is easy to use and deploy, and with the help of deployment systems such as Kubernetes [13], it is possible to efficiently run distributed training tasks in large-scale clus-ters. Our framework offers the following advantages:

- **Scalability**. Our framework is designed to be deployed in large-scale clus-ters, allowing efficient utilization of computational resources thus achieving significant training acceleration.
- **Modularization**. We modularize the MARL training process to simplify algorithms construction and provide support for distributed training.
- **Asynchronicity**. We decouple the modules to run the sampling and training process asynchronously, reducing the waiting time to achieve higher resource utilization and runtime speeds.
- **Flexibility**. Modules can be combined and flexibly deployed anywhere in the cluster to adapt to various cluster resource configurations.

2   Related Work

The success of Deep Reinforcement Learning(RL) is inseparable from huge data and computing power, which leads to huge demand for distributed learning that can speed up overall training and improve computational resource utilization.

Due to the structured computation pattern of RL algorithms, some successful RL methods are proposed for improving sample and training efficiency. Early algorithms improve sampling efficiency by interacting with multiple environments simultaneously, such as Advantage Actor-Critic (A2C) [11], which aggregates sample data and then performs SGD [16] iterations, using the updated strategy to continue collecting new samples. Asynchronous Advantage Actor-Critic (A3C) [14] uses multiple independent actors, each holding a policy copy, to perform environment simulation sampling, action inference, and gradient computation, respectively. GA3C [2], which is a hybrid CPU/GPU version of the A3C, introduces a separate learner component that uses the GPU for action generation and learning in an asynchronous implementation. These algorithms make previous non-distributed DRL methods distributed using one machine.

Based on these efficient algorithms, some frameworks extend to distributed training on multiple machines. Among them, IMPALA (Importance Weighted Actor-Learner Architecture) [6] uses a GA3C-like architecture where parallel actors communicate with environments, collect trajectories, and send them to the learners for parameter updating. Since gradient calculation is put on the learners' side, which can be accelerated with GPUs, the framework is claimed to scale to thousands of machines without sacrificing data efficiency. Based on IMPALA, SEEDRL (Scalable, Efficient, Deep-RL) [5] achieves further performance improvements through a centralized inference architecture and an optimized communication layer. The communication between learners and actors is mere states and actions reducing latency.

On the basis of these algorithms, a series of open-source distributed RL libraries and frameworks have been produced, some of which provide support for multi-agent reinforcement learning. RLlib [12] integrates a large number of RL algorithms into a high-performance, scalable distributed algorithm framework based on Ray [15]. However, its framework lacks the flexibility to control the details of distributed training to achieve targeted performance optimization, and code packaging is complex. MAlib [25] also develops a framework for distributed MARL algorithms based on population training with Ray. MARLlib [9] is a new distributed MARL library that combines the core advantages of Ray and RLlib, but does not provide a flexible distributed deployment scheme to effectively utilize distributed computing resources. There is still no flexible and scalable distributed training framework for multi-agent reinforcement learning algorithms. Our training framework is different from existing algorithm libraries in that we modularize the training process and run the modules asynchronously to achieve higher training efficiency; we use ZMQ, a high-performance asynchronous messaging library, instead of ray to build a flexible and scalable distributed deployment scheme.

3   Framework Design

In this section, we specifically describe the overall design and characteristics of SADMA. The overall framework is shown in Fig. 1. Based on multi-process techniques and the asynchronous messaging library ZMQ, we build a unified data transfer interface to facilitate efficient communication between processes to achieve compatibility with cross-process and cross-machine data transfer. We modularize the multi-agent reinforcement learning training process and employ asynchronous execution to reduce the waiting time in the original synchronous training process as much as possible. We perform a number of specific performance optimizations for sampling and training to further increase runtime speed and improve resource utilization. Our framework has great scalability and flexibility to adapt to different cluster resource configurations, and is able to support large-scale MARL training and effectively utilize cluster resources to reduce training time.

3.1   High-Performance Data Transfer Scheme

Cross-Process Data Transfer. In parallel computing, multiprocess programming has become a common way to fully utilize multi-core processors and improve program performance. However, for multi-agent reinforcement learning training tasks, frequent data transfers between processes are usually necessary, which requires efficient data transfer mechanisms to reduce the waiting time. We use cross-process data transfer scheme for modules running on the same machine. To handle CPU-side data, we build pipes for inter-process data transfer. To avoid unnecessary data copying, we utilize shared memory for frequently read and written data, such as replay buffers. As for GPU-side data, which are shared across processes, we exclusively transfer pointers to circumvent resource-intensive data transfers.

Cross-Machine Data Transfer. To achieve high-performance distributed training, improving the efficiency of cross-machine data transfer is paramount. Existing distributed reinforcement learning training frameworks typically employ Ray, an open-source unified compute framework, as their communication scheme. However, despite its user-friendliness, Ray is not lightweight and efficient enough. Since large-scale multi-agent environments may involve hundreds of agents with large observation dimensions, there is a high demand for distributed training data transfer. In pursuit of efficiency, we employ ZMQ, a lightweight and high-performance messaging library, to facilitate more expedited cross-machine data transfer. With the advantages of flexibility, reliability, high-performance and lightweight, ZMQ is ideally suited to handle the frequent data transfer requirements in large-scale multi-agent reinforcement learning training. Recently some researchers have also evaluated the speed benefits of ZMQ for communication [1]. We conduct a comparative analysis of the cross-machine transfer efficiency between ZMQ and Ray for various data sizes. Figure 2 shows that ZMQ

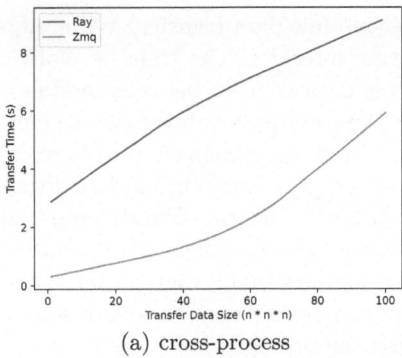

(a) cross-process

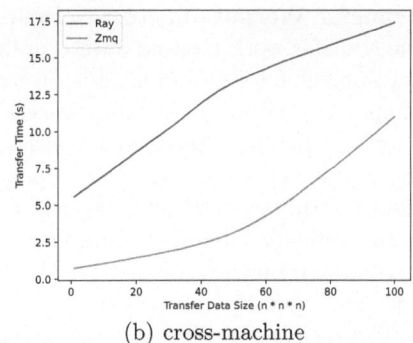

(b) cross-machine

Fig. 2. Cross-process and cross-machine data transfer speed comparison between ZMQ and Ray. We test the time consumption at different transfer data sizes. We create arrays of shape (N, N, N) and varied N from 1 to 100, with the horizontal axis representing the size of N, and transfer each array 1000 times.

is more efficient than Ray for both cross-process and cross-machine communication, especially for cross-machine transfers. This supports our choice of ZMQ as the efficient data transfer scheme.

Unified Transfer Interface Design. In order to flexibly adapt to single-machine and cross-machine data transfer, we unified the data transfer interface. We wrap these two data transfer schemes into a unified interface at the code level, which decides which scheme should be used for the current transfer based on the configuration. This unified design can bring many benefits. First, it simplifies programming at the code level so that users do not need to care about the tedious communication approach, and only need to set it in the configuration file. Second, it enhances the flexibility of our distributed training framework, enabling modules to be easily deployed across the distributed cluster without the need for custom communication implementations for each module.

3.2 Modular Design

In order to support distributed training, we modularize the training process so as to fully utilize the computational resources to run each module asynchronously to reduce the waiting time and improve the overall training speed. Our overall modularized design is shown in Fig. 1. The detailed functions of each module are described below.

Transfer Worker. In order to facilitate inter-module data transfer, we develop the transfer worker based on the unified transfer interface. The transfer Worker is responsible for cross-machine or cross-process data transfer between modules. It operates within a separate process and employs multiple sub-threads to concurrently handle inter-module data transfer operations, eliminating data waiting times that could otherwise impact the main program's execution. Benefiting from the unified transfer interface design, transfer worker can flexibly adapt to both single-machine and cross-machine inter-process communication scenarios. In combination with the transfer Worker, other modules enable high-performance and flexible data transfers that can be deployed in clusters of various resource configurations for efficient and convenient distributed training.

Sample Worker. Large-scale MARL tasks typically require massive amounts of interaction data for training. However, due to limitations in the inference speed of the environments, running a single environment for data sampling cannot efficiently provide the required training data in a timely manner. The prevailing approach is to parallelize multiple environments using multiprocessing techniques to accelerate the data sampling process. Hence, we construct the sample worker which is responsible for managing the interactions of multiple parallel environments.

Each sample worker contains a designated number of parallel environments that utilize multiprocessing techniques to fully leverage computing resources. In order to achieve better scalability and resource utilization, we separate and asynchronously execute environment interaction and policy inference. The sample worker refrains from conducting policy inference and instead focuses solely on managing the execution of environment instances. When interacting with the environment, the sample worker transfers all the environmental information to the inference worker via the transfer worker, and then the inference worker performs policy inference based on the transferred data and returns the corresponding actions to the sampler worker. After receiving the actions, the sample worker executes actions for corresponding environments and collects the information returned from the environment and transfers them to the inference worker again. All parallel environments interact synchronously.

Separating the environment execution from the policy inference can bring benefits to distributed training. Since policy inference involves neural network computation, which generally requires GPU, while environment execution only requires CPU, we can flexibly allocate computing resources to the inference worker and sampler worker for different cluster configurations to fully utilize the cluster resources.

Inference Worker. The inference worker is responsible for policy inference to provide actions for interacting with the environment. The inference worker creates the episode buffer for each environment it is responsible for, since complete episodes are often used as training data in MARL algorithms such as QMIX. The environment information transferred from the sample worker and the policy inference data are saved in the corresponding episode buffer after each interaction step. When an episode is finished, the full trajectory of the agent's interaction with the environment will be stored in the trajectory buffer in memory, which contains the observations, actions, rewards and other useful information at each step. In order to save unnecessary memory consumption, the number of episodes stored in the trajectory buffer can be less than the number of environments. The data in the trajectory buffer is ready and just waiting to be used for training.

In the case of on-policy algorithms such as IPPO [19], when the trajectory buffer reaches its capacity, it will no longer accept new trajectories from the episode buffer. If there is no free space in the trajectory buffer at the end of an episode in the episode buffer, the inference worker will be temporarily stopped until the data in the trajectory buffer are consumed. This limits the generation of outdated data, which can impact the performance of the on-policy algorithm. Although our framework runs asynchronously, there are still synchronization constraints for the On-policy algorithm, which allows us to approach the training bottleneck speed with the guaranteed quality of the sampled data.

Batch Worker. In the context of multi-agent reinforcement learning algorithms, the typical requirement is to train on a batch of episodes at once. To support large-scale distributed sampling, we allow the setup of multiple distributed inference workers. Once these episodes are collected, they must be organized into a batch and prepared for training on the GPU. Consequently, there is a need to transfer the data collected in the trajectory buffer to the trainer worker. To address this data management challenge, we introduce the batch worker that collaborates with the trainer worker.

The batch worker's role is to consolidate episode data from each inference worker into a batch and then transfer this batched data onto the GPU, placing it into the training buffer. The trainer worker, in turn, retrieves the training data directly from the GPU using data addresses. The batch worker runs asynchronously on a separate process without affecting the trainer worker. It operates as a data processing module, preparing data required for the upcoming training in advance while the trainer worker focuses on policy updates. This approach eliminates the need for the trainer worker to wait for data to be processed, resulting in significant time savings.

Trainer Worker The role of the trainer worker primarily centers around agent training and synchronization. With the presence of a batch worker, the trainer worker is relieved from the burden of tedious data processing. This streamlined workflow enables the trainer worker to devote undivided attention to agent training, resulting in improved efficiency. During each training step, the trainer worker acquires the pre-processed batch data from the training buffer and proceeds with the parameter update process. Subsequently, it dispatches the most recent parameters to each inference worker, ensuring parameter synchronization across the system. Both the trainer worker and the training buffer are located on the GPU, thus facilitating fast data communication. By design, the trainer

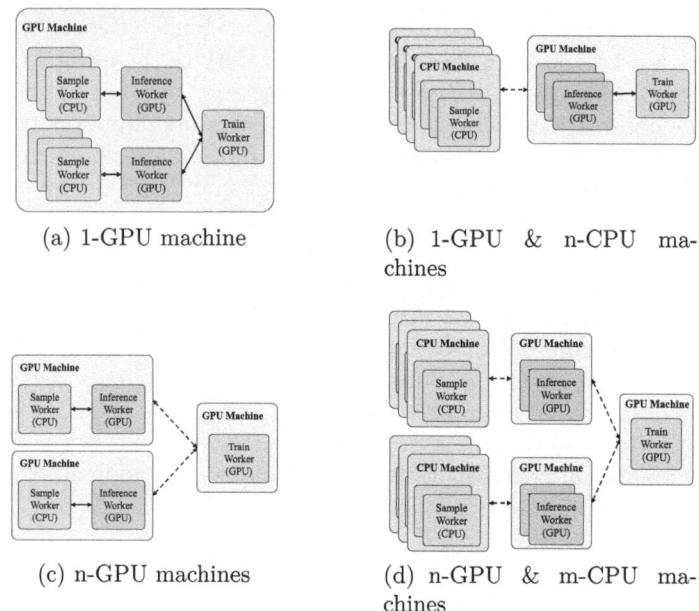

(a) 1-GPU machine

(b) 1-GPU & n-CPU ma-
chines

(c) n-GPU machines

(d) n-GPU & m-CPU ma-
chines

Fig. 3. Flexible distributed deployment in different cluster resource configurations. Solid arrows represent cross-process communication and dashed lines represent cross-machine communication

worker is devoid of superfluous functions, guaranteeing its efficient execution of training tasks. This optimization enhances the performance and responsiveness of the trainer worker, ultimately accelerating the overall training process.

3.3   Flexible Resource Allocation

Existing libraries usually do not focus on performance issues in large-scale distributed training scenarios, but more on algorithm integration and packaging. The most important difference between our framerwork and theirs is that we design our framework for deployment and performance issues in distributed training scenarios. This gives our framework a greater advantage for training multi-agent reinforcement learning algorithms in large-scale complex scenarios.

Benefiting from the modularized design and unified data transfer interface, each module can be flexibly combined with each other and assigned to different computing nodes in the cluster regardless of the hardware device restrictions. This facilitates deployment on clusters with different resource configurations. Our framework naturally adapts to different resource configurations and thus can fully utilize cluster resources to accelerate training. In the following we describe in detail several different configuration types supported by our framework, as shown in Fig. 3.

1-GPU Machine. Although our framework is designed for distributed training, considering that a single workstation may be sufficient for small-scale algorithm development, we still take into account the adaptation and runtime performance on a single machine, as shown in Fig. 3(a). In the single-computer case, the data between modules does not need to be transferred based on the network, but only needs to be considered for cross-process transfer. We use inter-process pipelines and shared memory to realize the communication, which ensures the efficiency of training.

1-GPU and N-CPU Machines. When there are limited GPU computing nodes, for example, there is only one GPU node and the rest are CPU nodes, as shown in Fig. 3(b). In this case, there are two general approaches. One is to run only multiple parallel environments on the CPU node, because the environments only need CPU resources to run. Then both the training module and the inference module are placed on the GPU node as its involved in the computation of the neural network. Another approach is to run the parallel environments and the corresponding inference modules on the CPU nodes and the GPU nodes perform only the training. Each of these two approaches has its own advantages. For the first scheme, since only the environment instance is running on the CPU node, there is no need to design the cross-node transfer of model parameters, which is time-consuming when the model parameters are large. However, the CPU node needs to wait for the GPU node to send back the inference results at every environment interaction, hence there is a delay. For the second scheme, since both the inference module and the environment run on the CPU node, there is no environment interaction delay as in the first scheme, but the network inference using the CPU will be slower, and it needs to communicate with the GPU node periodically to synchronize the model parameters. Existing libraries usually focus on algorithm encapsulation and integration, and do not provide optional distributed training schemes. Our framework, on the other hand, can flexibly adapt to a variety of different configurations and only requires modification of the configuration file without additional code changes.

N-GPU Machines. When all the computing nodes in the cluster have GPUs, our framework can more fully utilize GPU resources to accelerate training unlike MARLlib which is unable to utilize distributed GPU resources. Since the modules can be freely combined, we can run the parallel environment and the corresponding inference modules on multiple GPU nodes, as shown in Fig. 3(c). Moreover, in order to accelerate inference and improve GPU utilization efficiency, we can run multiple parallel environments with multiple inference modules on a single GPU node, and try to place each inference module on a different GPU card so as to make the load of GPU cards as balanced as possible. The training modules can also be deployed on any node with spare resources. This flexible configuration scheme can fully utilize the resources of each computing node, and thus can show advantages when facing distributed training of large-scale complex

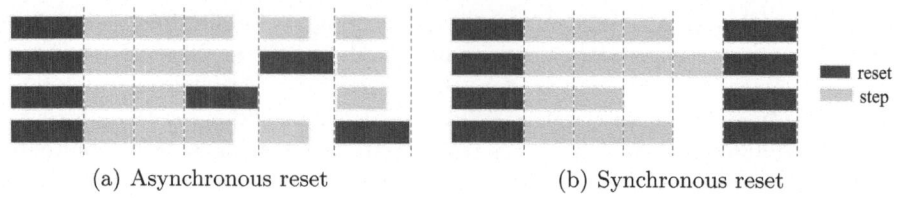

(a) Asynchronous reset   (b) Synchronous reset

Fig. 4. Synchronous and asynchronous environment reset.

tasks. Existing libraries, such as MARLlib, do not have the ability to utilize GPU resources across nodes, which limits their use in large-scale distributed training.

N-GPU and M-CPU Machines. When having multiple CPU nodes and GPU nodes, as shown in Fig. 3(d), our framework can flexibly deploy different computational tasks for different nodes' computational resources. We can run parallel environment instances on CPU nodes and then run inference modules on GPU nodes. And in order to improve resource utilization, we can group multiple CPU nodes, assign one GPU node to be responsible for inference, and run multiple inference module instances on this node for load balancing. For the training module, it can still be assigned to any GPU node with remaining resources. Moreover, when there are enough GPU nodes, the training module can also be deployed on a free GPU node and utilize multi-card accelerated training to cope with large-scale training data demand.

3.4   High-Performance Specific Optimization

To address the training process as well as our distributed framework, we use a series of targeted performance optimizations to improve the sampling speed and training speed. The specific optimization scheme is as follows.

Synchronous and Asynchronous Environment Reset. Our framework supports both synchronous and asynchronous environment reset modes. The difference between these two modes is shown in Fig. 4. When interacting with environments, we adopt batch inference to process information from multiple environments at the same time. In synchronous reset mode, we wait for the end of the episodes of all environments before resetting them, while in asynchronous reset mode, we reset an environment as soon as its episode ends. Both synchronous and asynchronous resets have their own advantages and disadvantages. When environment reset takes too long, adopting asynchronous reset mode may cause the overall interaction speed to decrease. This is because we need to wait for all environments to return information before performing policy inference, which can result in a long wait if an environment is being reset. In this case, synchronous reset mode may be better because it only needs to wait for the last environment to finish its episodes and spend one reset time to reset

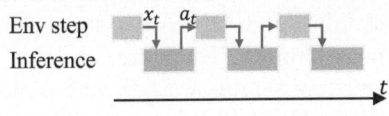

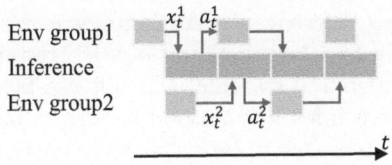

(a) Single-environment interactions   (b) Multi-environment interactions

Fig. 5. Illustration of single-environment and multi-environment group interactions. The blue rectangle represents the environment execution process and the orange rectangle represents the policy inference process. x_t ($Color\,figure\,online$) denotes the observation at the moment t and a_t denotes the action.

all environments, while asynchronous reset needs to wait for reset frequently. In contrast, asynchronous reset is more advantageous when the environment reset only consumes about the same amount of time as the environment execution. Therefore, when environment reset consumes a lot of time, it is suitable to adopt synchronous reset mode, while when environment reset consumes little time, it is advantageous to adopt asynchronous reset mode. Our framework supports both modes to deal with different application scenarios.

Multi-environment Group. The problem with synchronized environment interaction is that there is a sequential relationship between environment execution and policy inference. This results in sample workers and inference workers always having idle time and not being able to fully utilize compute resources. In order to achieve more efficient environment interaction, we use multi-environment groups to divide the environments managed in the sample worker into multiple groups, as shown in Fig. 5. When an environment group returns the environment information and waits for the inference worker's inference data, the rest of the environment groups perform the environment execution. When the inference worker finishes the inference, the rest of the environment groups will transfer the environment information immediately, so that the inference worker will not be in an idle state.

Batch Inference. Considering that multi-agent environments tend to have large observation dimensions due to a large number of agents and in order to speed up sampling, multiple sample workers are created in a distributed manner for sampling. However, if only one inference worker is allocated to these sample workers, since it is a synchronized environment interaction, it will result in the need to wait for the slowest environment to return observations. The existing practice of distributed reinforcement learning frameworks is to configure an inference worker for each sample worker to ensure efficient inference. However, since inference worker contains neural networks, too many inference workers can lead to a large amount of GPU resources consumption in the case of large-scale distributed training, which is not favorable for scalability. Therefore, we use the batch inference method to form a batch of multiple sample workers and assign an inference to be responsible for the interaction. This will bring flexibility and efficiency to the construction of the sampling process. This is not as fast as assigning an inference worker to each sample worker, since the time it takes for an environment to return batch information depends on the slowest environment, and the inference time increases due to the increase in the amount of data, but it allows the user to be more flexible and fully utilize the distributed computing resources. We can control GPU usage by controlling the number of inference workers. This design brings powerful scalability to distributed sampling.

4   Experiments

In this section, we evaluate the performance of the proposed SADMA framework. We choose to compare it with PyMARL2, a classic single-computer multi-agent reinforcement learning algorithm library, and MARLlib, the latest MARL algorithm library with distributed support, as baselines. In order to fully demonstrate the advantages of our framework, we test the efficiency under different computational resource scenarios on single-machine and multi-machine settings respectively. Considering that PyMARL2 itself does not provide a distributed deployment program, we only compare it with MARLlib in the multi-computer scenario. We use two different hardware configurations: (1) System#1: 128-core workstation with 8 GPUs; (2) System#2: a four-node cluster with each node owning 64-core and 4 GPUs. All the GPUs mentioned are of the same model (NVIDIA RTX3090). We describe the specific experimental setup and results below.

4.1   Throughput Comparisons

Throughput measures the sampling speed of the framework, which affects the overall training efficiency. Faster sampling speed reduces waiting time by providing the sample data needed for training in time. We compare to baselines under different resource configurations for single and multiple machines settings.

We choose the classical multi-agent reinforcement learning environment SMAC for testing. To increase the complexity of the environment interaction, we choose 27 m_vs_30m map in SMAC. Considering that multi-agent reinforcement learning includes on-policy algorithms like IPPO and off-policy algorithms like QMIX, these two categories of algorithms have different sampling processes, which may lead to different sampling speeds. We separately test the throughput under these two types of algorithms. In order to compare the sampling speed under different computational resource conditions, we gradually increase the CPU core utilization from 1 to 256 to test the throughput. To mitigate the

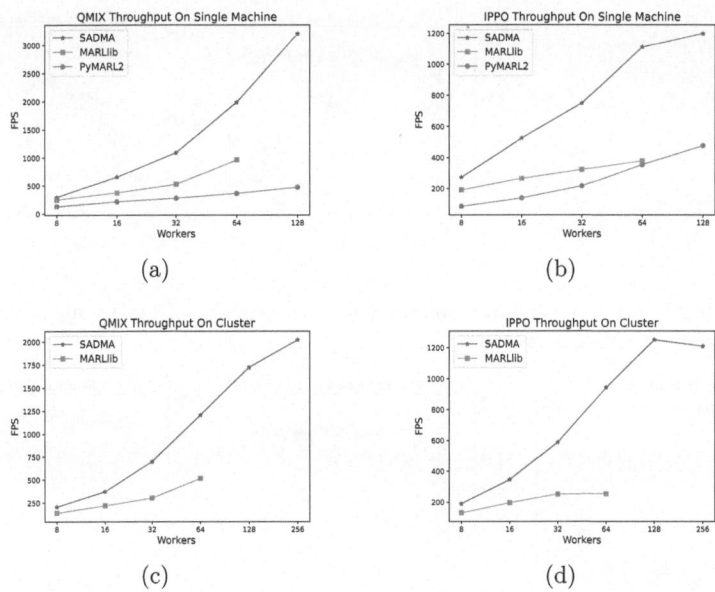

Fig. 6. Throughput comparison results. The horizontal coordinate represents the number of CPU cores used for sampling, with each core running one environment instance. Due to the high GPU memory usage of MARLlib, there is a memory overflow when setting the number of workers to 128, so we only tested to 64 workers.

impact of server performance fluctuations on the tests, we run the training program continuously for 5 minutes after it is fully initiated to calculate the average sampling speed.

Figure 6 shows the comparison results. It can be seen that the sampling speed of our framework is excellent on both single and multiple machines. Since PyMARL2 is a serial training process and does not set up different processes for sampling and training, its sampling speed is slower. Benefiting from the asynchronous training process and targeted optimization schemes, our framework can achieve higher sampling speeds. However, while MARLlib is capable of distributed parallel sampling, it does not have a targeted distributed optimization for the multi-agent reinforcement learning training process, resulting in poor performance and scalability. For the performance degradation at 256 workers in Fig. 6(d), we believe that this is due to the training speed bottleneck caused by setting the training batch of IPPO to 64. This means that in this case, the bottleneck of the whole system is no longer limited by the sampling speed, but by the policy training speed.

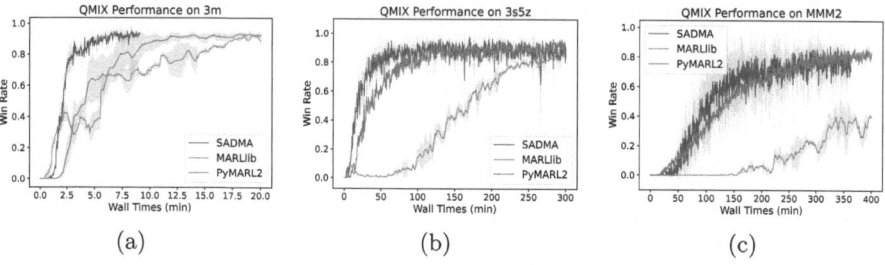

Fig. 7. Comparison of wall times required for convergence of QMIX algorithms with the same resource allocation.

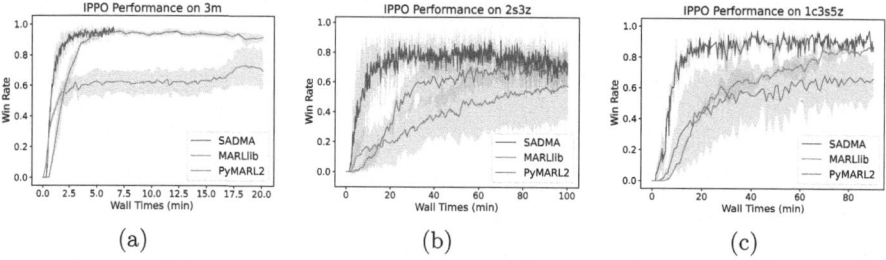

Fig. 8. Comparison of wall times required for convergence of IPPO algorithms with the same resource allocation.

4.2 Convergence Acceleration

Although our framework has a higher sampling speed, it remains a question whether this is effective in improving the wall times necessary for the algorithm to converge. Therefore, we compare the wall times of each framework to make the algorithm converge with the same resource configuration. For comparison with the convergence performance of the algorithm in PyMARL2, we test it on the single-machine configuration. We choose several maps in SMAC to test the convergence speed of each framework with the QMIX and IPPO algorithms. We uniformly set the number of workers to 8 and ensure that other parameters are consistent.

Figure 7 and Fig. 8 show the convergence of the QMIX and IPPO algorithm in each framework on different maps respectively. It can be seen that our curves are always above PyMARL2 and MARLlib, which indicates that our framework is able to effectively utilize the computational resources to improve the convergence speed of the algorithms under the same resource configuration. This demonstrates the efficiency of our framework. This is achieved by SADMA building an asynchronous training flow through efficient inter-process communication to increase the training speed. For off-policy algorithms such as QMIX, we decouple the environment sampling and training processes to run asynchronously, thus reducing the waiting time due to sampling.

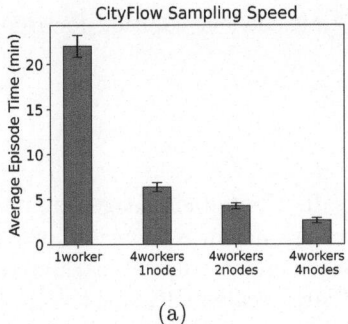
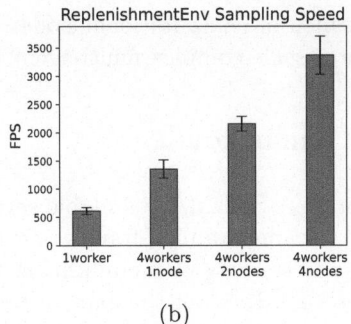

(a)   (b)

Fig. 9. Distributed sampling speed with different resource configurations. An episode in the CityFlow environment contains 242 steps.

4.3   Scalability Evaluation

In order to evaluate the scalability of SADMA for large-scale multi-agent environments, we construct two environments with more than 1000 agents. The first one is based on the CityFlow [23] environment with 1225 agents. Each agent controls an intersection, with each intersection having an 18-dimensional observation containing information about the distribution of vehicles in each lane, and an 8-dimensional discrete action control signal. The second one is a replenishment environment containing 1000 agents [20], where each agent needs to control one stock keeping unit (SKU) for storage, acquisition, and distribution to meet customer demands and optimize costs. The observation of each agent contains both SKU features and warehouse states totaling 87 dimensions. The agent needs to select actions in a 34-dimensional discrete action space to represent replenishment based on observations. Due to the large number of agents, running an episode of the environment takes a lot of time and memory. At the same time, single-step policy inference needs to compute the actions of all the agents, which leads to slower inference and larger GPU memory usage. In this case, SADMA can flexibly build a distributed training process similar to IMPALA, deploying the inference worker with the corresponding environment instances on the same compute node to ensure scalability. However, MARLlib cannot deploy the training flow flexibly.

Figure 9 shows the sampling speedup obtained by allocating different computational resources. For the CityFlow environment containing 1000+ agents, it is too slow to be able to develop and evaluate algorithms. While our framework can easily implement distributed scaling to accelerate training, opening up the possibility of researching large-scale complex muti-agent environments. For the Replenishment environment, where millions of steps are often required for good performance, the efficiency of sampling and training can be further improved with distributed scaling. The distribution flexibility of SADMA brings powerful scalability and compatibility, which can theoretically scale to hundreds or thousands of computational nodes, providing an efficient solution for research on large-scale complex multi-agent tasks.

5 Conclusion

We propose SADMA, a scalable asynchronous distributed multi-agent reinforcement learning training framework. Our framework achieves asynchronous sampling and training by modularizing the multi-agent reinforcement learning training process. In order to adapt to the needs of large-scale multi-agent body reinforcement learning training, we build a high-performance unified data transfer interface based on ZMQ and multi-process techniques, which makes it easy to deploy each module at any location in the cluster to fully utilize the computational resources. We also optimize the training process to further improve the speed. We compare the training efficiency of existing algorithm libraries under different resource configurations, and the results show that our framework is more efficient and scalable to satisfy the needs of large-scale distributed training. We hope to use our framework to build a generalized distributed multi-agent reinforcement learning algorithm library to accelerate the algorithm research and application. In future work, we will further improve our framework and add more algorithms and environment support.

Acknowledgement. This work was supported in part by National Key R&D Program of China under grant No.2021ZD0112700, NSFC under grant No.62125305, No.U23A20339, No.62088102, No.62203348.

References

1. Ahmad, M.F.: Public opinion and persuasion of algorithmic fairness: assessment of communication protocol performance for use in simulation-based reinforcement learning training. Int. J. Inf. Technol. **16**(2), 687–696 (2024)
2. Babaeizadeh, M., Frosio, I., Tyree, S., Clemons, J., Kautz, J.: Reinforcement learning through asynchronous advantage actor-critic on a gpu. arXiv preprint arXiv:1611.06256 (2016)
3. Berner, C., et al.: Dota 2 with large scale deep reinforcement learning. arXiv preprint arXiv:1912.06680 (2019)
4. Cao, Y., Yu, W., Ren, W., Chen, G.: An overview of recent progress in the study of distributed multi-agent coordination. IEEE Trans. Ind. Inf. **9**(1), 427–438 (2012)
5. Espeholt, L., Marinier, R., Stanczyk, P., Wang, K., Michalski, M.: Seed rl: scalable and efficient deep-rl with accelerated central inference. arXiv preprint arXiv:1910.06591 (2019)
6. Espeholt, L., et al.: Impala: scalable distributed deep-rl with importance weighted actor-learner architectures. In: International Conference on Machine Learning, pp. 1407–1416. PMLR (2018)
7. Hintjens, P.: ZeroMQ: Messaging for Many Applications. O'Reilly Media, Inc., Newton (2013)

8. Hu, J., Jiang, S., Harding, S.A., Wu, H., Liao, S.W.: Rethinking the implementation tricks and monotonicity constraint in cooperative multi-agent reinforcement learning. arXiv preprint arXiv:2102.03479 (2021)

9. Hu, S., et al.: Marllib: extending rllib for multi-agent reinforcement learning. arXiv preprint arXiv:2210.13708 (2022)

10. Huh, D., Mohapatra, P.: Multi-agent reinforcement learning: a comprehensive survey. arXiv preprint arXiv:2312.10256 (2023)

11. Konda, V., Tsitsiklis, J.: Actor-critic algorithms. Adv. Neural Inf. Process. Syst. **12** (1999)

12. Liang, E., et al.: Rllib: abstractions for distributed reinforcement learning. In: International Conference on Machine Learning, pp. 3053–3062. PMLR (2018)

13. Luksa, M.: Kubernetes in action. Simon and Schuster (2017)

14. Mnih, V., et al.: Asynchronous methods for deep reinforcement learning. In: International Conference on Machine Learning, pp. 1928–1937. PMLR (2016)

15. Moritz, P., et al.: Ray: A distributed framework for emerging {AI} applications. In: 13th USENIX Symposium on Operating Systems Design and Implementation (OSDI 2018), pp. 561–577 (2018)

16. Robbins, H., Monro, S.: A stochastic approximation method. Ann. Math. Stat. 400–407 (1951)

17. Samvelyan, M., et al.: The starcraft multi-agent challenge. arXiv preprint arXiv:1902.04043 (2019)

18. Vinyals, O., et al.: Alphastar: mastering the real-time strategy game starcraft ii. DeepMind Blog **2**, 20 (2019)

19. de Witt, C.S., et al.: Is independent learning all you need in the starcraft multi-agent challenge? arXiv preprint arXiv:2011.09533 (2020)

20. Yang, X., et al.: A versatile multi-agent reinforcement learning benchmark for inventory management. arXiv preprint arXiv:2306.07542 (2023)

21. Ye, D., Zhang, M., Yang, Y.: A multi-agent framework for packet routing in wireless sensor networks. Sensors **15**(5), 10026–10047 (2015)

22. Yuan, L., Zhang, Z., Li, L., Guan, C., Yu, Y.: A survey of progress on cooperative multi-agent reinforcement learning in open environment. arXiv preprint arXiv:2312.01058 (2023)

23. Zhang, H., et al.: Cityflow: a multi-agent reinforcement learning environment for large scale city traffic scenario. In: The World Wide Web Conference, pp. 3620–3624 (2019)

24. Zhang, K., Yang, Z., Başar, T.: Multi-agent reinforcement learning: a selective overview of theories and algorithms. In: Handbook of Reinforcement Learning and Control, pp. 321–384 (2021)

25. Zhou, M., et al.: Malib: a parallel framework for population-based multi-agent reinforcement learning. J. Mach. Learn. Res. **24**, 150–1 (2023)

Synergizing Trust and Autonomy: Gaia-X Enabled Multi-Agent Ecosystems for Advanced Freight Fleet Management

Dennis Maecker[1]([✉]) [iD], Felix Harenbrock[2] [iD], Henning Gösling[1] [iD], Timon Sachweh[3], and Oliver Thomas[1]

[1] German Research Institute for Artificial Intelligence, Osnabrück, Germany
{dennis.maecker,henning.gosling,oliver.thomas}@dfki.de
[2] Embeteco GmbH & Co. KG, Rastede, Germany
fh@embeteco.de
[3] TU Dortmund University, Dortmund, Germany
timon.sachweh@tu-dortmund.de

Abstract. This paper explores the integration of the Gaia-X framework into a Multi-Agent System (MAS) for managing a smart freight fleet, emphasizing identity and trust management. Focusing on a subsystem of delivery agents and autonomous robots, this study exemplarily illustrates how Gaia-X can be integrated in existing ecosystems consisting of software agents and appertaining services and assets. By utilizing Organizational Credential Managers (OCMs), mediator services and wallets, the paper addresses the challenges of credential management and connectivity for mobile edge devices like delivery robots. This integration showcases the potential of Gaia-X to improve the security and interoperability of smart freight systems, contributing to the advancement of trusted digital ecosystems in the logistics sector.

Keywords: Multi-Agent System · Autonomous Parcel Delivery · Data Ecosystems · Gaia-X · Smart Managed Freight Fleet

1 Introduction

The increasing demands on logistics due to the rise of e-commerce highlight the need for innovative solutions in last-mile delivery. Multi-Agent Systems (MASs) emerge as a viable solution, leveraging decentralized networks of autonomous delivery robots and other logistics assets to enhance delivery efficiency and adaptability in dynamic environments. These systems facilitate real-time decision-making and optimize delivery routes, addressing the complexities of urban logistics.

However, the decentralized nature of MASs, coupled with the diversity of stakeholders in the logistics ecosystem, presents challenges in data exchange, identity management, and trust. The introduction of the Gaia-X framework [3, 12] into MASs addresses these challenges by establishing a secure, interoperable, and transparent data infrastructure, ensuring data sovereignty and fostering trust among participants. Gaia-X's alignment with European values on data privacy and security further enhances the framework's suitability for complex logistics operations, providing a robust foundation for data exchange and collaboration within MASs.

This paper specifically focuses on a subsystem involving delivery agents and autonomous robots. By exploring the technical aspects of integrating Organizational Credential Managers (OCMs), mediator services, and digital wallets, the study elucidates the mechanisms through which Gaia-X facilitates interaction between agents and freight assets, ensuring secure credential management and reliable connectivity for mobile edge devices.

The paper begins with an introduction to the concept of an implemented Multi-Agent System (MAS) for smart freight management, focusing on the subsystem involving delivery robots (Sect. 2). It proceeds to discuss the Gaia-X framework, emphasizing its significance in enhancing trust and identity within the system. The Hyperledger Aries protocol is examined for its role in secure communications. Following this foundation, the paper details the proposed solution (Sect. 3), incorporating Organizational Credential Managers (OCMs), digital wallets, and mediator services to address the subsystem's challenges. The discussion (Sect. 4) assesses the implication of this work and outlines potential future developments, suggesting directions for advancing the integration of Gaia-X in MASs for logistics.

2 Background

This section first outlines the specific implementation of the MAS that has been developed within the research project and which serves as an example case for elaborating the introduction of the Gaia-X framework. Subsequently, the Gaia-X framework is introduced, focusing on the topics of digital identities and the required technologies.

2.1 The MAS Applied to Freight Fleet Management

The MAS that is used as an application case in this work was conceptualized within the Gaia-X 4 ROMS project, a consortium research endeavor dedicated to the application-oriented establishment of a connected and automated fleet management concept based on fleet assets along intermodal transport chains for parcel deliveries [16, 20]. Therein, a MAS enables the decomposition of complex problems and efficient distribution of both data and control across physical boundaries. The agents in the MAS are envisaged to be deployed on a decentralized server infrastructure. This innovative concept developed in the consortium research project is currently being realized through active collaboration with practitioners and software companies in the transportation sector, ensuring practical applicability and industrial relevance. In a business-focused point of view, the MAS under development can be regarded as a Software-as-a-Service (SaaS) solution, offering the smart management of freight assets not only to carriers of vehicle fleets (e.g., parcel delivery robots, telematics-enabled trailers, and swap-bodies), but also to operators of logistics infrastructure (e.g., workshops and depots). Within the system, agents coordinate tasks, such as parcel delivery orders, using the contract net protocol [26, 36]. Furthermore, the MAS is dependent on auxiliary services, such as Estimated-Time-of-Arrival (ETA) services, routing services as well as platforms for stakeholder interaction, such as operator cockpits or booking platforms for clients. The workshop agent further interfaces with the workshop staff by so-called Freight-Fleet-Glasses, an augmented-reality solution [15].

While the transactions along the transport chain necessitate various types of functions and interactions, the main task in this case is the allocation of orders, i.e., the transport of parcels, to resources. In the presented MAS, the orders are entering through an external booking platform and handled by a platform agent, that represents the platform. For each shipping order, a booking agent is initialized that further represents and manages this order. The booking agent then splits the shipping order considering the different legs along the parcel chain, i.e. pickup in the shipper's city, a freight transport to the recipients' city as well as delivery in the latter. The pickup and deliver orders are each released by a pool of PDR agents that represent the delivery robots in the respective cities. These agents continually optimize their routes and hence bid for the incoming order based on the associated cost when incorporating this order in the route. Similarly, the order for the freight transport is broadcasted to a pool of freight agents, each calculating the costs for placing the parcel optimally on their respective pallets. These pallets are further assigned to trailer agents through a new auctioning process, such that the trailers' space is utilized optimally, and the transport routes are as efficient as possible. Both trailer- and PDR agents exchange parcels at depots, hence there is a coordination mechanism with depot agents that assigns ramps and human resources to incoming vehicles, such that waiting and loading times are minimized.

The corresponding MAS is depicted in Fig. 1 together with its interfacing assets and service that are embedded with the MAS into a Gaia-X ecosystem. Hence, each interaction between agents of the MAS and external services and assets has to adhere to Gaia-X standards. In the further course of this work, elaborating the integration of Gaia-X services in this system, we will focus on the subsystem consisting of the parcel delivery robot (PDR) and its corresponding PDR agent to propose an exemplary solution to the Gaia-X requirements regarding identity and trust.

2.2 Trust and Identity Within the Gaia-X Framework

Trust within the context of software agents can have a wide variety of meanings, from which many of them target the behavior or performance of the agent, i.e., trust in the sense of accuracy or reliability [6, 32]. In the context of Gaia-X, trust is defined rather in the interaction between actors, covering a secure data exchange incorporating the concepts of verifiable identities, compliance standards and governance [13].

Gaia-X is a European initiative aimed at fostering innovation through data sharing, emphasizing data sovereignty, privacy, security, and interoperability [17, 31]. The project seeks to build trust within decentralized ecosystems by setting minimum participation requirements, ensuring shared governance and interoperability while giving users full control over their decisions. Cross Federation Service Components (XFSC) serve as the technical backbone, providing essential services and standards to facilitate secure collaboration among federations [9, 10].

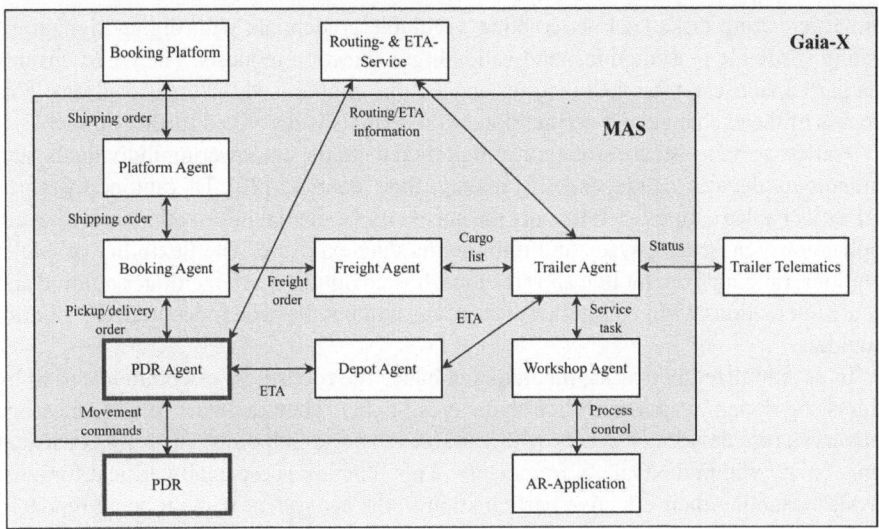

Fig. 1. The different types of software agents comprising the MAS developed in the consortium research project. Further depicted are the external services and platforms that are embedded into a Gaia-X ecosystem with the MAS. Highlighted is further the subsystem considered in this work, consisting of PDR and PDR agent.

Gaia-X aims to establish a secure and trustworthy digitalization framework by embracing the Self-Sovereign Identity (SSI) model [19], which allows individuals, organizations, or machines to manage their digital identities and credentials autonomously, without relying on centralized identity management systems. At the core of Gaia-X's SSI framework is the concept of Decentralized Identifiers (DIDs) [27], which are globally unique identifiers for entities within the ecosystem. These DIDs, along with Verifiable Credentials (VCs) [28], enable entities to maintain control over their identifiers and associated key materials, thereby enhancing privacy and security.

The W3C Triangle of Trust is fundamental in this context, comprising three main components: issuers, holders, and verifiers [14, 24]. Issuers create and issue verifiable credentials to holders, who are the entities that own and control these credentials. Holders can present their credentials to verifiers, who validate the authenticity and integrity of the credentials. As an example, a university (issuer) could issue a certificate to a student (holder) who stores it in a wallet. In this process, the university also stores cryptographic data in a data registry, which could be represented by a blockchain. An employer (verifier) could then request and verify the certificate from the student by checking it against cryptographic data in the data registry. In the Gaia-X ecosystem, this model ensures that all interactions are secure and trustworthy, as credentials are cryptographically signed and verifiable.

The Organizational Credential Manager (OCM) is a technology designed to establish trust among various participants in the decentralized ecosystem by managing the digital identities of participants [2]. It encompasses all trust-related functions necessary for managing and offering Gaia-X self-descriptions in the W3C Verifiable Credential format, covering tasks such as creating verifiable credentials with digital signatures, issuing verifiable presentations, and validating connection requests. The OCM ensures that participants can trust the identities and actions of others within the ecosystem. This process of the exchange and verification of credentials is described further in Sect. 3.

Wallets serve as secure storage for digital credentials, empowering individuals, and autonomous devices to independently manage their identities [30]. This autonomy is crucial, as it enables entities to share only the necessary credential information with relevant applications, ensuring privacy and minimizing data exposure. The flexibility of wallet solutions, ranging from mobile apps to cloud-hosted options [21], facilitates tailored and secure interactions within digital environments, without the need for centralized identity providers.

In decentralized networks, mediators enhance the robustness of communication by addressing dynamic addressability challenges [4, 11]. They facilitate reliable message delivery across devices or agents with variable network endpoints, ensuring consistent connectivity within the Gaia-X framework. This function is especially critical for edge devices, enabling their effective participation in the ecosystem without being hindered by fluctuating network conditions.

As one option for implementing the services, the Hyperledger technology is a viable option as it represents an open-source framework based on the SSI concept. Hyperledger Aries offers the protocols and tools for secure peer-to-peer communication and credential exchange [7], while Hyperledger Indy provides the blockchain infrastructure for decentralized identity management [1]. As a recent development, the Aries Askar implementation was introduced, representing a more performant and stable solution as compared to Indy [29, 33].

3 Integration of Gaia-X Services into the MAS

This chapter details the integration of Gaia-X services into the outlined MAS for parcel delivery, focusing on the fundamental workflow in digital identity management. It covers the identification of essential technologies and services, the establishment of secure connections, the issuing and managing of digital credentials, and the verification process to ensure the integrity and validity of these credentials within the network.

3.1 Identification of Services and Technologies

Regarding the subsystem that is considered in this work, consisting of a PDR and a PDR agent, it is first required to identify the necessary Gaia-X services that need to be deployed. As both the MAS and the fleet carrier for delivery robots represent different organizations, it is necessary to employ an OCM for each participant. This OCM then manages the credentials for each entity of the respective organization. Being developed within the Gaia-X project and building on the Hyperledger Aries framework, the OCM-engine implementation by the company Vereign was used [35]. This implementation is publicly available and comes preconfigured for connecting with the Hyperledger Indy test ledger BCovrin[1], developed by the Government of British Columbia. Further, the

---

[1] http://test.bcovrin.vonx.io/. Accessed: 2024–02-17.

OCM provides an extensive REST interface for interactions with the instance, such as for example the creation of credentials.

As the PDRs represent autonomously acting entities, each of them needs to be equipped with its own wallet to store its respective VCs. As a useful wallet technology, the Hyperledger Aries Cloud Agent Python (ACA-py) was determined, a Python wrapper for a light-weight Aries wallet agent [18]. ACA-py was initially developed by the same institution as the distributed test ledger and provides a similar API as compared to the OCM-engine, facilitating the interaction and data exchange.

As stated before, the physical PDR units act in a dynamic network environment, hence necessitating a solution for reliable connectivity and addressability. To address this, a mediator service needs to be deployed, that relays all messages between the OCM of the PDR fleet carrier to the respective wallets integrated on the PDR units. Here, the implementation of the mediator by Vereign is being further considered [34].

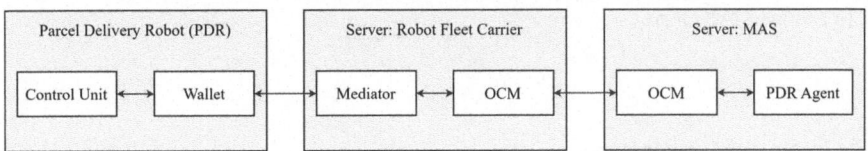

Fig. 2. Architectural overview of the Gaia-X compatible services to be integrated in the considered subsystem consisting of several environments, i.e., different servers and the PDR.

The overall architecture is depicted in Fig. 2. On the server that runs the MAS, the PDR agent interfaces with the appropriate OCM for credential management tasks. The OCM instance running on the server of the robot fleet carrier needs to be able to connect to the mediator instance for interfacing the robot's wallet as well as to the OCM instance on the MAS server in order to enable for instance the exchange of credentials in a later step. The wallet deployed on the PDR hardware is controlled by the control unit, managing its credentials, and initiating the connection to further resources, such as the mediator. A detailed description of the connection and credential-related mechanisms are provided in the next section.

3.2 Establishing Connections Between All Services

In order to obtain a public DID for the wallet that is deployed on the PDR, a new DID can be registered with the ledger from a seed. This DID is used for one wallet instance and is utilized for example in the provisioning process, i.e., the establishment of a wallet instance on the PDR unit.

To establish a system that is capable of exchanging VCs for the identification of participants and entities, it is necessary to establish connections in between all services, i.e., both the OCMs as well as the PDR's wallet and the corresponding mediator. This process is shown in Fig. 3 exemplarily for the connection between the two OCM instances. Using the REST API, a new connection request can be made at one of the OCMs. Accordingly, the respective OCM responds with an invitation URL. This invitation URL can then be passed on to the API of the second OCM, where the invitation can be accepted. If this process was executed successfully, the second OCM responds with a connection id that further identifies the connection that was established between the two instances. Similarly, this process can be repeated for the connections between the wallet and the mediator as well as between the mediator and the PDR fleet carrier's OCM.

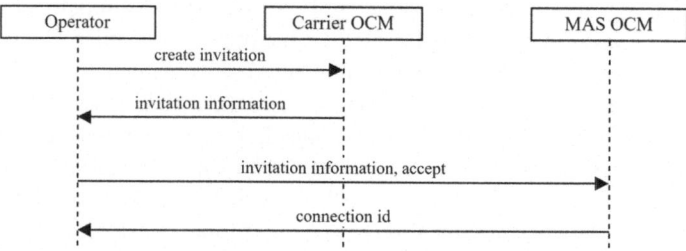

Fig. 3. Sequence diagram for connecting two instances, here as an example the robot fleet carrier's OCM and the MAS OCM.

3.3 Issuing of Credentials

After each instance of wallet and OCM are provisioned with a DID and all connections have been established as described before, verifiable credentials can now be issued. This process, depicted in Fig. 4, follows the proceedings of de Jong [8] and Nikita [22]. This is exemplarily described for the credentials to be held by the PDR, issued by the carrier's OCM.

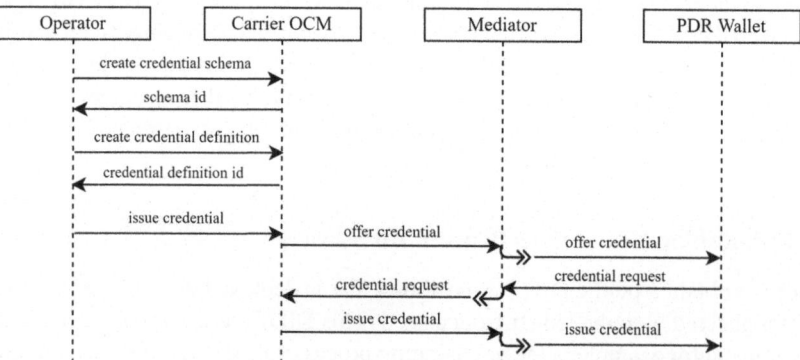

Fig. 4. Sequence diagram for the handling of credentials between two instances, here the carrier OCM and the PDR wallet. The process is instantiated by an operator. Messages between the OCM and the wallet are relayed by the mediator.

Assuming the OCM is controlled by an operator, first a credential schema and a credential definition have to be created. These are subsequently stored on the ledger. In a second step, the operator can initiate the issuing of credentials, resulting in a credential offer being sent to the holder (here the PDR wallet). The offer needs to be accepted by the PDR wallet, which then sends a credential request back to the carrier OCM. Following this step, the carrier OCM concludes the process by issuing credentials that can be stored on the PDR wallet. According to de Jong [9], the process of issuing a credential can also be initiated by the holder, i.e., the PDR wallet, by sending a credential proposal to the OCM which then answers with the credential offer.

3.4   Verification of Credentials

After an entity receives its digital credentials, the next step involves proving these credentials to relevant parties within the network. This process entails presenting cryptographic proof of the credentials, which are then verified against the public keys stored on the ledger. This verification ensures the credentials are valid and have been issued by a trusted authority.

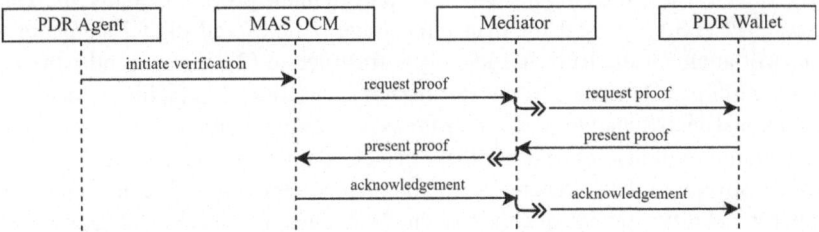

Fig. 5. Sequence diagram for the prove process of credentials, between the MAS OCM (verifier) and the PDR wallet (prover).

In the application case, the verification of credentials between the PDR and the PDR agent is of relevance. The protocol for credential verification [23] is adapted to the situation in this work and depicted as a sequence diagram below in Fig. 5. First, a request from the verifier (MAS OCM) to the prover (PDR wallet) describes the format and content that needs to be fulfilled by the prover. In a response to the request, the PDR's wallet presents the required proofs to the OCM, which subsequently verifies the proof using information on the distributed ledger and finally sends an acknowledgement back to the prover. Hence, the credentials of the PDR wallet have been verified. According to [23], the process above can also be initiated by the prover by sending an initial proposal to the verifier, which then answers with a request proof to the prover.

4   Discussion

Within this work, an application-oriented MAS, dedicated to freight fleet management is regarded with the aim to integrate it with auxiliary services and resources adhering to Gaia-X standards. A subsystem of a parcel delivery robot (PDR) and its respective agent representation, the PDR agent, are considered as an example case. The Gaia-X domain of trust and identity is considered as it represents an entry point for the realization of a decentralized, self-sovereign identity management system. After the crucial services, consisting of OCM, wallet and mediator were identified along with the corresponding implemented technologies, a workflow was presented in order to connect all employed Gaia-X services. Based on this, the process of issuing and verifying credentials in between the participants of the ecosystem was elaborated.

This study's value extends beyond theoretical implications, offering tangible benefits for industries employing physical entities as agents within MAS. The incorporation of the Gaia-X framework not only broadens the ecosystem to include a variety of stakeholders but also strengthens data sovereignty and collaborative efforts. Such advancements are pivotal for the practical application of MAS, ensuring robust and efficient operations across a spectrum of sectors, not limited to logistics. Moreover, the feasibility and industrial relevance of Gaia-X are demonstrated by application cases such as the Catena-X initiative in the automotive sector [5, 25], highlighting the practical impact and significance of our work.

After integrating the core components of the Gaia-X's trust and identity framework, further services are envisaged to be employed in the project. Notably, the Trusted Services API (TSA), pivotal for managing usage policies and digital signature validation, will augment the trust and identity infrastructure [2]. Concurrently, the inclusion of the Eclipse Dataspace Connector (EDC) is envisioned to facilitate secure inter-organizational data exchange, reinforcing the system's alignment with Gaia-X principles. The integration will also extend to other Gaia-X components, including the federated catalogue, sovereign data exchange, and compliance services [12], enhancing ecosystem interoperability. Specifically, the federated catalogue will enable the listing of MAS agents as bookable services, thereby allowing engagement from external entities such as delivery robot fleet operators with the data ecosystem.

Acknowledgments. This paper was written as part of the project Gaia-X 4 ROMS - Support and Remote Operation of Automated and Networked Mobility Services (FKZ: 19S21005C). The joint project is funded by the German Federal Ministry of Economics and Climate Protection (BMWK). The authors are responsible for the content of this article.

References

1. Bhattacharya, M.P., Zavarsky, P., Butakov, S.: Enhancing the security and privacy of self-sovereign identities on Hyperledger Indy Blockchain. In: 2020 International Symposium on Networks, Computers and Communications (ISNCC) (2020)
2. Binzer, M., et al.: GXFS - IDM & Trust. Architecture Overview (2021). https://www.gxfs.eu/idm-trust-architecture/. Accessed 17 Feb 2024
3. Braud, A., et al.: The road to European digital sovereignty with Gaia-X and IDSA. IEEE Network **35**(2), 4–5 (2021)
4. Capela, F.: Self-sovereign identity for the internet of things: a case study on verifiable electric vehicle charging. (2021): Rijksuniversiteit Groningen (2021)
5. Catena-X Automotive Network e.V. Catena-X uses this year's Gaia-X Summit for important announcements (2023). https://catena-x.net/en/news-dates/artikel/catena-x-uses-this-years-gaia-x-summit-for-important-announcements. Accessed 29 May 2024

6. Cheng, M., et al.: A general trust framework for multi-agent systems. In: Proceedings of the 20th International Conference on Autonomous Agents and MultiAgent Systems. 2021, International Foundation for Autonomous Agents and Multiagent Systems: Virtual Event, United Kingdom, pp. 332–340 (2021)

7. Chicano Valenzuela, D.: Identifying and tracking physical objects with hyperledger decentralized applications. Universitat Politècnica de Catalunya (2022)

8. de Jong, L.: Becoming a Hyperledger Aries developer: issue credentials V2 (2021). https://ldej.nl/post/becoming-a-hyperledger-aries-developer-issue-credentials-v2/. Accessed 17 Feb 2024

9. Eclipse foundation: eclipse XFSC creation review. n.d. https://projects.eclipse.org/projects/technology.xfsc/reviews/creation-review. Accessed 17 Feb 2024

10. eco – Verband der Internetwirtschaft. GXFS and the XFSC Toolbox. n.d. https://www.gxfs.eu/set-of-services/. Accessed 17 Feb 2024

11. Ferdous, M.S., Ionita, A., Prinz, W.: SSI4Web: A Self-sovereign Identity (SSI) Framework for the Web. In: Prieto, J., Benítez Martínez, F.L., Ferretti, S., Arroyo Guardeño, D., Tomás Nevado-Batalla, P. (eds.) Blockchain and Applications, 4th International Congress . BLOCKCHAIN 2022. Lecture Notes in Networks and Systems, vol. 595. Springer, Cham (2023). https://doi.org/10.1007/978-3-031-21229-1_34

12. Gaia-X: Gaia-X Architecture document, release 22.04. 2021, European Association for Data and Cloud, AISBL: Brussels (2024)

13. GAIA-X European association for data and cloud. Gaia-X trust framework (2022). https://docs.gaia-x.eu/policy-rules-committee/trust-framework/22.10/. Accessed 29 May 2024

14. GAIA-X European association for data and cloud. trust anchors. (2022). https://docs.gaia-x.eu/policy-rules-committee/trust-framework/22.10/trust_anchors/. Accessed 29 May 2024

15. Heinbach, C., Dreesbach, T., Thomas, O.: Freight Fleet Glasses – Augmented Reality Einsatz zur Unterstützung eines automatisierten und vernetzten Flottenmanagements. HMD Praxis der Wirtschaftsinformatik **60**(1), 89–109 (2023)

16. Heinbach, C., et al.: Smart managed freight fleet: Ein automatisiertes und vernetztes Flottenmanagement in einem föderierten Datenökosystem. HMD Praxis der Wirtschaftsinformatik **60**(1), 193–213 (2023)

17. Hoffmann, F., et al.: Developing GAIA-X business models for production. In: Proceedings of the Conference on Production Systems and Logistics: CPSL 2022, pp. 583-594 (2022)

18. Hyperledger: Hyperledger Aries Cloud Agent Python (ACA-Py). (2023). https://github.com/hyperledger/aries-cloudagent-python. Accessed 17 Feb 2024

19. Lange, C., Langkau, J., Bader, S.: The IDS information model: a semantic vocabulary for sovereign data exchange. In: Otto, B., ten Hompel, M., Wrobel, S. (eds.) Designing Data Spaces. Springer, Cham (2022). https://doi.org/10.1007/978-3-030-93975-5_7

20. Maecker, D., et al.: Exploring multi-agent systems for intermodal freight fleets: literature-based justification of a new concept. In: Wirtschaftsinformatik 2023 Proceedings, vol. 97 (2023)

21. Maier, B., Pohlmann, N.: Gaia-X secure and trustworthy ecosystems with self sovereign identity, in developing a decentralised, user-centric, and secure cloud ecosystem. 2021, eco – Verband der Internetwirtschaft (2021)

22. Nikita, K. Aries RFC 0036: Issue Credential Protocol 1.0. (2019). https://github.com/hyperledger/aries-rfcs/blob/main/features/0036-issue-credential/README.md. Accessed 17 Feb 2024

23. Nikita, K., Curran, S.: Aries RFC 0454: present proof protocol 2.0. (2021). https://github.com/hyperledger/aries-rfcs/tree/main/features/0454-present-proof-v2. Accessed 17 Feb 2024

24. Reed, D., Gisolfi, D.: ToIP foundation whitepaper: verifiable credential trust triangle. (2020). https://trustoverip.github.io/WP0010-toip-foundation-whitepaper/trust/vcred_trust_triangle/. Accessed 29 May 2024

25. Schlueter Langdon, C.: Catena-X With GAIA-X: will data space be the word of 2021? (2021). https://internationaldataspaces.org/catena-x-with-gaia-x-will-data-space-be-the-word-of-2021/. Accessed 29 May 2024

26. Smith, R.G.: The contract net protocol: high-level communication and control in a distributed problem solver. In: Readings Distributed Artificial Intelligence, A.H. Bond and L. Gasser, (eds.) Morgan Kaufmann, pp. 357–366 (1988)

27. Sporny, M., et al.: Decentralized Identifiers (DIDs) v1.0 – Core architecture, data model, and representations. W3C Recommendation (2022). https://www.w3.org/TR/2022/REC-did-core-20220719/. Accessed 17 Feb 2024

28. Sporny, M., et al.: Verifiable credentials data model 1.1. W3C recommendation (2022). https://www.w3.org/TR/2022/REC-vc-data-model-20220303/. Accessed 17 Feb 2024

29. Stephen, C., Grace, H.: 2022 Q2 Hyperledger Indy project update (2022). https://wiki.hyperledger.org/display/TSC/2022+Q2+Hyperledger+Indy. Accessed 17 Feb 2024

30. Stodt, F., Reich, C.: A review on digital wallets and federated service for future of cloud services identity management, in service computation. In: 2023: The Fifteenth International Conference on Advanced Service Computing. France (2023)

31. Tardieu, H.: Role of Gaia-X in the European data space ecosystem. In: Otto, B., ten Hompel, M., Wrobel, S. (eds.) Designing Data Spaces : The Ecosystem Approach to Competitive Advantage, pp. 41–59. Springer International Publishing, Cham (2022). https://doi.org/10.1007/978-3-030-93975-5_4

32. Tweedale, J., Cutler. P.: Trust in Multi-Agent Systems. Springer, Heidelberg (2006). https://doi.org/10.1007/11893004_62

33. Utku, S., Bahce, A.: A case study for mobile wallet implementation in self-sovereign identity infrastructure. J. Artif. Intell. Data Sci. 3(1), 1–16 (2023)

34. Vereign: AFJ-Mediator (2024). https://code.vereign.com/gaiax/ocm/ocm-engine. Accessed 1 Feb 2024

35. Vereign: organization credential manager engine (2024). https://code.vereign.com/gaiax/ocm/ocm-engine. Accessed 17 Feb 2024

36. Wooldridge, M.: An Introduction to Multiagent Systems. 2nd edn. Wiley, Chichester (2009)

Cognitive Planning for Persuasive Multimodal Interaction

Emiliano Lorini[1]([✉]), Magalie Ochs[2], and Nicolas Sabouret[3]

[1] IRIT, CNRS, Toulouse University, Toulouse, France
Emiliano.Lorini@irit.fr
[2] LIS, Aix-Marseille University, Marseille, France
[3] LISN, CNRS, Université Paris-Saclay, Gif-sur-Yvette, France

Abstract. This paper proposes guidelines for the design of embodied social agents endowed with cognitive planning capabilities to be used in the context of persuasive multimodal interaction. Cognitive planning is the kind of planning aimed at finding and then executing an informative plan with the goal of influencing the cognitive state or the behavior of the interlocutor. We show how the integration of elements from the motivational interviewing (MI) methodology and non-verbal behavior allows us to improve the persuasiveness of the agent.

1 Introduction

An agent's cognitive state encompasses its epistemic attitudes (e.g., beliefs and opinions), motivational attitudes (e.g., desires, moral values, preferences and intentions) and emotions. Their causal relationships as well as their causal influence on the agent's behavior are objects of study in cognitive psychology [1] and philosophy of mind [34]. Figure 1 provides a schematic representation of these causal relationships. For instance,

- the agent's preferences causally depend on both its endogenous intrinsic motivations (*alias* desires) and ethical values;
- the agent's intentions are the output of its decision-making process and causally depend on its beliefs and preferences;
- the agent's emotions are triggered by its beliefs, desires and moral concerns;
- the agent's emotions may affect its behavior by bypassing its deliberation process (e.g., fear triggered by the perception of a danger can cause an automatic response of escape).

Cognitive planning consists in an agent (the influencer) trying to find and then execute a plan aimed at changing the cognitive state or the behavior of another agent (the influenced or target agent). The concept of cognitive planning lies at the intersection between AI, cognitive sciences, social psychology and ethics. Thus, to be properly understood, it has to be investigated from an interdisciplinary perspective. From a human science point of view, cognitive

D. Briola et al. (Eds.): EMAS 2024, LNAI 15152, pp. 93–104, 2025.
https://doi.org/10.1007/978-3-031-71152-7_6

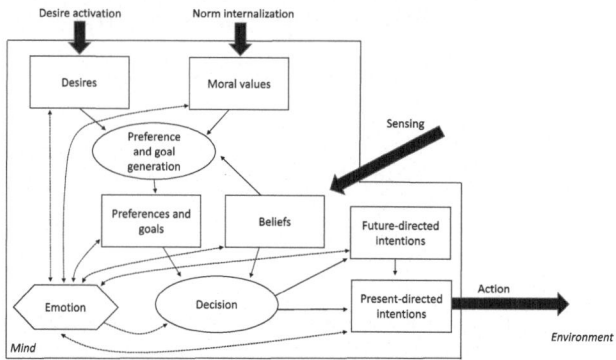

Fig. 1. Cognitive architecture [22]

planning is intimately related to theories of persuasion, social influence, nudging and attitude change [9,32,36]. From an AI point of view, cognitive planning can be seen as a generalization of epistemic planning [3,29]. It is not merely a belief state that the planning agent tries to induce but, more generally, a cognitive state or a behavior of the target agent. The goal of the planning agent is not necessarily communicative in the Gricean sense [17]. Moreover, the kind of communication involved in cognitive planning could be purely behavioral [5] without the use of a codified (verbal or non-verbal) language. For example, to dissuade Bob from disturbing her, Ann can decide to leave her office door ajar. Ann has not necessarily a communicative goal or intention. She may simply want Bob not to knock on her office door. To achieve her goal, she relies on Bob's deductive capabilities. Specifically, she knows that if Bob sees that the door is ajar, he will infer that Ann is busy and, consequently, he will refrain from knocking on the door since he does not want to disturb her when she is busy.

Cognitive planning has also several important ethical implications since building an artificial system with sophisticated persuasive capabilities can be potentially risky (e.g., the system could engage in a manipulative behavior or induce others to do dangerous or illegal actions or persuade them into false beliefs).

In this paper, we situate cognitive planning in the context of a human-machine interaction (HMI) in which the influencer is an artificial communicative agent and the target agent is a human. In particular, our aim is to provide the guidelines for designing, formalizing and then implementing an embodied agent endowed with cognitive planning and normative reasoning capabilities to be used in the context of persuasive multimodal interaction. We will show that in order to develop such agent for HMI applications, it is necessary to integrate logic-based automated reasoning with machine learning techniques in a principled manner at different levels of the design process. The paper is organized as follows. In Sect. 2, we offer a bird eye view of the overall methodology. Then, we illustrate how cognitive planning can be modeled and automated in an artificial agent using logic-based methods (Sect. 3), and how to relate cognitive planning to a psychological theory of attitude change in the context of persuasive verbal communication (Sect. 4). Then, in Sect. 5, we move from verbal to non-verbal communication: we explain how to use machine learning methods to identify the degree of persuasiveness of a non-verbal message and to endow the agent with persuasive non-verbal capabilities. Finally, Sect. 6 is devoted to the problem of evaluating the persuasiveness of a virtual agent. In Sect. 7, we conclude by illustrating some challenges for future research.

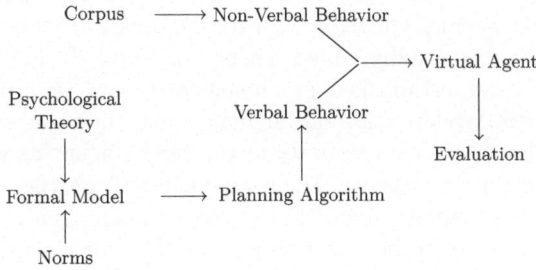

Fig. 2. Overview of the methodology

2   Methodological Foundation

Figure 2 schematically presents a general methodology for designing cognitive planning systems for persuasive multimodal interaction. The integration of verbal and non-verbal communication is a key feature of the methodology. Indeed, several research studies, particularly in the human-human interaction field, have explored the efficiency of behavioral cues to increase persuasiveness (e.g. [4]). In the domain of virtual agents, empirical research has shown the importance of combining non-verbal cues with verbal ones to create a persuasive virtual agent [8,15]. On the verbal side, the agent should be able to generate and put into place dialogue plans depending on the context of interaction. Such functionality of the artificial agent can be achieved satisfactorily by leveraging on logic-based reasoning and planning methods. On the non-verbal side, it is crucial to identify the multimodal cues that should be coupled with the agent's dialogue moves to increase the persuasiveness of its message. This necessarily requires an empirical analysis.

There is an important difference between the two levels. While the agent's generation of dialogue plans relies on psychological theories (top-down approach), the specification of the non-verbal behavior is grounded on an empirical corpus-based analysis (bottom-up approach). This difference is justified by two aspects. On the one hand, there is no well-established theory of non-verbal persuasive communication which clearly identifies the behavioral signals (types, duration, frequencies, combinations) increasing the persuasiveness of the message. Thus, we can only exploit inductive methods, namely, apply machine learning methods to an existing corpus of non-verbal communication in order to predict the persuasiveness of non-verbal signals. On the other hand, we have well-established psychological theories and methods validated by experts for attitude change and persuasion based on verbal communication. Thus, we can rely on them to attain a fine-grained control of the verbal output by the cognitive planning agent. In particular, for the planning agent to be able to generate effective persuasion or influence plans, it should have both i) information about the target agent's overall cognitive state as well as ii) a theory of the causal relationships between the target agent's epistemic and motivational attitudes, emotions and behavior. The latter is usually called Theory of Mind (ToM) [16] and should be grounded on a well-established psychological theory. A crucial step of the design process is to develop a formal language with the right expressiveness to be able to formalize the cognitive state of the target agent as well as the principles of the psychological theory. Such language will be then used to specify the theory-grounded planning algorithm of the artificial agent, namely, the generative component of its verbal communication. The formal model will also be used to formalize the normative and ethical requirements with which the agent is expected to comply, during its interaction with the human. This is to guarantee that it will behave ethically and will refrain from performing obnoxious actions. The norm-aligned verbal behavior generated by the planning module should be appropriately coupled and synchronized with the agent's non-verbal behavior. A user perceptive study should be conducted at the end of the process to evaluate the effectiveness and persuasiveness of the agent's multimodal communication.

In the rest of the paper, we will illustrate the methodology in more detail partially drawing on the experience of a project we have worked on over the last few years. The name of the project is CoPains (Cognitive Planning in Persuasive Multimodal Communication)[1]. The work carried out in the project covers only some aspects of the methodology sketched in Fig. 2 and of the integration between logic and machine learning which, as underlined in the introduction, we deem fundamental. For instance, the normative and ethical aspects of cognitive planning and persuasive communication were not explored in detail in the CoPains project. Therefore, we will not focus on them in the rest of the article.

3   Formal Model of Cognitive Planning

In the CoPains project we generalized epistemic planning, in which only epistemic attitudes (beliefs and knowledge) of agents are modeled, to cognitive planning in which the global cognitive state of the target agent is taken into consideration and influenced by the planning agent. A logical language for cognitive planning was developed [11,12]. The language builds on previous work in epistemic logic in which multi-relational Kripke models are replaced by knowledge bases, in order to facilitate the modeling and implementation of artificial rational

---

[1] https://www.irit.fr/CoPains/.

agents endowed with cognitive attitudes and with a theory of mind [23–27]. The main advantage of knowledge bases over Kripke models is their computational groundedness and succinctness which make them well-suited for implementation in multi-agent applications.

The language distinguishes two concepts of belief: explicit and implicit belief. An agent's explicit belief corresponds to a piece of information in the agent's belief base, while an agent's implicit belief corresponds to a piece of information that is deducible from the agent's explicit beliefs. It treats the artificial agent, or more simply the machine, and the human agent in an asymmetric way. On the one hand the language allows us to represent both the explicit and implicit beliefs of the machine, captured respectively by the operators $\triangle_m$ and $\square_{\mathfrak{h}}$. On the other hand only the explicit beliefs of the human are representable, captured by the operator $\triangle_{\mathfrak{h}}$. This asymmetry is justified by the fact that the human is by definition resource-bounded and has no deductively closed beliefs. On the contrary, the artificial agent has perfect deductive capabilities, exemplified by the notion of implicit belief, that can be exploited to reason about the human's mind and, consequently, to plan communicative actions aimed at influencing it.

We explored a variety of algorithmic solutions for implementing cognitive planning in an artificial conversational agent including a SAT-based approach and a QBF-based approach. We combined the logic-based cognitive planning module of the conversational agent with its belief revision module. This step was key to come up with a conversational agent that is able to deal with the two fundamental aspects of dialogue, namely, to compute a communicative action or plan and to revise its beliefs in the light of the interlocutor's response.

Two applications were explored during the CoPains project: the first one in the domain of sport recommendation, and a second one in the domain of human-machine collaborative gaming. In the first application, the artificial agent has to motivate the human to practice a physical activity regularly and to help her to find the sport that best suits her preferences and needs. In the second application, the agent has to play a collaborative card game with the human in which reasoning about the human's beliefs and performing informative actions aimed at changing her beliefs play a crucial role. Here, we focus on the first application whose details can be found in [28]. In the next section we will show how the psychological theory of attitude change was imported into the formal model of cognitive planning to endow the agent with an in-depth and theoretically grounded knowledge of how to motivate the human to engage in a regular physical activity. More details about the second application can be found in [13, 21].

4   Formalization of the Psychological Theory

There exists numerous psychological theories in the literature that could serve as a basis for designing the persuasive verbal behavior of an artificial agent whose ultimate goal is to induce attitude or behavior change in its human interlocutor. In the CoPains project we relied on Motivational Interviewing (MI) [30], a counseling method aimed at empowering the individual by raising her ability to recognize her internal motivators, make reflected decisions and monitor their progress. MI is based on motivation theories to convert the willingness to change into intention and action [18]. The MI communication process leads the person to explore her values, feelings and beliefs about the risky behavior so as to resolve any ambivalence that may arise between desires and inhibitors of change. Throughout the conversation, the MI practitioner infuses a collaborative spirit (partnership) with a non-judgmental and accurate empathetic stance (acceptance). Resolving conflicting motivations through evocation is a central component of MI. Thus, the interviewer's attitude should reflect compassion, respect the interlocutor's opinions and state of readiness to change, avoiding the temptation to give a premature advice. It assumes that people progressively go through various states of mind throughout the process. At the beginning of a session, an individual may express more thoughts in favor of the old habit than the desired one (called sustain talk). The success of the intervention resides in the practitioner's ability to highlight that the weight of the benefits of change is greater than the status quo using the client's own arguments.

Most psychological theories of attitude change and persuasion, including MI, make use of "mentalistic" concepts such as belief, desire, preference and intention, so-called cognitive attitudes, and explain human behavior in the light of these cognitive attitudes. For this reason, the language and algorithm of cognitive planning described in Sect. 3, in which cognitive attitudes are explicitly represented, have proven to be particularly suitable for formalizing the MI theory and making it operational. They were used to make the artificial planning agent capable of i) ascribing and reasoning about the cognitive attitudes of the human, and ii) predicting the effects of its informative actions on the human's cognitive state and behavior, in accordance with the psychological theory. For example, in light of the MI theory, the artificial agent knows that to motivate the human to practice regular physical activity, it has to make her aware of the fact that her sedentary lifestyle is in conflict with her desire to be healthy. Thus, to achieve its goal of inducing a behavior change in the human, the artificial agent forms the subgoal of making the human aware of the inconsistency between her actual behavior (i.e., the human has a sedentary lifestyle) and desires (i.e., the human desires to be healthy). Such form of awareness is captured by the following formula of the logical language:

$$\mathsf{AwareIncon}(\mathfrak{h}, \neg\mathsf{does}(\mathfrak{h},pa), he) =_{def} \mathsf{des}(\mathfrak{h}, he) \wedge$$
$$\triangle_{\mathfrak{h}}\mathsf{nec}(he, \mathsf{does}(\mathfrak{h},pa)) \wedge$$
$$\triangle_{\mathfrak{h}}\neg\mathsf{does}(\mathfrak{h},pa).$$

According to the previous abbreviation, the human is aware of the inconsistency between not practicing regular physical activity and the desire to be healthy, noted $\mathsf{AwareIncon}(\mathfrak{h}, \neg\mathsf{does}(\mathfrak{h},pa))$, if and only i) she desires to be healthy (i.e., $\mathsf{des}(\mathfrak{h}, he)$), ii) she believes that practicing regular physical activity is a necessary condition for being healthy (i.e., $\triangle_{\mathfrak{h}}\mathsf{nec}(he, \mathsf{does}(\mathfrak{h},pa))$), and iii) she believes she doesn't practice regular physical activity (i.e., $\triangle_{\mathfrak{h}}\neg\mathsf{does}(\mathfrak{h},pa)$). Full details about the logical encoding of this aspect of MI in the scenario of application of the CoPains project are provided in [28, Section 6]. Another important aspect of MI that was not formalized in [28] is the principle that to induce a behavior change in the human, one has to make her aware of being able and having the potential to make that change. This is called self-efficacy belief in psychology [2]. To formalize it, it would be necessary to extend the language of cognitive attitudes developed within the CoPains project with notions of ability and know-how [37].

As emphasized in Sect. 2, the psychological theory and its encoding in the formal model of cognitive planning only handle the verbal aspect of persuasive communication. To handle the non-verbal aspect, we mainly relied on machine learning methods which is what we report in the next section.

5   Persuasive Non-verbal Behavior

Developing a persuasive behavior model implies several challenges, and in particular the precise identification of the behavioral cues associated to persuasion. Indeed, even if the literature in psychology highlights certain cues, the existing research is not sufficient to create a computational model of non-verbal persuasive behavior. One method to identify how a virtual agent should behave to be perceived as persuasive consists in exploring the persuasiveness of human communication in audiovisual corpora. Machine learning techniques are particularly relevant for this task, provided that a corpus with annotations of perceived persuasiveness is available. The POM corpus [31] is, to the best of our knowledge, the only multimedia corpus with annotations of perceived persuasiveness. The POM corpus contains web videos of individuals discussing diverse topics in front of a camera. In a machine learning approach, particular attention must be paid to the interpretability of the model to be able to identify features that can be easily understood and controlled on virtual agents. Different classifiers could be considered such as the traditional SVMs or Random Forests particularly suitable to handle high-dimensional data with a high generalization power [14,33]. In the CoPains project, we have explored different sets of features and classifiers on the POM corpus to identify the important behavioral cues of persuasion including facial expressions (AUs), head movements and vocal cues [7].

Once the behavioral cues of persuasion have been identified, the next step is to construct the computational model to automatically generate the behavior of a persuasive virtual character. In the CoPains project, on the basis of the persuasive behavioral cues identified from the POM corpus, we have proposed a dictionary to establish reference points that reflect persuasive non-verbal behavior. A convolution-based model, based on this dictionary, was then developed and integrated in a tool to compute the persuasive behavior of the virtual agent based on a video of a neutral face. The tool that we have developed, called THRUST (from neuTral Human face to peRsUaSive virTual face), automatically generates the head movements and facial expressions of a persuasive virtual character. The tool is designed to automatically convert a human's video into a video of a virtual character that exhibits a persuasive non-verbal behavior. Specifically, the tool extracts automatically the human's head movements and facial expressions, applies modifications based on a proposed computational model, and reproduces the resulting head and facial movements on a virtual face. In the next section, we deal with the issue of evaluating the persuasiveness of a virtual agent.

6   Evaluation of Virtual Persuasiveness

The persuasiveness of a virtual character's behavior must be evaluated through subjective and objective measures. The subjective evaluation refers to the perception of the agent's persuasiveness and believability whereas objective evaluation aims at assessing the change in the user's attitude (see, e.g., [35]). The importance of the subjective evaluation must not be underestimated. It consists in measuring to which degree the behavior of the agent is perceived by users as a persuasive behavior. The most popular method for this consists in asking participants to watch pre-recorded videos of the agent interacting with a user and to indicate their perception through direct questions on the virtual speaker's persuasiveness (e.g. "Did you find the character in the video persuasive?"). The advantage of such videos is twofold. First, it is easier to build an online experimentation and access enough participants for statistical evaluation of the results (which is always a difficulty in subjective studies). Secondly, we can verify that the videos are correctly classified as persuasive or non-persuasive by the classifier described in Sect. 5. However, the real challenge is to conduct the evaluation in a situation in which the user interacts actively with the virtual agent and not just passively by watching videos. This can be difficult to achieve in practice.

Note that in all cases, a control condition must also be built, in which the agent does not include any persuasive component: the verbal behavior simply follows a predefined list of questions and the non-verbal behavior uses either no transformation or randomly generated non-verbal cues. The subjective evaluation then validates the proposed approach showing that the videos or interaction sessions are perceived as significantly more persuasive than the ones obtained without the model. Testing each modality separately is also interesting to understand what is most important in the user's perception. However, it increases the number of conditions, and by consequence the number of required participants (the standard is to have a minimum of 30 participants per condition). It is also recommended that we evaluate the virtual agents' behavior considering different human videos as input, both female and male, to show that the model provides persuasive output whatever human is in the input video and whatever agent gender in output. Videos generated with virtual agents with different appearances must be evaluated to completely assess the efficiency of the model.

The objective evaluation also raises several challenges by itself. Two different things can be objectively measured: the behaviour change intention (declarative/subjective measure) after the intervention, and the actual behavior change in the long term with objective measures (*e.g.* number of steps per day, time of physical activity per week, *etc.*). In the CoPains project, we measured physical activity through the Global Physical Activity Questionnaire (GPAQ) endorsed by the World Health Organization [6]. This measure of the activity planning gives some view of the intention to change. We also measured the self-efficacy feeling [19], i.e., the individual's belief in his or her capacity to produce specific attainments (in our case, having a regular physical activity).

The real challenge however is to conduct ecological studies, i.e., having people use the agent outside of the laboratory (which is what we did in the CoPains project). Such evaluation situation is prone to system errors (bugs or misconception), irregular use of the system by the other, or other external disruptions. In such ecological conditions, the interaction with the persuasive agent can have a significant positive effect on barrier self-efficacy, but only a limited one on activity planning [20]. This remains however the ultimate goal of persuasive agents.

7   Challenges

We conclude by briefly discussing some challenges for future research in the area of cognitive planning and persuasive multimodal communication: i) developing a model of verbal persuasive communication based on reinforcement learning (RL), as an alternative to the planning model; ii) proposing a number of benchmarks for persuasive communication; iii) exploring the connection between cognitive planning and Large Language Models (LLMs).

RL-Based Model of Verbal Persuasive Communication. A conversational agent must have a policy or a criterion for selecting the communicative action or plan to be executed in a given situation. In the CoPains project we explored a solution based on automated planning . A challenge for future research is to come up with a solution based on RL, and to compare the planning approach with the RL approach. In the RL approach, the information about the human interlocutor's cognitive state should be part of the state description in a Markov decision process (MDP) which represents the communicative interaction between the agent and the human. Indeed, in a conversational setting the result of a communicative action depends not only on the properties of the environment but also on the interlocutor's cognitive state. Therefore, the probabilistic state transition function in the MDP should take the latter into account. A challenging task will be the integration of the MDP and the logical language for representing the cognitive state of the human we discussed in Sect. 3. A model-free approach such as Q-learning seems the most appropriate in this setting since in principle the artificial agent should not know the probabilities of the transitions, namely, the probability that a certain communicative action will produce a certain effect on the cognitive state of the human depending on her initial cognitive state.

Benchmarks and Metrics. In connection with the previous challenge, future research will be devoted to proposing a number of benchmarks through which to compare the performance of the various models of verbal persuasive communication. For instance, to compare the planning model and the RL model, one shall evaluate the persuasiveness of the planning-based communication module in comparison to the RL-based communication module through controlled experiments on human subjects by using both objective and subjective measures. As discussed in Sect. 6, an objective measure corresponds to *how effective* the artificial agent is in persuading the human to change her beliefs, intentions and behavior. A subjective measure corresponds to *how persuasive* the artificial agent is perceived by the human. A challenging task will be to come up with general metrics for *persuasive effectiveness* and *perceived persuasiveness* that can be used to evaluate models of persuasive communication of different natures, including the planning vs the RL model.

Cognitive Planning and LLMs. Conversational agents based on LLMs exhibit extraordinary capacities to understand the human interlocutor's utterances and to interact with her in a meaningful and informative way. Nonetheless, they have no representation of the human's cognitive state and have no control on the effects of their actions on it, e.g., on the emotions and stress they may induce in the human. This is what the cognitive planning approach provides: a top-down goal-driven approach to communication in which what the agent should do/not do in a given situation depends on its representation of the human interlocutor's cognitive state and on its theory of the interlocutor's mind. So, a crucial challenge is to combine logic-based cognitive planning models with LLMs for natural language processing (NLP) to be able to exploit the potentialities of both approaches. This challenge is particularly timely, as recent LLM-based agents [38] offer some promising perspectives of integration between logic-based models and natural language communication. The integration can occur at both levels, the reception and the transmission level. For example, it is in principle possible to request to the LLM to extract a formal representation of the human's natural language utterance which can then be processed by the agent's logic-based reasoning module. The planning module can then compute the high-level informative act in response to the user's message which can in turn be transformed, using a second request to the LLM, into a contextualized natural language utterance. Additionally, sentiment analysis models [10] could be exploited to analyze the emotional content of the generated utterance (e.g., to verify the absence of "stressful" markers and expressions).

Acknowledgments. Support from the the ANR project CoPains ("Cognitive Planning in Persuasive Multimodal Communication") is gratefully acknowledged.

References

1. Albarracín, D., Sunderrajan, A., Lohmann, S., M. Sally Chan, D.J.: The psychology of attitudes, motivation, and persuasion. In: Albarracín, D., Johnson, B.T. (eds.) The Handbook of Attitudes, Volume 1: Basic Principles, 2nd edn., pp. 1–42. Routledge (2018)
2. Bandura, A.: Self-Efficacy: The Exercise of Control. Freeman, New York (1997)
3. Bolander, T., Andersen, M.B.: Epistemic planning for single- and multi-agent systems. J. Appl. Non-Classical Logics **21**(1), 9–34 (2011)
4. Burgoon, J.K., Birk, T., Pfau, M.: Nonverbal behaviors, persuasion, and credibility. Hum. Commun. Res. **17**(1), 140–169 (1990)

5. Castelfranchi, C., Pezzulo, G., Tummolini, L.: Behavioral Implicit Communication (BIC): communicating with smart environments. Int. J. Ambient Comput. Intell. (IJACI) **2**(1), 1–12 (2010)
6. Chauvin, R., Clavel, C., Sabouret, N., Ravenet, B.: A virtual coach with more or less empathy: impact on older adults' engagement to exercise. In: Proceedings of the 23rd ACM International Conference on Intelligent Virtual Agents, pp. 1–9 (2023)
7. Cherni, A., Bertrand, R., Ochs, M.: From neutral human face to persuasive virtual face, a new automatic tool to generate a persuasive attitude. In: Advances in Signal Processing and Artificial Intelligence (ASPAI 2022) (2022)
8. Chidambaram, V., Chiang, Y.H., Mutlu, B.: Designing persuasive robots: how robots might persuade people using vocal and nonverbal cues. In: Proceedings of the Seventh Annual ACM/IEEE International Conference on Human-Robot Interaction, pp. 293–300 (2012)
9. Cialdini, R.B.: Influence: Science and Practice. Allyn & Bacon (2001)
10. Clavel, C., Callejas, Z.: Sentiment analysis: from opinion mining to human-agent interaction. IEEE Trans. Affect. Comput. **7**(1), 74–93 (2015)
11. Fernandez Davila, J.L., Longin, D., Lorini, E., Maris, F.: A simple framework for cognitive planning. In: Proceedings of the Thirty-Fifth AAAI Conference on Artificial Intelligence (AAAI 2021), pp. 6331–6339. AAAI Press (2021)
12. Fernandez Davila, J.L., Longin, D., Lorini, E., Maris, F.: Logic-based cognitive planning for conversational agents. Auton. Agent. Multi-Agent Syst. **38**(1), 20 (2024)
13. Fernandez Davila, J.L., Longin, D., Lorini, E., Maris, F.: A logical modeling of the Yōkai board game. AI Communications, The European Journal on Artificial Intelligence (forthcoming)
14. Forman, G., Cohen, I.: Learning from little: comparison of classifiers given little training. In: Boulicaut, J.-F., Esposito, F., Giannotti, F., Pedreschi, D. (eds.) PKDD 2004. LNCS (LNAI), vol. 3202, pp. 161–172. Springer, Heidelberg (2004). https://doi.org/10.1007/978-3-540-30116-5_17
15. Ghazali, A.S., Ham, J., Barakova, E.I., Markopoulos, P.: Poker face influence: persuasive robot with minimal social cues triggers less psychological reactance. In: 2018 27th IEEE International Symposium on Robot and Human Interactive Communication (RO-MAN), pp. 940–946. IEEE (2018)
16. Goldman, A.I.: Simulating Minds: The Philosophy, Psychology, and Neuroscience of Mindreading. Oxford University Press (2006)
17. Grice, H.P.: Studies in the Way of Words (3rd edition). Harvard University Press (1989)
18. Hardcastle, S.J., Hancox, J., Hattar, A., Maxwell-Smith, C., Thøgersen-Ntoumani, C., Hagger, M.S.: Motivating the unmotivated: how can health behavior be changed in those unwilling to change? (2015)
19. Kim, J., Eys, M., Robertson-Wilson, J.: 'if they do it, so can i': a test of a moderated serial mediation model of descriptive norms, self-efficacy, and perceived similarity for predicting physical activity. Psychol. Health **36**(6), 701–718 (2021)
20. Koring, M., Richert, J., Lippke, S., Parschau, L., Reuter, T., Schwarzer, R.: Synergistic effects of planning and self-efficacy on physical activity. Health Educ. Behav. **39**(2), 152–158 (2012)
21. Longin, D., Lorini, E., Maris, F.: Beliefs, time and space: a language for the yōkai board game. In: Proceedings of the 23rd International Conference on Principles and Practice of Multi-Agent Systems (PRIMA 2020). LNCS, vol. 12568, pp. 386–393. Springer, Cham (2020). https://doi.org/10.1007/978-3-030-69322-0_28

22. Lorini, E.: Logics for games, emotions and institutions. IfCoLog J. Logics Appl. **4**(9), 3075–3113 (2017)
23. Lorini, E.: In praise of belief bases: Doing epistemic logic without possible worlds. In: Proceedings of the Thirty-Second AAAI Conference on Artificial Intelligence (AAAI-18), pp. 1915–1922. AAAI Press (2018)
24. Lorini, E.: Exploiting belief bases for building rich epistemic structures. In: Moss, L.S. (ed.) Proceedings Seventeenth Conference on Theoretical Aspects of Rationality and Knowledge (TARK 2019). EPTCS, vol. 297, pp. 332–353 (2019)
25. Lorini, E.: Rethinking epistemic logic with belief bases. Artif. Intell. **282**, 103233 (2020)
26. Lorini, E., Rapion, E.: Logical theories of collective attitudes and the belief base perspective. In: Proceedings of the 21st International Conference on Autonomous Agents and Multiagent Systems (AAMAS 2022). ACM (2022)
27. Lorini, E., Romero, F.: Decision procedures for epistemic logic exploiting belief bases. In: Proceedings of the 18th International Conference on Autonomous Agents and Multiagent Systems (AAMAS 2019), pp. 944–952. IFAAMAS (2019)
28. Lorini, E., Sabouret, N., Ravenet, B., Fernandez Davila, J., Clavel, C.: Cognitive planning in motivational interviewing. In: Proceedings of the 14th International Conference on Agents and Artificial Intelligence (ICAART 2022), pp. 508–517. SCITEPRESS (2022)
29. Löwe, B., Pacuit, E., Witzel, A.: DEL planning and some tractable cases. In: van Ditmarsch, H., Lang, J., Ju, S. (eds.) LORI 2011. LNCS (LNAI), vol. 6953, pp. 179–192. Springer, Heidelberg (2011). https://doi.org/10.1007/978-3-642-24130-7_13
30. Miller, W.R., Rollnick, S.: Motivational Interviewing: Helping People Change. Guilford press (2012)
31. Park, S., Shim, H.S., Chatterjee, M., Sagae, K., Morency, L.P.: Computational analysis of persuasiveness in social multimedia: A novel dataset and multimodal prediction approach. In: Proceedings of the 16th International Conference on Multimodal Interaction, pp. 50–57 (2014)
32. Rashotte, L.: Social influence. In: Ritzer, G., Ryan, J.M. (eds.) Concise Blackwell Encyclopedia of Sociology. Blackwell (2009)
33. Salperwyck, C., Lemaire, V.: Impact de la taille de l'ensemble d'apprentissage: une étude empirique. Conférence Internationale Francophone sur l'Extraction et la Gestion de Connaissance (2011)
34. Searle, J.: Rationality in Action. MIT Press, Cambridge (2001)
35. Siegel, M.S.: Persuasive robotics: how robots change our minds. Ph.D. thesis, Massachusetts Institute of Technology (2008)
36. Thaler, R.H., Sunstein, C.R.: Nudge: Improving Decisions About Health, Wealth, and Happiness. Yale University Press (2008)
37. Wang, Y.: A logic of goal-directed knowing how. Synthese **195**(10), 4419–4439 (2018)
38. Xi, Z., et al.: The rise and potential of large language model based agents: a survey. arXiv preprint arXiv:2309.07864 (2023)

A Novel Bidding Strategy for PDAs Using MCTS in Continuous Action Spaces

Sanjay Chandlekar[1,2]([✉]) [ID] and Easwar Subramanian[2] [ID]

[1] IIIT Hyderabad, Hyderabad, India
sanjay.chandlekar@research.iiit.ac.in
[2] TCS Innovation Labs, Hyderabad, India
easwar.subramanian@tcs.com

Abstract. Bidding in a periodic double auction (PDA) is challenging due to its sequential nature, where one needs to consider current as well as future auctions to decide the bids. Monte-Carlo Tree Search (MCTS), which is a state-of-the-art online planning algorithm for tackling sequential problems, seems a perfect fit for bidding in PDAs. However, the success stories of MCTS are largely limited to discrete action spaces, and its efficacy diminishes when dealing with continuous actions. Conventional methods often resort to overly simplistic discretizations that limit exploration and fail to provide valuable insights into unexplored actions. In this work, we propose a novel bidding strategy for PDAs, Regression-MCTS, that is built upon MCTS for a continuous action space of bid prices. Unlike conventional methods, our novel MCTS method leverages information obtained from explored actions to enhance the understanding of the larger action set within the continuous domain to place bids in the auctions, thus generalizing the information about action quality between a wider action space for faster learning. To test the efficacy of our proposed method, we design an efficient PDA simulator that closely resembles real-world PDAs. Our analysis verifies that the increase in the number of rollouts improves its performance. Furthermore, our experimental results demonstrate that our approach outperforms existing MCTS-based bidding strategies and the majority of state-of-the-art PDA bidding strategies, showcasing its superior performance in PDAs.

Keywords: MCTS for Continuous Action Space · Online Planning · Bidding Strategy for PDA

1 Introduction

Auctions play a pivotal role in computer science and its associated domains, serving as dynamic mechanisms for the allocation of resources and the facilitation of transactions. Their significance spans a broad spectrum, from the allocation of computational resources in cloud computing to the distribution of spectrum in wireless networks. Double auctions, in particular, are widely used in industries like stock trading and energy markets, with significant economic influence. For instance, Stock Exchanges facilitate daily transactions worth trillions of dollars, while energy markets in Europe alone witness volumes exceeding 1000 TWh, translating to billions of dollars in cash flow through energy trades [1]. Given this economic impact, the development of bidding strategies capable of optimizing procurement costs holds paramount importance, promising significant improvements in both profitability and operational efficiency.

However, despite the prevalence of double auctions, the design of optimal bidding strategies remains a formidable challenge, particularly in complex domains such as the energy market. In this context, trades often occur through periodic double auctions (PDAs), where participants can procure energy several hours ahead of the delivery hour, necessitating strategic planning across current and future auctions, with each decision influencing subsequent steps. Consequently, the decision-making process for bidding strategies becomes intricate, demanding innovative approaches to navigate the complexities of real-time bidding dynamics effectively. For such sequential decision-making problems, Monte Carlo Tree Search (MCTS) emerges as a fitting framework capable of constructing trees that encompass entire decision-making trajectories, comprehensively capturing process dynamics. Renowned for its efficacy in sequential decision-making tasks, MCTS gained widespread recognition after its pivotal role in AlphaGo's triumph over the world champion in Go [2]. However, MCTS's application predates its Go breakthrough, primarily in game-playing.

Numerous variations aiming to enhance search efficiency and reduce computational overhead have since been proposed. MCTS's advantage lies in its ability to blend the precision of tree search with the generality of random sampling. Nevertheless, its performance in continuous spaces remains a subject of exploration, particularly in real-world problems with continuous action spaces, like determining velocity and acceleration in autonomous driving or setting bid prices in auctions. In these contexts, sequential decision-making is paramount, with each action step affecting the problem state in the future. While MCTS appears well-suited for such tasks, its adaptation to continuous action spaces requires further investigation and refinement.

In the literature, addressing the challenge of applying MCTS to continuous action space problems involves several approaches, including (i) Discretization, (ii) Unpruning or Progressive Widening, (iii) Policy Optimization, and (iv) Action Optimization. Discretization simplifies the continuous action space by discretizing it into a finite set of actions. However, this method constrains MCTS to operate within a fixed action set, limiting its ability to explore all potential outcomes and failing to provide insights into unexplored actions. Progressive Widening addresses the fixed action set limitation by dynamically expanding the action space with more and more simulations. Nevertheless, it also faces constraints due to discretization, restricting thorough exploration of potential outcomes. These techniques share a common limitation: they do not leverage insights gained from explored actions to inform the exploration of unexplored actions or enhance knowledge about previously explored ones.

Given the impracticality of exhaustively exploring all available actions in continuous space, any MCTS algorithm operating in this domain must generalize the action space based on exploration. Policy optimization and action optimization exhibit this generalization capability. Specifically, action optimization (techniques like KR-UCT) aims to enable insights across the entire continuous action space with each action MCTS sample using the environment knowledge, whereas policy optimization methods take a hybrid approach where they build the MCTS tree in a continuous action space and update the policy gradient using the sampled MCTS trajectories to train a parametric model; thereby outperforming discretization and progressive widening methodologies. However, both the above methods are curated for specific problem settings and may not be directly extendable to other problem settings.

In this study, we delve into the realm of continuous action spaces to explore the potential of MCTS, presenting a novel bidding strategy tailored for PDAs. Our strategy, named Regression-MCTS (R-MCTS), harnesses MCTS to derive optimal bidding prices from the continuous action space of prices. Unlike conventional approaches that limit exploration to discrete sets of candidate actions, R-MCTS considers the entirety of the continuous action space, leveraging a predefined set of candidate actions as initialization. Inspired by the KR-UCT method, the core of our strategy lies in generalizing action value estimates across the entire parameter space, facilitating information sharing and enabling exploration beyond the initial candidate set. This adaptability proves invaluable, especially in scenarios with imperfect domain knowledge.

Central to our approach is the generalization of action value estimates over the bid price parameter space for PDAs, achieved by assigning a clearing probability to each action in the action space at each level of the Monte-Carlo tree, reflecting the likelihood of bid clearance. As simulations progress, each exploration updates the clearing probabilities for all previously considered actions at any given level, enhancing MCTS's knowledge incrementally with each iteration. To evaluate the effectiveness of our method, we develop a comprehensive PDA simulation that closely replicates real-world dynamics. This simulation serves as a rigorous testing ground, enabling a comparative analysis of our proposed strategy against state-of-the-art MCTS approaches and top-performing PDA bidding strategies. Below, we outline our contributions:

- We investigate the efficacy of MCTS in continuous action spaces, specifically for the context of placing bids in a periodic double auction.
- Introducing R-MCTS, a novel method designed to navigate the continuous action space of bid prices, harnessing insights gleaned from explored actions to update knowledge about previously visited actions, facilitating enhanced generalization of the action space and accelerating MCTS learning.
- With comprehensive performance analysis, we demonstrate the effectiveness of R-MCTS. Our evaluation encompasses comparisons against several state-of-the-art MCTS methods, as well as various PDA bidding strategies, leveraging a simulated PDA environment as our experimental test bed.

2 Related Work

Some attempts have been made previously to extend the vanilla MCTS to continuous action spaces. One of the early works is done in HOO [5], which deals with continuous arms by utilizing a tree of coverings of the action space and is inspired by the bandit framework. HOOT [3] improvises on vanilla MCTS by replacing the UCB1 action selection rule with HOO. Alternatively, HOLOP [6] embraces a different strategy by modeling this as a continuous bandit problem, where actions correspond to plans, leveraging HOO. Alternative strategies, such as the progressive widening method, have also been expanded to address stochastic continuous state and action planning predicaments by employing double progressive widening [7], which applies progressive widening to both states and actions. To amplify the efficacy of MCTS integrated with progressive widening, cRAVE [8] integrates the RAVE heuristic [10] using Gaussian convolution, thereby promoting information exchange among actions throughout the entire subtree. Additionally, KR-UCT [11] is another notable approach fostering information sharing among actions within the same node through kernel regression, and it generates new actions guided by kernel density estimation. KR-UCT has showcased superior performance compared to cRAVE in simulated curling environments, earning its acknowledgement as state-of-the-art. The work by Couetoux [9] provides an excellent overview of the MCTS literature.

MCTS-based strategies have also found application in the domain of simultaneous ascending auctions [18,19], negotiations [20] and sponsored search auctions [21]. Apart from these, MCTS-based strategies have contributed to the domain of PDAs as well, many interesting MCTS strategies are proposed in the framework of the Power Trading Agent Competition (PowerTAC) [13]. This competition, which closely simulates real-world smart grid scenarios, hosts an annual tournament attracting various teams who deploy broker agents equipped with bidding strategies for energy procurement from the wholesale market PDAs. Notably, SPOT [14], a prominent broker agent in the PowerTAC literature, introduced an MCTS-based bidding strategy augmented with heuristic techniques. Inspired by the success of SPOT's MCTS strategy, Tuc_Tac [17] developed its own MCTS bidding strategy, which bears significant resemblance to SPOT's approach. However, both strategies operate within discretized action spaces, crucial for determining bid prices and quantities in auctions. Specifically, they employ bid price predictors to anticipate suitable bid prices for all auctions. These predicted bid prices serve as input for MCTS, which subsequently determines multipliers and quantity fractions from a discrete set of actions. These multipliers are then applied to the predicted bid price to establish lower and upper bounds for bid prices, within which they place multiple bids for the selected bid quantity. However, all these methods are either limited by the discrete nature of action space or curated for specific problem settings and may not be directly extendable to other problem settings.

3   Background

We start by outlining the foundational algorithms that R-MCTS will build upon and introducing the problem domain for which the proposed strategy is designed.

3.1   MCTS for Discrete Action Spaces

MCTS is a powerful algorithm in the realm of artificial intelligence and computer science, particularly acclaimed for its effectiveness in decision-making and problem-solving in complex, strategic environments. Originally developed for game-playing scenarios, MCTS has since found applications in various domains, from robotics to optimization. Unlike traditional tree search methods, MCTS employs a stochastic sampling approach to traverse the search space, effectively balancing exploration and exploitation. By simulating numerous random playouts from each node of a decision tree and updating statistics accordingly, MCTS gradually refines its understanding of the problem landscape, ultimately guiding toward optimal or near-optimal solutions.

MCTS is a simulation-based search approach to planning in finite-horizon sequential decision-making settings. The core of the approach is to iteratively simulate executions from the current state to a terminal state, incrementally growing a tree of simulated states (nodes) and actions (edges). Each simulation starts by visiting nodes in the tree and selecting which actions to take based on a *selection function* and information maintained in the node. Consequently, it transitions to a successor state. When it encounters a node that is not fully expanded, then the node is *expanded* by adding a new leaf to the tree. Then, a *simulation* is performed from the new leaf to a terminal state. The value of the terminal state is then returned as the value for that new leaf and the information stored in the tree is updated.

The most widely used selection function for MCTS is Upper Confidence Bounds Applied to Trees (UCT) [12]. In UCT, each node maintains the mean of the rewards received for each action, $\bar{v}_a$, and the number of times each action has been selected, n_a. It initially tries each action once and then chooses the next action based on the size of the one-sided confidence interval on the reward, computed using the Chernoff-Hoeffding bound as shown below,

$$argmax_a \left[\bar{v}_a + C \sqrt{\frac{log \sum_b n_b}{n_a}} \right] \qquad (1)$$

This bound is controlled by the constant C, which determines the exploration-exploitation trade-off and is typically fine-tuned for the specific domain. However, one of the primary limitations of discrete MCTS methods is the fixed size of the action space, which is addressed by progressive widening methods.

3.2 MCTS for Continuous Action Spaces: Simple Progressive Widening (SPW)

In continuous MCTS, the vanilla UCT no longer works since each action should be tried at least once and there are infinitely many actions to be considered. Progressive widening addresses this challenge by maintaining a finite list of actions to be explored and incrementally adding new child action nodes v_c to this list based on visitation counts. Specifically, a new child node is added whenever the following condition is met:

$$n(v_c)^\alpha \geq |children(v_c)|$$

Here, $\alpha \in (0, 1)$ is a parameter controlling the growth rate, $n(v_c)$ is the visit count of the node v_c's and $|children(v_c)|$ is the size of node v_c children list. This ensures that before adding a new action to the list, the current set of actions gets visited sufficient times. When a new node v_d is created, a new action particle is either sampled from a probability distribution $a \sim \pi_{sampler}(\cdot|s)$ or deterministically generated (e.g., to expand the action space coverage). This generated action particle is stored in $action(v_d)$, and the process iterates accordingly.

3.3 Periodic Double Auction

The wholesale market of a smart grid comprises large power-generating companies, also known as GenCos, which produce energy in bulk and offer it at wholesale prices. Energy in this market is traded through an auction mechanism, specifically a *day-ahead periodic double auction* involving GenCos and energy brokers. Here, *day-ahead* signifies that brokers engage in buying or selling energy for future delivery timeslots, typically ranging from 1 to 24 hours ahead. These auctions occur periodically, with clearing taking place after each hour. In most cases, a specific type of double auction known as a *k-double auction* is employed, which is considered for this work as well, as described below.

k-Double Auction: A k-double auction is a type of auction where potential buyers submit bids and potential sellers submit asks to the auctioneer. The auctioneer then aggregates these bids and asks, determining each player's *clearing quantity* and *clearing price* using predefined allocation and payment rules. The clearing price represents the price at which the auctioneer clears the market by matching buyers' bids with sellers' asks. The clearing quantity for each player denotes the number of items they receive (for buyers) or sell (for sellers) after the auction clears, as determined by the allocation rule. Additionally, the payment rule specifies the payment each player makes or receives at clearing time (buyer pays, seller earns). In our context, if a buyer's bid b exceeds the seller's bid s, the clearing price is calculated as $kb + (1 - k)s$ for some fixed $k \in [0, 1]$. Here, we consider $k = 0.5$, meaning the clearing price is the mean of b and s.

Figure 1 provides an illustrative example of market clearing in a typical PDA using the k-double auction mechanism. During each auction instance, buyers and sellers submit their bids and asks to the auction, following the convention

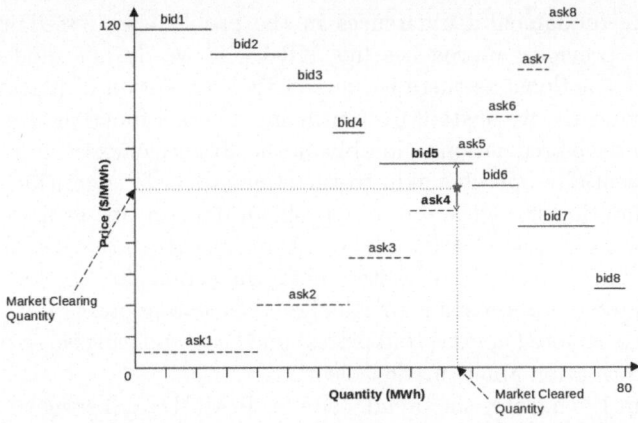

Fig. 1. Market Clearing Example: Partial bid5 and full ask4 are the last to clear

where bids contain a positive energy amount and negative price, while asks include a negative energy amount and positive price. Bids, or asks without price details (known as market orders), are sorted first as they are treated as the highest bid amount or lowest ask amount. Demand and supply curves are then constructed from these bids and asks. As illustrated in the figure, asks are sorted in increasing order of prices (forming the supply curve), while bids are sorted in decreasing order of prices (forming the demand curve). The clearing price occurs at the intersection of these curves. If there is no unique price intersection, the clearing price is calculated based on the lowest successful bid (b) and the highest successful ask (s) price, following the definition of a k-double auction.

In this work, we adhere to the *uniform payment rule*, where all successful buyers[sellers] pay[receive] the same clearing price, regardless of their bid[ask] values. The cleared quantity for a buyer[seller] matches its bid[ask] energy amount in the case of full clearing and partially in the case of partial clearance.

4   Regression-MCTS (R-MCTS)

In this section, we present our proposed method, R-MCTS, which operates within a continuous action space by leveraging domain knowledge to generalize explored actions. Our algorithm draws inspiration from KR-UCT's concept of facilitating information sharing among all considered actions, aiding in action space generalization and insights into unexplored actions. Additionally, to accommodate continuous action spaces, we employ the SPW technique. This involves initiating each node with a shallow action space and progressively expanding it as the node is visited repeatedly. Both initially provided candidate actions and progressively added actions, along with their estimated values, collectively form a single dataset at each node for R-MCTS.

Given the fundamental differences in the problem addressed in this work compared to previous approaches like KR-UCT, we do not model execution uncertainty for actions, as there is none in their execution of placing bids in a PDA. Consequently, we abstain from utilizing a kernel function to gain insights into similar unexplored actions. Notably, in the absence of execution uncertainty, KR-UCT essentially operates akin to the standard UCT algorithm with SPW, potentially limiting its efficacy in our problem domain. Instead, we utilize the knowledge of the market clearing of the bids to strengthen the insights about the actions that have already been visited; here, the actions are the bid prices. The core idea behind our approach is to calculate the clearing probability, $p\_cleared$, for each of the explored actions (bid prices) and keep updating these probabilities with new information about market clearing.

Algorithm 1 delineates the pseudocode for R-MCTS, adhering to the conventional four-step process of MCTS: selection, expansion, simulation, and backpropagation. The primary procedure, R-MCTS, is invoked on the root of the search tree for a fixed number of rollouts determined by a computation budget, returning a list of bid prices for the buyer. The functions $generate\_sellers()$ and $clone\_buyers()$ emulate the sellers and buyers (including R-MCTS and random buyers) of the PDA, respectively. Thus, these modeled sellers and buyers facilitate the simulation of PDA scenarios during the rollout process.

The modeled sellers primarily comprise GenCos, which follow a quadratic supply curve along with some noise. To model these GenCos, we take help from the PowerTAC simulator that simulates such GenCos. The PowerTAC simulator generates GenCos ask with the help of pre-defined quadratic functions along with some nice to infuse stochasticity in the asks. We utilise the same set of quadratic functions along with noise in our simulator to model the GenCos. On the other hand, the modeled buyers consist of a clone of R-MCTS alongside ZI buyers that place bids randomly. The simulator also allows one to choose from a set of baseline buyers (see Sect. 6.2) instead of the ZI buyer to play against R-MCTS during the simulation. Throughout the rollout process, we replicate the actual market scenario using these modeled sellers and the same number of modeled buyers as in the original PDA, trading for demands identical to the original demands of buyers. Specifically, if in the actual market scenario, the R-MCTS is competing against n buyers where each of these buyers has their own demands; in the simulation, too, we replicate a similar scenario by cloning the same n number of competing buyers with their actual demand. The seller, too, would have similar asks and corresponding prices as to the actual market scenario. Since we may not have information about the opponents' actual bidding strategies, during the rollout, the ZI buyers or any other baseline buyers function as opponents of R-MCTS. This setup enables R-MCTS to assess the market scenario and make decisions accordingly. Further insights into the proposed algorithm are provided below.

Algorithm 1. R-MCTS($rem\_quant, cur\_ts, delv\_ts$)

1: $bids \leftarrow []$, $root \leftarrow$ Node()   # initialise bids list and root node
2: $rem\_auctions \leftarrow delv\_ts - cur\_ts$ # number of auctions remaining in a PDA
3: **if** $rem\_quant > 0$ **then**
4:     **while** i in NUMBER_OF_ROLLOUTS **do**
5:         $visited \leftarrow []$, $rewards \leftarrow []$, $cur \leftarrow root$ # initialise lists of visited, rewards
6:         $visited \leftarrow [visited; root]$
7:         $list\_of\_sellers \leftarrow$ generate_sellers()
8:         $list\_of\_buyers \leftarrow$ clone_buyers()
9:         **while** not cur.is_leaf(rem_quant) **do**
10:             $cur \leftarrow$ select(rem_quant)   # see algorithm 2
11:             $cur.p\_cleared \leftarrow$ get_pcleared($rem\_auctions, cur.action$)
12:             cp, cq, rem_quant $\leftarrow$ perform_auction($cur.action$, rem_quant, $list\_of\_sellers, list\_of\_buyers$)   # clearing the current auction round
13:             $rewards \leftarrow [rewards; cp]$
14:             $visited \leftarrow [visited; cur]$
15:         **end while**
16:         $cur\_cost, cur\_quant \leftarrow cur$.simulation($rem\_quant, rem\_auctions$)
17:         $root \leftarrow$ backpropogation($rewards, visited, cur\_cost, cur\_quant$)
18:     **end while**
19:     $lp \leftarrow root$.best_action()
20:     $bids \leftarrow [bids;$ Bid(buyer_ID, lp, rem_quant)]   # limit order
21: **else**
22:     $bids \leftarrow [bids;$ Bid(buyer_ID, NULL, rem_quant)]   # market order
23: **end if**
24: **return** $bids$

Algorithm 2. select($node, rem\_quant$)

1: **if** $number\_of\_visits(node)^\alpha \leq number\_of\_children(node)$ **then**
2:     $A \leftarrow$ actions considered in $node$
3:     $action \leftarrow argmax_{a \in A} \mathbb{E}(v|a) + C\sqrt{\frac{log \sum_{b \in A} number\_of\_visits(b)}{number\_of\_visits(a)}}$ # UCB-select
4: **else**
5:     new $action \leftarrow$ child of $node$ by taking an action using $p\_cleared$ data
6:     $node.children \leftarrow [node.children; action]$ # SPW-select: expanding action space
7: **end if**
8: $new\_state = node.action$
9: **return** new_state

Calculation of Clearing Probabilities: The function $p_{cleared}(s, action)$ is estimated from the past auction statistics as:

$$p_{cleared}(s, action) = \frac{\sum_{ac \in auction[s], ac.CP < action} ac.cleared\_amount}{\sum_{ac \in auction[s]} ac.cleared\_amount} \quad (2)$$

where $auction[s]$ represents the collection of all past auctions in the current state s, with CP denoting the clearing prices of those auctions. Here, the state is defined by the number of auctions remaining in the PDA or the level in the

Monte-Carlo tree, denoted as *rem_auctions* and computed based on current and delivery timeslots (Line 2). Essentially, this formula calculates the clearing probability of any *action*, which represents a bid price, by considering what fraction of the total quantity traded in the current state (s) had a clearing price (CP) less than the given *action*. In simple terms, the formula calculates, historically, how much quantity has been traded at a price less than *action* price, which indicates the probability or likelihood of a bid at *action* price getting cleared. A higher price would have a $p_{cleared}$ value close to 1 as, historically, most of the quantity would have been sold at a comparatively lesser price and vice versa. In Algorithm 1, the *get_pcleared(rem_auctions, cur.action)* function executes the above-mentioned calculations for each action or bid price selected during the rollouts (Line 11).

4.1   Selection and Expansion Phase

The selection phase locates the leaf node in the current tree (the node that has not been expanded yet) and then we perform the expansion phase to expand the tree from that node (Lines 9–15). Our algorithm invokes the *select* method (Line 10), which determines the next node to traverse by utilizing two selection modes: UCB-select and SPW-select, as depicted in Algorithm 2. UCB-select adheres to the UCB formula at each decision node, aiding the algorithm in selecting from previously explored actions. At each node, crucial metrics such as the number of visits, the action that led to the current node, the average unit purchase cost (mean utility $\mathbb{E}(v|a)$), and a set of child nodes b are maintained. As iterations progress and outcomes are revisited, their mean utilities and visit counts are updated accordingly. These updated estimates are then integrated into their respective roles within the UCB formula, guiding the selection of actions for further refinement. The scaling constant C plays a pivotal role, governing the tradeoff between exploring less-visited actions and refining the value of more promising actions.

SPW-select is triggered when the condition for SPW 3.2 is satisfied (Line 1), indicating that a node has been visited sufficiently many times compared to its number of children. This condition signifies the necessity to expand the action space for the current node. This decision is based on maintaining the number of outcomes in a node bounded by some exponential function of the number of visits to the node. To execute the SPW step, a random policy is employed to select an action beyond the initial action space. Alternatively, domain knowledge can be utilized for selecting a new action.

During the SPW stage, we leverage the knowledge of $p_{cleared}$ data in the current state of the node to introduce a new action into the action space. Given that PDA allows a buyer to bid for 24 rounds per auction, our strategy varies based on risk tolerance. In early rounds, we opt for actions with lower $p_{cleared}$, taking higher risks to procure the required quantity at lower prices. As the auction progresses towards its final rounds, we adopt a more conservative approach, prioritizing actions with higher $p_{cleared}$ to ensure procurement certainty, as shown in Fig. 2. This strategy enables R-MCTS to explore risky actions (or bid prices)

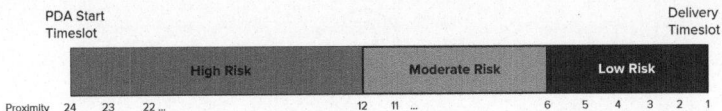

Fig. 2. Tactics to Adjust Risk between Auction Rounds

initially and transition towards more assured options as the auction progresses. Once the new action is chosen, it is added to the list of children of the current node, and the function returns the next state after executing the selected action.

Once the algorithm reaches a leaf node in the tree, it expands the tree by selecting an action and conducting auction clearing (*perform_auction()*) for that chosen action. This process results in transitioning to the next state, which becomes a child of the current node. Subsequently, the simulation phase is conducted from this new state.

4.2   Simulation and Backpropagation Phase

When a new outcome is integrated into the tree, a complete search ensues to reach a terminal state using a default policy, which can be a random policy as well. We simulate the remaining rounds of the auction from the state generated during the expansion phase and record the procurement cost along with the quantity purchased by R-MCTS (Line 16). During the simulation phase, at each of the remaining auction states (*rem_auctions*), we conduct auction clearing (*perform_auction()*) and record intermediate procurement costs. Additionally, we update the remaining quantity of all the brokers for the subsequent state based on the market clearing in the current state. Subsequently, all the intermediate procurement costs and cleared quantities of R-MCTS are aggregated and returned as the output of the simulation phase. This output is then utilized to update $\mathbb{E}(v|a)$ and the visit count of the visited nodes along the selected path through the tree during the backpropagation phase (Line 17).

4.3   Final Selection Phase

Once the computational budget is exhausted, determined either by the number of iterations or by a pre-allocated time limit, we utilize the search results to select an action for execution. The chosen action is the one at the root with the highest mean utility, indicating the lowest unit purchase cost.

Figure 3 shows an intermediate state of R-MCTS. Each node contains VC, act, MU, |C| denoting the visit count of the node, action or limitprice that leads to the node, mean utility, and number of children, respectively. Below, we provide implementation details of R-MCTS with the help of the example given in Fig. 3.

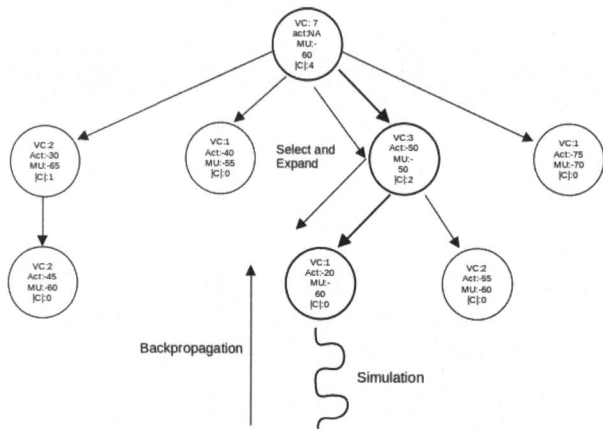

Fig. 3. Pictorial Representation of R-MCTS Displaying all the Phases

5   Example Walk-Through of R-MCTS

In this section, we explain the working of the proposed Algorithm 1 in more detail with the help of an example shown in Fig. 3. At the start, the tree is empty. The algorithm starts with initialising the *root* node of the tree and the list of *bids*. Then, it creates the search tree based on the current auction round (*rem_auctions*). After that, if the remaining quantity (electricity) to purchase for the broker is positive, then it starts the ROLLOUT routine; otherwise, it places a market order to see the quantity (if the remaining quantity is negative, that means the broker has extra quantity and it needs to be sold). In the rollout routine, the algorithm performs $NUMBER\_OF\_ROLLOUTS$ iterations; the number of iterations depends on the available computation budget.

During the rollout process, the algorithm initialises the essential data structures to store the list of visited nodes (*visited*) and rewards (*rewards*). Here, the *reward* is the average clearing price of PDA during each rollout process. A new node *cur* is created and assigned to the *root* node of the tree; this node helps the algorithm to traverse the search tree. The rollout routine starts with adding the *root* node in the *visited* list. Then, to simulate the rollout process, it generates the list of sellers and list of buyers as described in Sect. 4. After this, the algorithm follows the standard four-step process of MCTS: selection, expansion, simulation and backpropagation. First is selection, followed by expansion, combined in the algorithm (line no. 9 to 15). Then, the simulation step (line no. 16) and the backpropagation step (line no. 17). This four-step process is repeated at each iteration of the rollout process.

In our example, in the first iteration of rollout, there is only a single node in the tree. Thus, the selection process would select that node and expand the tree from that selected node. In order to expand the tree, the algorithm selects an action (a bid price) and places a bid in the PDA. The auction clearing mechanism collects this bid along with bids and asks from the generated sellers and buyers. The mechanism determines the clearing price cp, clearing quantity cq and remaining quantity rem_quant for all the players in this auction. After this, a new node is added to the search tree and is added to the *visited* list. The cq is a reward and is added to the *rewards* list. The visit count for the new node becomes 1 (initially 0 and gets incremented by 1 after each visit. After the expansion step, the simulation step occurs, where the tree is traversed till all rounds of auction get exhausted. During each round, a PDA auction occurs exactly as discussed above, and the cp,cq and rem_quant are recorded. Finally, once the simulation is over, the reward is calculated as the average clearing price during the simulation using the data of cp and cq, which is then added to the *rewards* list. Finally, the backpropagation step takes place, and all the visited nodes get updates with their respective rewards; also, $p\_cleared$ of each visited node gets updated based on auction data till the current iteration.

The above process is repeated multiple times to expand the tree in breadth and depth directions. Once the rollout process is over, the algorithm selects the *best_action* from the *root* node of the tree, which is the action that leads to the child node having the lowest average clearing price. Once the action is known, a bid is placed in the actual market PDA.

6   Experimental Evaluation

In this section, we conduct experiments to assess the performance of R-MCTS within continuous action spaces. As R-MCTS deals with a continuous action space, it can effectively handle any number of actions by expanding the tree in breadth. Specifically, we apply R-MCTS to the domain of PDAs, where it generates bid prices from a continuous range of feasible prices. To facilitate our evaluation, we have developed an efficient PDA simulator that faithfully replicates real-world PDA dynamics. This simulator serves as our testing platform to thoroughly examine R-MCTS and compare it against baseline strategies. We begin by detailing the experimental setup, followed by descriptions of each of the opponent baseline strategies. Finally, we present results alongside discussions.

6.1   Experimental Setup

To thoroughly evaluate the proposed R-MCTS, we conduct a comprehensive analysis alongside state-of-the-art MCTS strategies and efficient PDA bidding strategies. Our experiments are organized into three sets. Set-1 focuses on examining the learning capabilities of R-MCTS by analyzing its performance relative to the number of rollouts. Specifically, we compare the average purchase cost of R-MCTS across varying rollout numbers to ascertain whether increased rollouts lead to improved performance. Set-2 involves comparing the purchase cost of R-MCTS against various other MCTS-based bidding strategies in 1v1 games (only two buyers in PDAs, R-MCTS and one of the opponent strategies) under different demand scenarios (low, medium, high, and extreme). By performing these experiments, we aim to demonstrate the efficacy of our proposed approach against state-of-the-art MCTS methods. Similarly, Set-3 entails a comparison of R-MCTS against potent bidding strategies from the PowerTAC literature in 1v1 games across all four demand scenarios. This experiment assesses the performance of our strategies against some of the best PDA bidding strategies.

By conducting these comparisons across different demand levels, we aim to test the efficacy of our strategies under diverse circumstances. Each experiment is executed 100 times to ensure robust results, with mean values presented in the results. Below, we provide detailed explanations for each set of experiments.

Experiment Set-1: In this set of experiments, we engage R-MCTS as the sole participant in a PDA. Each iteration involves randomly generating demand for the strategy from a Gaussian distribution. To fulfil this demand, R-MCTS conducts a series of rollouts to familiarize itself with the environment and determine optimal bidding strategies. The purpose of these experiments is to assess the learning proficiency of R-MCTS across varying numbers of rollouts, ranging from low to high. Specifically, we explore the following rollout numbers: $\{1, 5, 10, 50, 100, 500, 1000\}$. For each rollout quantity, we record the unit purchase cost of R-MCTS, and the corresponding graph is depicted in Fig. 4. This analysis provides insights into how the performance of R-MCTS evolves with increasing rollout numbers.

Experiment Set-2: This set of experiments aims to assess the performance of the R-MCTS bidding strategy against various other MCTS-based strategies. To achieve this, we leverage several state-of-the-art MCTS methods to design bidding strategies. Specifically, we implement bidding strategies based on Vanilla-MCTS and MCTS-SPW [7]. Additionally, we incorporate the SPOT [14] agent, renowned as one of the top-performing strategies in PowerTAC tournaments. Each of these strategies engages in 1v1 competition against R-MCTS. Following each individual bidding round, we record the average unit purchase costs of each opponent, including R-MCTS. These experiments are conducted across four different demand levels: (i) Low, (ii) Medium, (iii) High, and (iv) Extreme. R-MCTS's results are computed based on 500 rollouts. The resulting graph is presented in Fig. 5.

Experiment Set-3: The third set of experiments mirrors Set-2, albeit with a broader scope. Here, we compare the R-MCTS bidding strategy against a comprehensive array of efficient bidding strategies drawn from the PowerTAC literature. These strategies embody some of the most effective approaches for PDAs, encompassing diverse attributes such as learning-based strategies using Reinforcement Learning, Heuristics-based methods, and more. Specifically, we include ZI, ZIP, VV21 and SPOT strategies in our evaluation. Similarly to Set-2, each of these strategies engages in 1v1 competition against R-MCTS across all four demand levels. We meticulously record the average unit purchase costs of each opponent alongside R-MCTS following individual bidding rounds.

R-MCTS's results are derived from 500 rollouts. The comparative performance graph is displayed in Fig. 6.

6.2 Baseline Strategies

Below, we provide concise descriptions of the baseline strategies employed as opponents in our experiments. These strategies are categorized into two groups: MCTS-based strategies and PowerTAC bidding strategies.

MCTS-based Strategies

MCTS-Vanilla: MCTS-Vanilla is an MCTS method utilizing a discrete and fixed-size action space, constructed iteratively through a search tree as detailed in Sect. 3.1. For designing a bidding strategy for PDAs, MCTS-Vanilla discretizes the action space of bid prices. Each action within this space is defined by two multipliers, α_1 and α_2, applied to the lower and upper bounds of feasible bid prices, respectively. The resulting bid is then placed in the PDA, with the remaining quantity placed as bid quantity across all auction instances. Procurement cost, determined by the bid price, serves as a reward propagated back through the tree.

MCTS-SPW: MCTS-SPW (Simple Progressive Widening) extends MCTS-Vanilla to accommodate continuous action spaces better. While still maintaining a discrete action space, MCTS-SPW dynamically grows its size with the number of rollouts. In the context of designing a bidding strategy for PDAs, MCTS-SPW initializes the action space with randomly sampled bid prices. With more and more rollouts, it explores actions outside the initial action space while striking a balance between exploration and exploitation. Like MCTS-Vanilla, it allocates the remaining quantity as a bid quantity across all auction instances.

SPOT: SPOT [14] employs an MCTS-based bidding strategy; additionally, SPOT integrates several heuristic techniques to optimize bid prices and strategically place multiple bids in auctions. Specifically, it calculates the standard deviation of clearing prices σ offline and incorporates an external limit price predictor that provides limit-price μ. Utilizing a discrete action space, each action includes two multipliers for the limit-price (Δ_{min} and Δ_{max}) and a fraction γ for bid quantity. MCTS selects an appropriate action, and multiple bids are strategically placed within the price range of $\mu + \Delta_{min} * \sigma$ and $\mu + \Delta_{max} * \sigma$ to procure a total fraction of γ of the remaining quantity.

PowerTAC Bidding Strategies

ZI: Instead of considering market conditions, the ZI strategy randomly chooses a bid price within a set range (between a minimum and maximum allowed value) for each auction in a PDA. This strategy involves submitting a single bid with a randomly chosen price for each auction, along with the remaining desired quantity as the bid quantity in all instances.

ZIP: The ZIP agent [15] keeps a scalar variable m representing the profit it aims to achieve, which gets combined with a unit limit price to calculate a bid price p. Small increments adjust the price for each trade with the help of a δ by comparing the submitted bid price and the clearing price. The initial bid price μ is decided randomly at the start of the game and the profit margin is set to -1% of μ, resulting in the initial bid price being $p = \mu * 0.99$. Both δ and μ are updated after each auction to improve future bids. Like ZI strategy, ZIP agent submits the entire remaining quantity as the bid quantity for each auction.

VV21: VV21 [16] is a heuristic strategy that models the cost curve of GenCos derived from uncleared ask information available in PDAs. This strategy aims to identify the price corresponding to the buyer's bid quantity (based on demand forecasts of both the buyer and the market) on the cost curve. It then sets this price as the upper bound on limit prices and places multiple bids below it. This approach facilitates procurement of the majority of the quantity from other buyers' asks in the market, potentially at lower prices, with GenCos considered as suppliers of last resort. VV21 places bids for all the remaining quantity by dividing it into multiple bids.

6.3   Results and Discussion

Below, we present the results of each of the three experiments mentioned above, averaging over 100 random rollouts.

Experiment Set-1: Figure 4 depicts the results from Set-1 experiments, illustrating the impact of the number of rollouts on the average unit procurement cost of R-MCTS. As evident in the graph, there exists an inverse relationship between the number of rollouts and the procurement cost: as the number of rollouts increases, R-MCTS enhances its performance and procures the demand at lower prices.

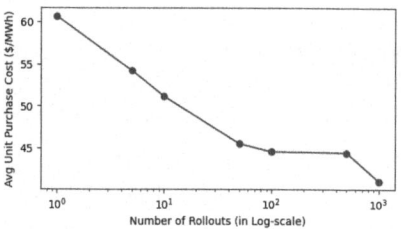

Fig. 4. Rollouts vs Average Unit Purchase Cost for R-MCTS

Consequently, the efficacy depends on the number of rollouts feasible within the system. The result can also be viewed as an effect of number of actions on the average unit procurement cost. The higher the number of rollouts, the broader the breadth of the Monte-Carlo tree, which would mean that more number of actions under any tree node can be explored. As results suggest, increase in number of rollouts leads to decrease in the procurement cost, which signifies the impact of exploring more and more number of actions in order to generalize the continuous action space.

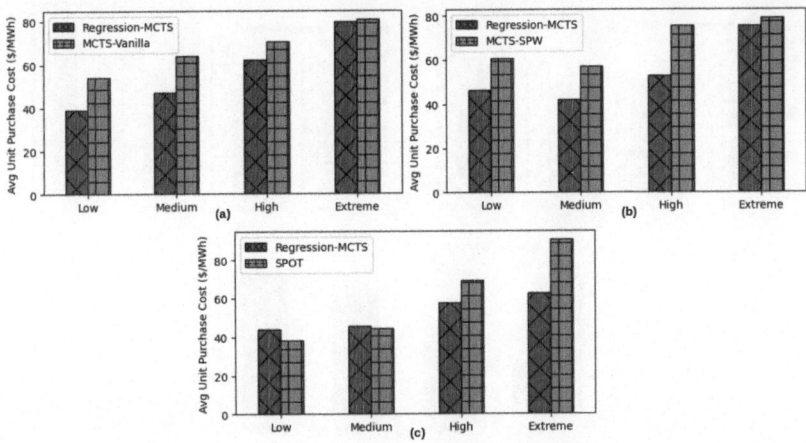

Fig. 5. Comparing R-MCTS vs MCTS-based Bidding Strategies in Low, Medium, High and Extreme Demand Scenarios (((a) vs MCTS-Vanilla (b) vs MCTS-SPW (c) vs SPOT))

Experiment Set-2: Figure 5 illustrates the results of Experiment Set-2, comprising three graphs that compare R-MCTS against three opponents across four different demand scenarios. Specifically, Fig. 5(a) compares the R-MCTS against MCTS-Vanilla, Fig. 5(b) against MCTS-SPW, and Fig. 5(c) against SPOT. As depicted in Figs. 5(a) and 5(b), R-MCTS consistently outperforms MCTS-Vanilla and MCTS-SPW across all demand levels-low, medium, high, and extreme. With the exception of extreme demand, R-MCTS achieves significantly lower procurement costs compared to MCTS-Vanilla and MCTS-SPW across all scenarios. Similarly, as evident in Fig. 5(c), except for low-demand, R-MCTS matches SPOT's performance in medium-demand scenarios and outperforms SPOT by a substantial margin in high and extreme-demand scenarios.

Experiment Set-3: Figure 6 presents the results of Experiment Set-3, comprising three graphs comparing R-MCTS against three opponents across four different demand scenarios. Specifically, Fig. 6(a) compares R-MCTS against MCTS-ZI, Fig. 6(b) against MCTS-ZIP, and Fig. 6(c) against VV21. As depicted in Fig. 6(a), R-MCTS consistently outperforms ZI across all four demand levels. Similarly, as shown in Fig. 6(b), except for extreme demand scenarios, R-MCTS outperforms ZIP by a substantial margin and nearly matches its performance in extreme demand scenarios. A possible explanation for ZIP outperforming R-MCTS in an extreme demand scenario may be that ZIP maintains a profit margin while placing bids, and its unit procurement costs show very low variance; however, R-MCTS has small but increasing variance as we move from low demand to extreme demand. Thus, ZIP's ability to maintain a steady procurement cost helps it to perform slightly better than R-MCTS. Finally, as illustrated in Fig. 6(c), while VV21 outperforms R-MCTS in low and medium-demand scenarios, R-MCTS maintains its performance in high and extreme-demand scenar-

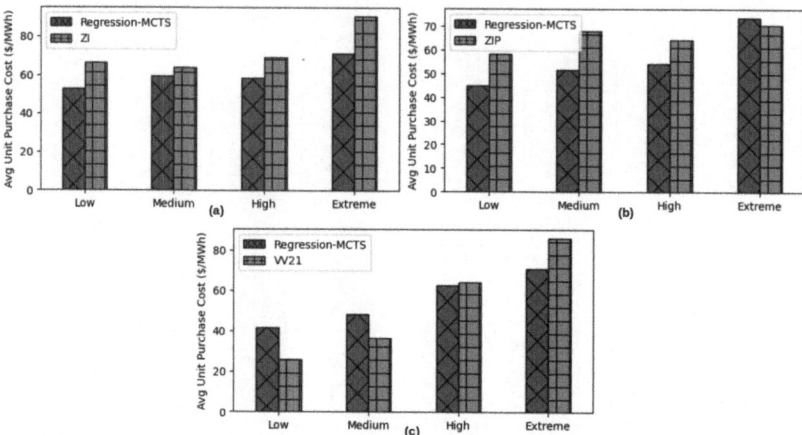

Fig. 6. Comparing R-MCTS vs PowerTAC Bidding Strategies in Low, Medium, High and Extreme Demand Scenarios (((a) vs ZI (b) vs ZIP (c) vs VV21))

ios, surpassing VV21 by a considerable margin. Notably, VV21 is regarded as the best strategy for PowerTAC PDA, and our proposed strategy proves to be more robust across different demand scenarios.

The series of experiments conducted above underscore the effectiveness of our proposed R-MCTS method in the continuous action space of bid prices for PDAs. It shows performance enhancement with an increasing number of rollouts. Furthermore, our method consistently outperforms several top-tier MCTS-based and PowerTAC PDA bidding strategies across different demand levels, underscoring its robustness in adapting to varying demand scenarios.

7   Conclusion

In this work, we delve into the underexplored realm of Monte Carlo Tree Search (MCTS) for continuous action spaces, presenting a novel bidding strategy named R-MCTS that extends MCTS to the continuous action space of bid prices, aiming to improve auction bidding strategies. By leveraging information from explored actions, R-MCTS enhances understanding of the larger action space within the continuous domain, facilitating more informed bidding decisions. Specifically, we utilize clearing probabilities of bid prices calculated based on MCTS's previous auction bids, thereby generalizing information about action quality. To evaluate our method's effectiveness, we developed a realistic PDA simulator closely resembling real-world scenarios. Our analysis reveals that increasing the number of MCTS rollouts enhances performance. Moreover, R-MCTS outperforms existing MCTS-based baseline bidding strategies and many state-of-the-art PDA bidding strategies, showcasing its superior performance in PDAs.

References

1. Nord Pool AS: Anual Report. https://www.nordpoolgroup.com/49eea7/globalassets/download-center/annual-report/annual-review-2020.pdf Accessed 26 Feb 2024
2. Silver, D., Huang, A., Maddison, C.: Mastering the game of Go with deep neural networks and tree search. Nature **529**, 484–489 (2016)
3. Mansley, C., Weinstein, A., Littman, M.: Sample-based planning for continuous action Markov decision processes, In: ICAPS, vol. 21, no. 1, pp. 335–338 (2011)
4. Bubeck, S., Munos, R., Stoltz, G., Szepesvari, C.: X-Armed bandits. J. Mach. Learn. Res. 1655–1695 (2011)
5. Bubeck, S., Munos, R., Stoltz, G., Szepesvari, C.: Online optimization in X-armed bandits. In: NIPS, pp. 201–208 (2008)
6. Weinstein, A., Littman, M.L.: Bandit-based planning and learning in continuous-action Markov decision processes. In: ICAPS (2012)
7. Couetoux, A., Hoock, J., Sokolovska, N., Teytaud, O., Bonnard, N.: Continuous upper confidence trees. In: LION 2011: Proceedings of the 5th International Conference on Learning and Intelligent Optimization, Italie (2011)
8. Couetoux, A., Milone, M., Brendel, M., Doghmen, H., Sebag, M., Teytaud, O.: Continuous rapid action value estimates. In: The 3rd Asian Conference on Machine Learning (ACML2011), vol. 20, pp. 19–31, Taoyuan, Taiwan, Province De Chine. JMLR (2011)
9. Couetoux, A.: Monte carlo tree search for continuous and stochastic sequential decision making problems. Data Structures and Algorithms [cs.DS]. Université Paris Sud - Paris XI (2013)
10. Gelly, S., Silver, D.: Monte-Carlo tree search and rapid action value estimation in computer Go. Artif. Intell. **175**(11), 1856–1875 (2011)
11. Yee, T., Lis'ylis'y, V., Bowling, M.: Monte carlo tree search in continuous action spaces with execution uncertainty. In: The Proceedings of the Twenty-Fifth International Joint Conference on Artificial Intelligence, pp. 690–696 (2016)
12. Kocsis, L., Szepesvári, C.: Bandit based monte-carlo planning. In: Fürnkranz, J., Scheffer, T., Spiliopoulou, M. (eds.) ECML 2006. LNCS (LNAI), vol. 4212, pp. 282–293. Springer, Heidelberg (2006). https://doi.org/10.1007/11871842_29
13. Ketter, W., Collins, J., Reddy, P.: Power TAC: A competitive economic simulation of the smart grid. In: Energy Economics, pp. 262–270 (2013)
14. Chowdhury, M., Kiekintveld, C., Tran, S., Yeoh, W.: Bidding in periodic double auctions using heuristics and dynamic monte carlo tree search. In: International Joint Conferences on Artificial Intelligence Organization, pp. 166–172 (2018)
15. Cliff, D.: Minimal-intelligence agents for bargaining behaviors in market-based environments. In: Technical Report HPL-97-91, Hewlett Packard Labs (1997)
16. Chandlekar, S., Pedasingu, B.S., Subramanian, E., Bhat, S., Paruchuri, P., Gujar, S.: VidyutVanika21: An Autonomous Intelligent Broker for Smart-grids. In: Proceedings of the Thirty-First International Joint Conference on Artificial Intelligence, pp. 158–164 (2022)
17. Orfanoudakis, S., Kontos, S., Akasiadis, C., Chalkiadakis, G.: Aiming for half gets you to the top: winning PowerTAC 2020. In: European Conference on Multi-Agent Systems, pp. 144–159 (2021)
18. Pacaud, A., Marceau, C., Aurelien, B.: Monte carlo tree search bidding strategy for simultaneous ascending auctions. In: 20th International Symposium on Modeling and Optimization in Mobile, Ad hoc, and Wireless Networks (WiOpt). IEEE (2022)

19. Pacaud, A.: Bidding efficiently in simultaneous ascending auctions using monte carlo tree search. In: Institut Polytechnique de Paris (2024)
20. Buron, C.L.R., Guessoum, Z., Ductor, S.: MCTS-based automated negotiation agent. In: Baldoni, M., Dastani, M., Liao, B., Sakurai, Y., Zalila Wenkstern, R. (eds.) PRIMA 2019. LNCS (LNAI), vol. 11873, pp. 186–201. Springer, Cham (2019). https://doi.org/10.1007/978-3-030-33792-6_12
21. Shen, W., et al.: Reinforcement mechanism design- with applications to dynamic pricing in sponsored search auctions. In: Proceedings of the AAAI Conference on Artificial Intelligence, vol. 34, no. 2 (2020)

Jadex BDI Agents Integrated with MATSim for Autonomous Mobility on Demand

Marcel Mauri[(✉)], Ömer Ibrahim Erduran, and Mirjam Minor

Department of Computer Science, Goethe University Frankfurt, Frankfurt am Main,
Germany
{mauri,erduran,minor}@cs.uni-frankfurt.de

Abstract. This paper presents our extension for the BDI-ABM interface, which provides a connection layer for BDI agents to interact with
Agent-based Models (ABM) such as simulation platforms in an integrated Multi-Agent System (MAS). We introduce a new version of the
ABM-Jadex layer, which allows attaching BDI Agents developed with
Jadex, an Agent Development Framework, to the MATSim traffic simulation environment. We introduce cognitive vehicle agents capable of
negotiating among themselves via the contract net protocol. The scalability of the integrated MAS architecture is tested in the first experiments
simulating the behavior of a fleet of autonomous e-trikes.

Keywords: BDI Agent · BDI-ABM Framework · Traffic Simulation ·
Jadex · Agent Development Framework

1 Introduction

Sustainable mobility is one of the global challenges. Large-scale systems with
agent-based technology can contribute to reducing traffic emissions [4]. Simulations of vehicle agents may facilitate better decisions in urban development,
usage of multi-modal mobility, or traffic operation. Platforms like Grab[1] have
recently emerged and launched mobility services with fleets of public and private vehicles. The Grab app connects passengers with private hire, taxi, and
coach drivers. However, it takes seven minutes according to Grab's web page
to be matched with an appropriate vehicle when using its ride-sharing service
GrabShare which takes more than one booking in one ride than one.[2] Cognitive
software agents with negotiation capabilities may provide a more efficient, scalable solution for transport tasks, especially for *Autonomous Mobility on Demand*

---

[1] https://www.grab.com/, last access: 04/16/2024.
[2] https://www.grab.com/sg/inside-grab/stories/grabshare-weve-revamped-our-
carpooling-service/, last access: 04/16/2024.

An earlier version of this paper had been presented at the LWDA 2023 workshop in
Marburg, Germany [23].

D. Briola et al. (Eds.): EMAS 2024, LNAI 15152, pp. 125–143, 2025.
https://doi.org/10.1007/978-3-031-71152-7_8

(AMoD) scenarios. An AMoD system consists of a fleet of autonomous vehicles
that pick up passengers and transport them to their destination [41]. Cognitive software agents like BDI agents have been applied in a wide range of real-
world domains and scenarios for solving different challenges [4,15,16,22]. BDI
agents are based on the human reasoning cycle, translating into beliefs, desires,
and intentions [17]. Since our use case requires several actions to be performed
simultaneously, such as negotiating, maintaining battery power and performing
driving operations, BDI agents were selected as a suitable architecture.

Many agent development platforms supporting BDI agents provide a simulation environment. Frequently, those simulations are rather simplified and closely
application-specific. In contrast, stand-alone simulation platforms are mostly
limited to simple agent types and do not support BDI agents. This makes it
difficult to carry out more complex simulations with BDI agents. Singh et al.
[35] open an alternative strand of research. They integrate agent development
platforms following the BDI agent architecture [17] with rich, agent-based simulation platforms. Figure 1 illustrates how the cognitive BDI agents in the upper
layer interact with each other and the simulation platform. The spotlights indicate that a cognitive vehicle agent receives sensory inputs from its particular
avatar in the simulation and decides its actions.

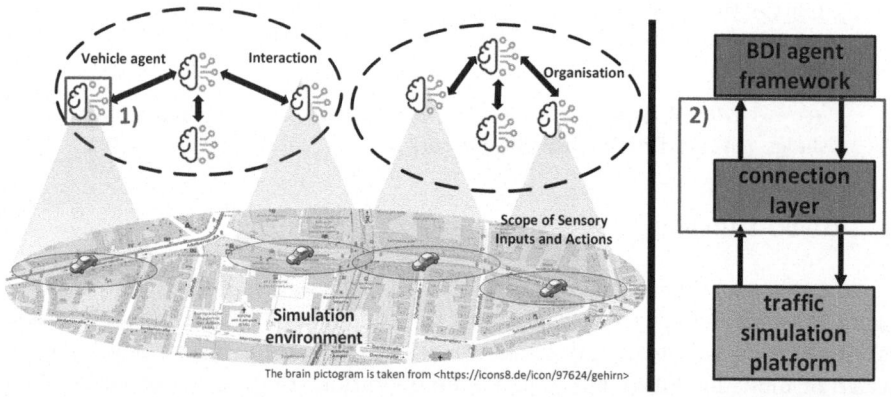

Fig. 1. Contributions marked in red: (1) Development of BDI vehicle agents interacting
with each other. A fleet can be considered as an organization of agents. (2) a connection
layer to the MATSim simulation environment (based on Klügl [20]).

The main contribution of this paper is twofold (cmp. Fig. 1):

1. the *design of self-managing vehicle agents* for AMoD applications following
   the BDI paradigm and using the contract net protocol (CNP) to negotiate
   workloads among themselves.
2. the *synchronization between a BDI agent development framework and a traffic
   simulation platform* building upon the results of Singh et al. [35].

We use mainly open-source tools and framework solutions to implement the integration according to two MAS components. For the *Agent Development Framework* (ADF) we choose Jadex [28]. It is a proven framework that supports BDI agents and is Java-based. A preliminary version of the vehicle agents implemented in Jade [5] has been published in previous work [15]. Jade does not provide libraries for BDI, which made our own implementation too inflexible and difficult to maintain. We decided to redesign the cognitive agents in a native BDI agent framework. Of the established ADFs, we opted for Jadex over other frameworks such as Jill since Jadex provides a well-structured documentation with a large community. In addition, with regard to our future plans for this project Jadex seems more promising for implementing a complex range of functions, including support for the CNP [37] for the communication between agents and the potential for a straight-forward integration of standard machine learning components.

MATSim [40] is used as the simulation platform. MATSim is an agent-based traffic simulation platform, widely used and based on Java. To connect these two platforms, we build upon the already existing BDI-ABM framework [35] and add a new interface for integrating Jadex and MATSim which is not yet included. BDI-ABM has been used to train approximately 60 emergency management specialists from 20 different agencies on bushfire evacuation recently [33]. There is already an integration between an outdated version of Jadex and another simulation platform. Due to the numerous changes on the Jadex framework this version is no longer executable. The intended application scope of the integrated MAS is a broad range of scenarios in AMoD, including ride-hailing, last-mile delivery, or disposal logistics. For the experimental evaluation, we have chosen an AMoD test scenario with a fleet of autonomous e-Trikes.

The remainder of this paper is structured as follows: Sect. 2 presents the related works. The idea and the design of the BDI-ABM integration in general is covered in Sect. 3. Section 4 contains the concept design and the implementation of the integration layer. The conceptual framework of the Jadex vehicle agent is covered in Sect. 5. In Sect. 6, the first experimental results toward scalability of the fleet size for elastic demands are described based on real-world data from a ride-hailing scenario. Section 7 concludes and discusses future work.

2   Related Work

Integrating autonomous software agents into simulation environments has been researched extensively. Software agents have been covered in survey works focusing on the different development frameworks as well as the extensibility of the cognitive architecture [1,9,13,21]. For example, the works of *Timoteo et al.* [39] and *Sadeghi Garjan et al.* integrate software agents, built with Jade in [31], and the traffic simulation SUMO[3]. *Timoteo et al.* provides a generic interface with functionalities for messaging and information exchange between agents and the traffic simulation. However, the current version is incompatible with MATSim

---

[3] https://sumo.dlr.de/docs/index.html, last access: 04/16/2024).

and further implementation is needed to attach it. In addition, no concrete ADF connection is considered. The code is not maintained regularly. *Sadeghi Garjan et al.* integrate Jade agents with SUMO. Although the approach of connecting an ADF and a traffic simulation environment is similar, their presented framework is not open-source. Our work differs in the tool selection and considered frameworks since we require BDI agents. The application of the CNP net protocol for transportation scheduling has been investigated by *Fischer et al.* [19] and *Dorer and Calisti* [12]. The development of software agents is a well-researched field with a plethora of Agent development frameworks proposed by different research labs and organizations. *Silva et al.* cover the BDI agent architecture in their survey [32] and point out several research directions. The main contribution of this paper extends the BDI-ABM environment [35]. This work is grounded in several research papers mentioned in this section. The concepts and fundamental approach of BDI-ABM is presented by *Padgham et al.* in [25]. Here, the authors present multiple layers for integrating different agent development frameworks that especially implement the BDI Agent architecture, with Agent-based Models (ABM) such as simulation platforms.

On a high level, the BDI-ABM framework contains several integration layers for different ADFs implemented in Java. Especially, the framework contains a generic layer, which represents a connection layer for different ADF and simulation environments. For each ADF and simulation environment, a specific layer is developed, which interacts via BDI-ABM. According to *Singh et al.* [35], the mentioned layer provides the possibility to connect other simulation environments as well.

In this context, ABMs provide the environment, where the agents can interact. Thus, research has been conducted in the application scenario of emergency evacuation and multi-modal transportation at a city-wide level [33]. One of the layers connects the simulation environment MATSim [26] with the agent development framework Jill. A Jadex layer is also considered in BDI-ABM. However, the layer is customized for an older version of Jadex and only works with the simulation environment Repast [24] and not with MATSim. There is also no demonstration or example freely available that demonstrates the interaction of Jadex with those simulation environments. In addition it does not support the connection to the current versions of Jadex BDI agents, called *BDIv3*. Thus, we developed a novel integration layer for the connection of Jadex and MATSim. MATSim is a mature and powerful traffic simulator that can be used for large-scale traffic simulations, primarily to assess the likely results of various infrastructure or road network changes.

3   Background

BDI-ABM is listed as a plugin for MATSim providing the connection of BDI agents to MATSim [26,36]. One application of BDI-ABM is in the Emergency Evacuation Scenario (EES) [34,35], where agents in Jill are combined with MATSim by using the BDI-ABM framework. The integration of Agent development frameworks and traffic simulation has also been conducted by *Soares et al.* by integrating Jade platform and the Sumo traffic simulation [38]. Developing a simulation environment for software agents represents the same challenge as developing cognitive agents. *Ricci et al.* use an *Artifact-based approach* [29,30]. *Davoust et al.* consider an *Unmanned aerial vehicle* (UAV) scenario where the agents interact with the simulation environment [10]. Here, the focus is set on the computational performance of executing the framework.

3.1 Traffic Simulation

In our considered domain of traffic simulation, we focus on AMoD settings, where the vehicle agents transport customers from a starting position to their desired destination. MATSim is an activity-based, extendable, multi-agent simulation framework implemented in Java, which is open-source [40]. MATSim is developed using the concept of agent-based modeling that is specified for transport simulation. This framework is designed for large-scale scenarios and is usually used to model a single day. With MATSim, it is possible to simulate traffic, taxi fleets, mobility as a service as well as different modes of transportation. By using MATSim, different modes of Mobility on Demand systems can be simulated. In the current version of MATSim[4] the contribution package DVRP provides the necessary components for setting up a ride-sharing or ride-hailing simulation. In addition, the contribution DRT provides ride-pooling including vehicle agents with additional capacities. It is built on top of the DVRP package. Recent work that investigates scenarios on Mobility on Demand is from *Bischoff et al.*, where ride-pooling and shared taxi fleets are simulated on a city-wide scale analyzing the fleet performance [6–8]. Other mentionable work investigating ride-pooling by using MATSim is from *Zwick et al.* [43] and *Kaddoura & Schlenther* [18]. Our work differentiates from the previously mentioned works since we do not consider MATSim solely, but rather in combination with the external BDI agent platform Jadex. Jadex is responsible for the decisions that are made during the simulation. Therefore, the mentioned AMoD and Mobility as a Service (MaaS) components in MATSim are not considered in our work.

3.2 Interface for Cognitive Agents

In the conceptual framework of BDI-ABM [35], the agents in the simulation have a *"brain"* in the BDI system, which is the decision-making component, and a *"body"* in the ABM system which carries out actions. An agent in this integrated framework will be situated in an environment where it can perceive environmental input via percepts, and act, via actions. These activities of perceiving and acting will happen inside the ABM, where the "body" interacts with the physical world of the domain. To be precise, as shown in Fig. 1 with the arrows of action and percept, the perceptions from the ABM will be communicated to the "brain" on the BDI side. The "brain" will use its decision-making mechanism to select

---

[4] version 15.0, https://github.com/matsim-org/matsim-libs (last access: 04/16/2024).

the suitable action based on the input from percepts, the chosen action will be delivered back to the ABM to be carried out. It is defined in the conceptual framework that a percept going into BDI from ABM does not have to be identical to the percepts in ABM. The percept in BDI is a high-level percept composed of lower-level observations of the environment, which are the percepts represented in ABM. Similarly, an action going from the BDI agent to its ABM counterpart must typically be decomposed into a sequence of lower-level environment actions that the ABM agent knows how to perform. In terms of data transfer between the BDI and ABM systems, two key optimizations for this integrated framework are defined. The first one is that a single data container is passed between the systems in each simulation cycle. The data container bundles the messages for all agents and delivers them all together to the other system to simplify the syn-chronization between the systems. The second one is that not every percept is computed and pushed to the BDI system on every cycle. The reason is the BDI agent processes information contextually and only certain information is useful in certain situations. From the technical point of view, the framework consists of three distinct layers (see right-hand side of Fig. 1). First is a generic layer, which realizes the conceptual model from the previous section. The second layer is the system layer, which provides the code necessary for linking a particular BDI or ABM system into the generic layer. With this layer, built on top of the generic layers, specific BDI systems like Jadex and Jill, as well as ABM systems (i.e. MATSim), can receive and send percepts and actions back and forth. The last layer is the application layer, which provides the application-specific code includ-ing agent behavior and reasoning. Overall, the BDI application provides action decisions to the ABM and the ABM provides observations and environmental information of interest to the BDI module.

4   Jadex-MATSim Integration Layer

The Jadex-MATSim integration framework is inspired by the already existing Jill-MATSim integration framework [36]. Figure 2 shows the new integration lay-ers with the existing components depicted in grey color. The BDI-ABM layer synchronizes the mutual control taken by the cognitive side (Jadex agents) and the simulation side (MATSim). The `Dataserver` component controls the access to a shared memory structure called `AgentDataContainer`. The `Dataserver` grants read/write access to the cognitive side via the `TakeControl BDI` com-mand and withdraw it via the command `TakeControl ABM`, which provides the simulation side with read/write access. Intermediate results from the reasoning cycles of the BDI side are stored in `AgentDataContainer` to be shared with the simulation and the simulation outputs and vice versa.

The `JadexModel` is responsible for initializing the BDI agents and controls the incoming and outgoing data from and to Jadex. To connect the vehicle agents with the BDI-ABM layer, the `SimSensoryInputBroker` and the `SimActuator` play the role of mediators. The mediators are required because Jadex active

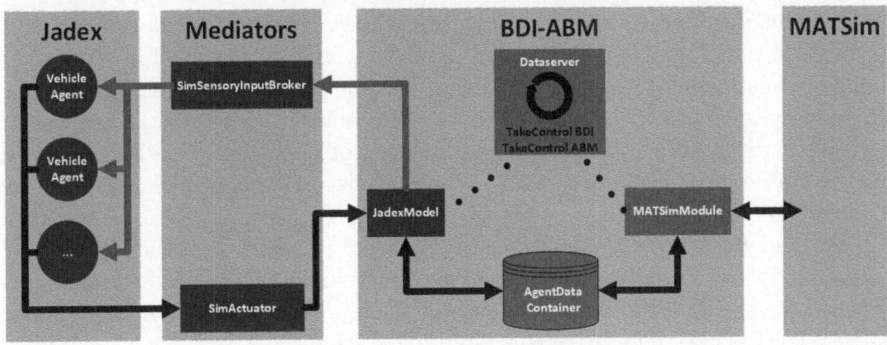

Fig. 2. Simplified illustration of the connection between Jadex and MATSim by BDI-ABM

components like the vehicle agents cannot be accessed directly by external (non-Jadex) components [27]. The `SimActuator` is used by the vehicle agents to write the actions (`drive-to`) into the `AgentDataContainer`.

The `SimSensoryInputBroker` distributes the incoming data from the BDI-ABM (MATSim) side. The entries of the `AgentDataContainer` are directly written into the beliefs of the respective vehicle agents. Once the `SimActuator` has collected new `drive-to` commands from the vehicle agents, the `JadexModel` will update the content of the `AgentDataContainer` and notify the `Dataserver` to pass control to the MATSim side again. The `MATSimModule` [25] will then translate the BDI-actions from the `AgentDataContainer` into low-level actions for MATSim. This means that the updates are performed in a non-equidistant manner.

Unlike the Jill-MATSim integration framework, our Jadex-MATSim integration layer allows agents to continue other non-driving related activities when the control is currently at the MATSim side. All other actions such as communication, negotiation, and calculations are carried out independently of the cycle described in Fig. 2.

5   BDI Vehicle Agents

The agent framework we have developed consists of different types of agents. The geographical environment is divided into multiple zones, each with a responsible area agent. Vehicle agents are autonomous vehicles that are distributed in the application area. All vehicle agents are designed to be homogeneous and cooperate with each other to improve the results of the entire fleet.

They can check in and out at their area agents when they enter or leave their zone and send an update with their current location after every completed journey. When a customer requests a trip, it is delegated to the area agent whose area of responsibility the starting position of the trip is located.

The area agent sends the request to the vehicle agent which is located closest to the start position. The vehicle agent will then evaluate how well it is suited to fulfill the customer's request considering the amount of already accepted trips, the battery level (etc.). Depending on the outcome, it processes the request or negotiates with other vehicle agents in its area of operation to delegate it to a more suitable one. Therefore, it can request a list of other vehicle agents from its associated area agent.

The vehicles will use the contract net protocol (CNP), a negotiation protocol according to the definition of [37]. Thus, the vehicle agents are self-managed. When there are no customers, they drive to safe parking spaces, and when their battery level is low, they drive to a charging station.

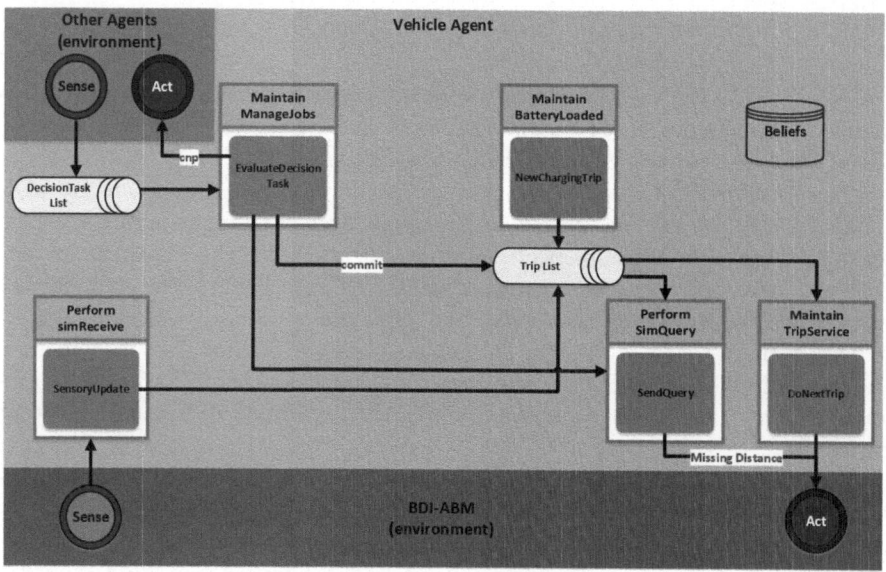

Fig. 3. The components of the vehicle agent architecture

Jadex agents implement a BDI architecture using beliefs, goals, and plans. Beliefs represent the current knowledge of the agent. Desires are goals that are desirable for the agent in general while intentions are a subset of the desired goals for which the agent has committed. Goals in Jadex are used to implement both desires and intentions. Depending on the current state of a goal its theoretical meaning [17] may change between a desire only (inactive goal) or a desire and an intention (active goal). Jadex supports multiple types of goals for different purposes. There are performance goals that will only be executed once and maintain goals that will be triggered by a condition repeatedly. Plans describe the sequence of actions that are executed to achieve a goal.

Figure 3 shows the newly designed architecture of a vehicle agent. The design comprises five goals: `ManageJobs`, `BatteryLoaded`, `TripService`, `SimQuery` and `SimReceive` and their corresponding plans. Vehicle agents have an interface to the BDI-ABM Layer and a second interface for communication with other Jadex agents. Vehicle agents exchange messages with corresponding area agents and other vehicle agents. Incoming jobs are stored inside the `DecisionTaskList`. Every entry in this list is a not yet evaluated `DecisionTask`. A `DecisionTask` contains information about a trip that has been requested by a customer (start time, start position, end position, etc.). As long as this list is not empty the `ManageJobs` goal is active. The corresponding plan `EvaluateDecisionTask` iterates through the entries and determines by their actual progress state the next needed action. We decided against a design in which every `DecisionTask`/ `Trip` will cause the generation of a separate goal/plan that handles its processing. Our approach achieves the same functionality but is easier to handle.

For newly received jobs a utility score is calculated. This score determines how well this vehicle agent is suited to perform this ride. The agent self-assesses three relevant criteria in its utility function, namely the length of the journey to the customer $u_{distance}$, the battery conditions $u_{battery}$, and the punctuality $u_{punctuality}$. The journey to the customer *journey* is measured by the estimated distance d the agent has to drive to reach the customer. This calculation is based on the assumed position at which the agent is expected to be before starting the journey to the customer. This can be the final position of the previously planned *journey*, the location of a charging station, or simply the agent's current location. The Euclidean distance approximates the distance between geolocations specified by decimal degrees with a 1-meter variation in every 2,500-meter distance (cmp. the discussion in [16]). $u_{distance}$ is calculated as follows:

$$u_{distance}(trip) = max\{0, 100 - \frac{journey}{dmax}\} \tag{1}$$

where *dmax* denotes the maximum possible distance between two points at the borders of the territory to normalize the distance values.

The battery conditions are scored as follows. The current battery level from the agent's beliefs is discharged by the estimated battery power consumption for serving the entire trip list committed so far and the job under consideration resulting in an approximate value of *battery*. Assuming a linear decrease of battery during traveling, the battery consumption in terms of several charge units is directly derived from the travel time. The *travel time* between two geolocations l_x, l_y at a constant velocity v is estimated as:

$$travel\_time(l_x, l_y) = \frac{d(l_x, l_y)}{v} \tag{2}$$

We consider a battery factor B_{factor} to rate battery lifetime-friendly thresholds higher:

$$B_{factor} = \begin{cases} 1.0, & battery > 80\% \\ 0.75, & 80\% \geq battery > 30\% \\ 0.1, & battery \leq 30\% \end{cases} \tag{3}$$

These thresholds are also used in other works [2,11,42]. An estimated *battery* beyond the threshold gets a higher score to create incentives for the trip to reach the threshold. The function of the battery utility in light of the agent's current beliefs is defined as follows:

$$u_{battery}(trip) = \begin{cases} -\infty, & battery < 0 \\ B_{factor} * battery, & else \end{cases} \tag{4}$$

The punctuality is scored using the estimated arrival time at the prospective customer and its eventual delay *delay* (approximated using *travel_time*, cmp. Eq. (2)) behind the desired arrival time:

$$u_{punctuality}(trip) = \begin{cases} 100, & delay < \theta \\ 100 - \frac{100(delay-\theta)}{\theta}, & \theta \leq delay \leq 2\theta \\ 0, & else \end{cases} \tag{5}$$

where θ is a threshold the customer is ready to wait without any penalty.

Any distance that has not yet been calculated and is missing in the agent's belief database can be requested from the BDI-ABM environment. The requests are handled by the goal `SimQuery` and its plan `SendQuery`. On the current state of the implementation the goal `SimQuery` is not yet implemented. Currently, all distance calculations on the Jadex side are based on the Euclidean distance, as the agent does not know the actual path their counterparts will take in MATSim.

If the utility score is below a previously defined threshold the agent which calculated the low score will start the CNP to delegate the trip. Before starting, it first requests a list of the vehicle agents registered with its associated area agent. The call for proposals (cfp) will be sent to all other vehicle agents in that area. Cfps are treated similarly to DecisionTasks and are stored inside the `DecisionTaskList`. Any further step of the CNP will also be executed by `EvaluateDecisionTask`. All recipients (contractors) must then calculate how suitable they are for the job and send their proposals back to the sender (manager). The recipients are forced to take part in CNP but are able to communicate their possible usuitability by y low score (especially see Eq. (2))

When the manager has received all proposals it will send an accept/ reject to the contractors and delegate the `DecisionTask`. In our CNP implementation, the manager will always take part as a contractor too. In this way, we can ensure that the most suitable vehicle agent always receives the order and that a sensible decision is made for the entire fleet. Especially if the other agents' proposals are even worse than the manager's or if there are no other agents at all. There are currently no unexpected events or the possibility that the CNP will not be completed. In future updates, we will add a robustness component to our agent that will enable it to make correct decisions even in error cases (e.g. connection loss).

If the utility score of a `DecisionTask` is above the threshold or the agent has received an acceptance regarding a completed CNP the agent will commit it and create a corresponding trip. There are different subtypes of trips. Besides the customer trips that contain information about a trip that was requested by a customer, there are charging trips.

In the current state, each vehicle estimates what the charge level of its battery will be when all committed trips are finished. This estimate is refreshed every time a new trip is committed. If it falls below a charge threshold the goal `BatteryLoaded` is triggered. The corresponding plan `NewChargingTrip` will generate a charging trip that contains information for a `drive-to` to a charging station. Depending on the type, a trip can contain one or more coordinates. While a charging trip just needs the coordinates of the charging station a customer trip needs the start position and the end position of a trip. Trips are stored in the `TripList`, which contains a sorted list of all committed trips that have not yet been started. Any newly created trip will be sent to a scheduler that will insert the new trips into the `TripList` and reschedule the entire list if needed. In the current state of our framework, we can only use FIFO scheduling to insert charging trips into the `TripList`. Future planning will be able to take various criteria into account to ensure that all journeys can still be made and that the remaining battery level is sufficient.

When the `TripList` is not empty the `TripService` goal is activated. The corresponding plan `DoNextTrip` takes the next trip from the `TripList` and sends a `drive-to` command to the BDI-ABM framework which will cause the MATSim counterpart of the agent to drive to the specified location. When a `drive-to` command is sent the internal progress of this `CurrentTrip` is updated. As long as there is no feedback from the BDI-ABM framework the agent will not perform any other `drive-to` operations. Any information sent from the BDI-ABM framework to the Jadex vehicle agent is handled by the `SimReceive` goal. The plan `SensoryUpdate` processes all incoming information from the simulation side. This information could include, for example, the result of a `drive-to` with the new position of the vehicle or a requested distance. After the vehicle has received the confirmation that the last drive operation on the simulation site is finished `DoNextTrip` can resume its work. If the vehicle should break down every Trip inside the `TripList` will be terminated and will be considered as failed. The vehicle will then continue its journey on a full battery.

6   Experimental Evaluation

The experimental evaluation investigates the following hypotheses:

H1 The customer satisfaction increases due to the capability to negotiate and delegate trips via CNP.

H2 The average travel distance per satisfied customer remains stable despite negotiation.

H3 Fewer agents are required to do the work due to negotiation.

Two measures are defined as evaluation criteria for the agent's behavior. The *order dropout rate ODR* measures the rate of trip requests that have been dropped. The threshold θ specified for calculating the estimated punctuality (see Eq. (5)) is also used during driving simulation. If the delay when arriving at the customer is above θ the customer is deemed to be missed. In this case, the vehicle agent drives to the start position of the next trip from the `TripList`. ODR is a measure of customer satisfaction. The *average travel distance ATD* measures the average travel distance to serve a trip. MATSim records the travel distances when simulating a trip between two geolocations. The ATD is calculated by dividing the overall travel distance from MATSim by the number of successfully served trips for the entire fleet. ATD is a significant factor of the traffic emissions (for a sample calculation see Chapter 18 of the MATSim book of Horni et al. [26]).

6.1 Experimental Data

In our experiments, we consider three trip request data sets each containing up to 1000 trip requests from a single day. The dataset has its origin in an open-source bike-sharing data set by Deutsche Bahn[5]. In this historical dataset, we extracted all trips that have their start and end positions inside the considered network area. Furthermore, we generated valid start and end coordinates for the data set to create a free-floating scenario. Precisely, the original data set contains trip request coordinates from a station-based bike-sharing system and gets new coordinates from a range across the campus map. Thus, we get trip request coordinates starting and ending in a free-float manner [16]. The amount of trip requests for a single day is also increased intentionally since the performance of the MAS can be observed clearly when a high capacity utilization arises during processing. The simulation takes place on a university campus map and simulates a day starting from 0:00 am to 11:59 pm. The campus map is extracted from OpenStreetMap[6]. To run our framework, we create a MATSim scenario with the required files [3]. Our MATSim scenario comprises the following data:

- *Population file*: Definition and starting position of the MATSim agents,
- *Network file*: Road network layer with roads of the university campus area,
- *Configuration file*: Configuration file for starting a MATSim simulation.

The sequence of data processing is conducted as follows: First, the trip request dataset is processed by the area agent. It delegates each trip request to the nearest vehicle agent which in turn processes it by its internal reasoning architecture. The Jadex agents send their `drive-to` operations to the equivalent MATSim agents. After completing the trip, the simulation updates the BDI agents by sending back status information concerning the driven trips including their

---

[5] https://data.deutschebahn.com/dataset/data-call-a-bike.html,   last   access: 03/05/2024.

[6] https://openstreetmap.org.

routes and the travel time. In this manner, the data set is processed in a single simulation run representing a whole day of 24 h. The code is available on GitHub[7].

6.2 Experimental Runs

To show the influence of the total number of agents and the influence of the CNP, we set up ten different experimental configurations and ran each with all three datasets (1000 trip data files described above). The 10 configurations consist of five different numbers of vehicle agents (8, 10, 12, 14, and 16), each once with and once without the ability to use the CNP to delegate trips that received a low utility score (cmp. Tables 1 and 2).

Each component of our utility function, $u_{distance}$, $u_{battery}$, $u_{punctuality}$ is weighted with 1/3 and will result in a total score between 0 and 100. The commitment threshold is set to 50, any value greater than or equal to 50 will commit the trip. Any value below this will start the CNP, with the other agents' bids based on the same utility function. To ensure that the trip is always delegated to the most suitable agent, the manager agent of the CNP will always be a participant too. It is therefore possible for the CNP to delegate a trip to an agent even if the score is less than 50. θ is set to 10 min. If a vehicle arrives at the customer's location later than 10 min after booking, the trip is treated as failed. The journey to the end of the trip will not be made in these cases. When the battery has dropped below zero this causes a breakdown of the vehicle. Thus, we estimate the battery level after having served all trips in the `TripList` regularly for each commitment of a new trip. If the estimated battery level is below a threshold of 40%, we will generate a charging trip.

6.3 Experimental Results

The experimental results are measured by ODR and ATD as described above. The presented results are the average form of the results gained by simulating the three datasets. Figure 4 depicts the number of served trips, missed trips, and charging trips for the ten configurations of experimental runs. Having a look at the pie charts from up to down, the ODR decreases with an increasing number of agents as expected (see also last column in Table 1). Comparing the pie charts on the left-hand side for the configurations without negotiation (Fig. 4a, 4c, 4e, 4g, 4i) versus those including negotiation on the right-hand side (Fig. 4b, 4d, 4f, 4h, 4j), the ODR decreases due to the negotiation capabilities for each pair of configurations. For all ten configurations, we can observe that for the same number of agents, the ODR with negotiation is always lower than with negotiation. For larger agent populations, the ODR decreases further. Obviously, at some point, the amount of work per agent becomes so low that the ODR values converge against zero for all configurations. Hypothesis H1 is confirmed by the experimental results.

---

[7] "https://github.com/oemer95/ees"   &   https://github.com/oemer95/bdi-abm-integration, branch: "emas24".

Table 1. Simulation results: Average Order dropout rate (ODR)

config	served trips	missed trips	charging trips	ODR
$nearest_8$	748	252	261	25.2%
$with\_neg_8$	826	174	260	17.4%
$nearest_{10}$	804	196	258	19.6%
$with\_neg_{10}$	875	125	253	12.5%
$nearest_{12}$	852	139	239	13.9%
$with\_neg_{12}$	910	86	227	8.6%
$nearest_{14}$	881	125	245	12.5%
$with\_neg_{14}$	934	61	234	6.1%
$nearest_{16}$	893	89	235	8.9%
$with\_neg_{16}$	961	44	228	4.4%

The ATD values are listed in Table 2. Since the configurations with negoti-ation capabilities serve more trips, they drive longer distances to do this work. Despite the narrow scheduling approach (FIFO), the differences are smaller than expected. This might be due to the fact, that the configurations without nego-tiation (*nearest*) assign the agents in a simple greedy manner. Only the current position of the agent at the time of assignment is considered. It is completely ignored that the agent travels further when serving the trips committed so far. As a consequence, the journey to the customer under consideration in the nearest configurations might be sub-optimal. Having a look at the ATD values (travel distance per successfully served trip), Table 2 shows a slight decrease in the travel distances due to negotiating. Hypothesis H2 is confirmed. An improved schedul-ing method would potentially reduce the total distances further. At the moment, bookings in advance are not yet allowed. Introducing pre-bookings might have an additional positive impact on the total distances driven.

Hypothesis H3 can be discussed as well using the ODR results. Comparing the pie charts from Fig. 4 gives an impression of the savings in terms of the number of agents required to do the work. The results provide a first hint towards the confirmation of H3. Larger experiments with even more data sets, further sizes of agent populations, a more sophisticated utility function, and a scheduling algorithm would hopefully allow us to confirm H3 with higher evidence.

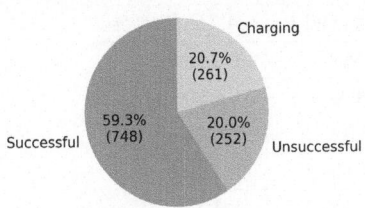

(a) 8 Agents without negotiation

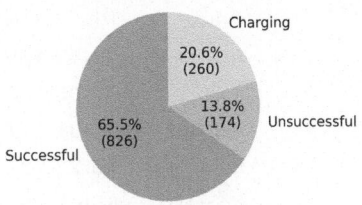

(b) 8 Agents with negotiation

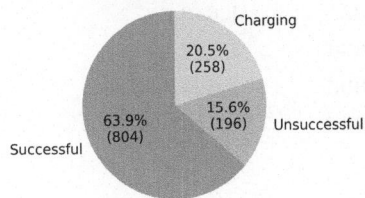

(c) 10 Agents without negotiation

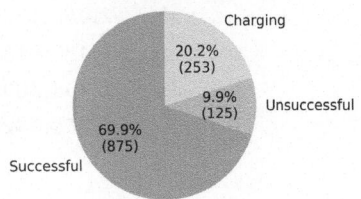

(d) 10 Agents with negotiation

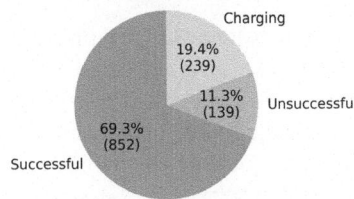

(e) 12 Agents without negotiation

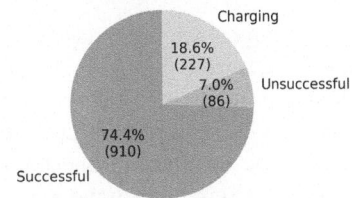

(f) 12 Agents with negotiation

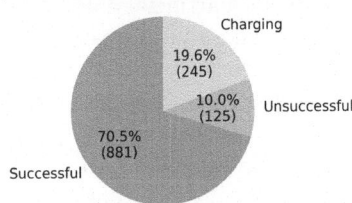

(g) 14 Agents without negotiation

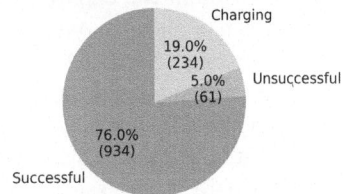

(h) 14 Agents with negotiation

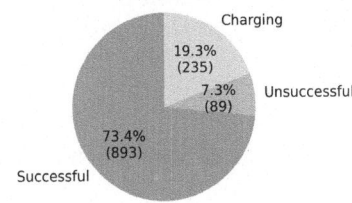

(i) 16 Agents without negotiation

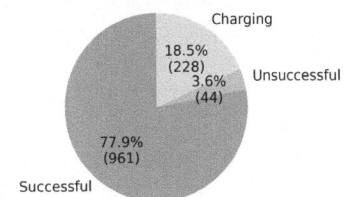

(j) 16 Agents with negotiation

Fig. 4. Average values of 3 data sets of processed trips of each configuration

Table 2. Simulation results: Average travel distance (ATD)

config	total distance (meters)	served trips	ATD (meters)
$nearest_8$	**1,442,185**	**748**	**1,928**
$with\_neg_8$	**1,535,585**	**826**	**1,859**
$nearest_{10}$	**1,461,647**	**804**	**1,815**
$with\_neg_{10}$	**1,522,737**	**875**	**1,740**
$nearest_{12}$	**1,467,224**	**852**	**1,722**
$with\_neg_{12}$	**1,500,483**	**910**	**1,649**
$nearest_{14}$	**1,452,130**	**881**	**1,648**
$with\_neg_{14}$	**1,483,613**	**934**	**1,588**
$nearest_{16}$	**1,454,333**	**893**	**1,629**
$with\_neg_{16}$	**1,454,542**	**961**	**1,514**

7   Discussion of Results and Future Work

In this paper, we have designed, implemented, and tested two components of a
MAS framework for AMoD applications. In detail, we have specified goals and
plans for the architecture of BDI vehicle agents. We have defined a utility function for CNP-based communication between vehicle agents considering battery
conditions, estimated punctuality, and length of the journey to the customer as
decision criteria. We have extended the BDI-ABM integration framework by a
Jadex-MATSim connection layer to achieve an integrated MAS framework with
reasoning-simulation capabilities. The experiments with artificial data of a simulated e-trike service (based on a real data set from a bike-sharing scenario) show
very promising results. A reduction of resources such as vehicles and energy
(cmp. H2, H3) becomes apparent. This might have a significant impact on the
development of future AMoD services based on MAS technology.

The integration of both ADF and simulation environment is part of a larger
project, where other research areas of Multi-agent systems are considered. The
project is ongoing work with still some minor open issues. Soon, a more sophisticated scheduling of trips within the vehicle agent's trip list will be implemented
based on distance values received from MATSim. Further, the process of charging and the charging infrastructure will be investigated more in-depth. Larger
experiments on the scalability and robustness of the MAS in case of breakdown
and connectivity losses will be conducted.

For future work, we plan to extend the cognitive agents with Machine Learning algorithms to investigate *Neuro-symbolic Agents* as well as their explain-
ability [14]. Furthermore, we will design an experimental setup and run ride-
hailing scenarios with different configurations. Other application scenarios like
ride-pooling and waste collection by a fleet of trucks will be investigated using
the presented framework in this paper. We think that our MAS framework with

its reasoning-simulation integration contributes some foundational methods to achieve more sustainable solutions for mobility in the future.

Acknowledgements. The authors would like to thank Mahkamjon Raupov and Olena Tsvietkova who contributed to the implementation and evaluation of the work.

References

1. Abar, S., Theodoropoulos, G.K., Lemarinier, P., O'Hare, G.M.: Agent based modelling and simulation tools: a review of the state-of-art software. Comput. Sci. Rev. **24**, 13–33 (2017)
2. Ahadi, R., Ketter, W., Collins, J., Daina, N.: Siting and sizing of charging infrastructure for shared autonomous electric fleets. In: AAMAS (2021)
3. Axhausen, K.W., ETH Zürich: The Multi-Agent Transport Simulation MATSim. Ubiquity Press (2016)
4. Bazzan, A.L., Klügl, F.: A review on agent-based technology for traffic and transportation. Knowl. Eng. Rev. **29**(03), 375–403 (2014)
5. Bellifemine, F., Caire, G., Greenwood, D.: Developing multi-agent systems with JADE. Wiley series in agent technology, Chichester, reprint. edn. (2008)
6. Bischoff, J., Kaddoura, I., Maciejewski, M., Nagel, K.: Simulation-based optimization of service areas for pooled ride-hailing operators. Procedia Comput. Sci. **130**, 816–823 (2018)
7. Bischoff, J., Maciejewski, M.: Proactive empty vehicle rebalancing for Demand Responsive Transport services. Procedia Comput. Sci. **170**, 739–744 (2020)
8. Bischoff, J., Maciejewski, M., Nagel, K.: City-wide shared taxis: a simulation study in Berlin. In: 2017 IEEE 20th International Conference on Intelligent Transportation Systems (ITSC), pp. 275–280. IEEE, Yokohama (Oct 2017)
9. Cardoso, R.C., Ferrando, A.: A review of agent-based programming for multi-agent systems. Computers **10**(2), 16 (2021)
10. Davoust, A., et al.: An architecture for integrating BDI agents with a simulation environment. In: Dennis, L.A., Bordini, R.H., Lespérance, Y. (eds.) EMAS 2019. LNCS (LNAI), vol. 12058, pp. 67–84. Springer, Cham (2020). https://doi.org/10.1007/978-3-030-51417-4_4
11. Dlugosch, O., Brandt, T., Neumann, D.: Combining analytics and simulation methods to assess the impact of shared, autonomous electric vehicles on sustainable urban mobility. Inform. Manage. **59**, 103285 (2020)
12. Dorer, K., Calisti, M.: An adaptive solution to dynamic transport optimization, pp. 45–51. AAMAS 2005, Association for Computing Machinery, New York, NY, USA (2005)
13. Dorri, A., Kanhere, S.S., Jurdak, R.: Multi-agent systems: a survey. IEEE Access **6**, 28573–28593 (2018)
14. Erduran, Ö.I.: Machine learning for cognitive BDI agents: a compact survey. In: ICAART (1), pp. 257–268 (2023)
15. Erduran, Ö.I., Mauri, M., Minor, M.: Negotiation in ride-hailing between cooperating BDI agents. In: Proceedings of the 14th International Conference on Agents and Artificial Intelligence, vol. Volume X, pp. 425 –432. Scitepress, Online Streaming (2022)

16. Erduran, Ö.I., Minor, M., Hedrich, L., Tarraf, A., Ruehl, F., Schroth, H.: Multi-agent learning for energy-aware placement of autonomous vehicles. In: 2019 18th IEEE International Conference On Machine Learning And Applications (ICMLA), pp. 1671–1678. IEEE, Boca Raton, FL, USA (2019)

17. Georgeff, M., Pell, B., Pollack, M., Tambe, M., Wooldridge, M.: The belief-desire-intention model of agency. In: Müller, J.P., Rao, A.S., Singh, M.P. (eds.) ATAL 1998. LNCS, vol. 1555, pp. 1–10. Springer, Heidelberg (1999). https://doi.org/10.1007/3-540-49057-4_1

18. Kaddoura, I., Schlenther, T.: The impact of trip density on the fleet size and pooling rate of ride-hailing services: a simulation study. Procedia Comput. Sci. **184**, 674–679 (2021)

19. J.P.M., Pischel, M.: Cooperative transportation scheduling: an applicationdomain for dai. Appl. Artif. Intell. **10**(1), 1–34 (1996)

20. Klügl, F.: Multiagentensysteme. In: Handbuch der Künstlichen Intelligenz, pp. 755–781. De Gruyter Oldenbourg, Berlin/Boston, 6. auflage edn. (2021)

21. Kravari, K., Bassiliades, N.: A survey of agent platforms. J. Artif. Soc. Soc. Simul. **18**(1), 11 (2015)

22. Malas, A., Falou, S.E., Falou, M.E., Itmi, M., Cardon, A.: Solving on-demand transport problem through negotiation. In: Proceedings of the Summer Computer Simulation Conference, pp. 1–7 (2016)

23. Mauri, M., Erduran, Ö.I., Anh, T.P.D., Minor, M.: Integrating BDI Agents with the MATSim traffic simulation for autonomous mobility on demand. In: Leyer, M., Wichmann, J. (eds.) Lernen, Wissen, Daten, Analysen (LWDA) Conference Proceedings, Marburg, Germany, October 9-11, 2023. CEUR Workshop Proceedings, vol. 3630, pp. 247–258. CEUR-WS.org (2023). https://ceur-ws.org/Vol-3630/LWDA2023-paper23.pdf

24. North, M., et al.: Complex adaptive systems modeling with repast simphony. Complex Adapt. Syst. Model. **1** (2013). https://doi.org/10.1186/2194-3206-1-3

25. Padgham, L., Nagel, K., Singh, D., Chen, Q.: Integrating BDI Agents into a MATSim Simulation. ECAI (2014)

26. Padgham, L., Singh, D.: Making MATSim agents smarter with the belief-desire-intention framework. In: ETH Zürich, Horni, A., Nagel, K., TU Berlin (eds.) The Multi-Agent Transport Simulation MATSim, pp. 201–210. Ubiquity Press (2016)

27. Pokahr, A.: Aktive Komponenten: Ein integrierter Entwicklungsansatz für verteilte Systeme. Ph.D. thesis, Hamburg University (2017)

28. Pokahr, A., Braubach, L., Jander, K.: The Jadex Project: Programming Model. In: Ganzha, M., Jain, L. (eds.) Multiagent Systems and Applications: Volume 1:Practice and Experience, pp. 21–53. Springer, Heidelberg (2013). https://doi.org/10.1007/978-3-642-33323-1_2

29. Ricci, A., Croatti, A., Bordini, R.H., Hübner, J.F., Boissier, O.: Exploiting Simulation for MAS Programming and Engineering-The JaCaMo-sim Platform. EMAS, p. 19 (2020)

30. Ricci, A., Piunti, M., Viroli, M.: Environment programming in multi-agent systems: an artifact-based perspective. Auton. Agent. Multi-Agent Syst. **23**(2), 158–192 (2011)

31. Sadeghi Garjan, M., Chaanine, T., Pasquale, C., Paolo Pastore, V., Ferrando, A.: Agamas: A new agent-oriented traffic simulation framework for sumo. In: Malvone, V., Murano, A. (eds.) Multi-Agent Systems, pp. 396–405. Springer Nature Switzerland, Cham (2023). https://doi.org/10.1007/978-3-031-43264-4_25

32. Silva, L.d., Meneguzzi, F., Logan, B.: BDI agent architectures: a survey. In: Proceedings of the Twenty-Ninth International Joint Conference on Artificial Intelligence, pp. 4914–4921. International Joint Conferences on Artificial Intelligence Organization, Yokohama, Japan (2020)

33. Singh, D., Ashton, P., Kuligowski, E., Pawan, G.: Bushfire evacuation decision support system use in incident management training. Aust. J. Emerg. Managem. **37**, 73–76 (2022)

34. Singh, D., Padgham, L.: Emergency Evacuation Simulator (EES) - a tool for planning community evacuations in Australia. In: Proceedings of the Twenty-Sixth IJCAI, pp. 5249–5251. Melbourne, Australia (Aug 2017)

35. Singh, D., Padgham, L., Logan, B.: Integrating BDI agents with agent-based simulation platforms. Auton. Agent. Multi-Agent Syst. **30**(6), 1050–1071 (2016)

36. Singh, D., Padgham, L., Nagel, K.: Using MATSim as a component in dynamic agent-based micro-simulations. In: Engineering Multi-Agent Systems, vol. 12058, pp. 85–105. Springer International Publishing, Cham (2020)

37. Smith: The contract net protocol: high-level communication and control in a distributed problem solver. IEEE Trans. Comput. **C-29**(12), 1104–1113 (1980)

38. Soares, G., Kokkinogenis, Z., Macedo, J.L., Rossetti, R.J.F.: Agent-Based Traffic Simulation Using SUMO and JADE: An Integrated Platform for Artificial Transportation Systems. In: Behrisch, M., Krajzewicz, D., Weber, M. (eds.) Simulation of Urban Mobility, vol. 8594, pp. 44–61. Springer, Berlin Heidelberg (2014). https://doi.org/10.1007/978-3-662-45079-6_4

39. Timóteo, I.J., Araújo, M.R., Rossetti, R.J., Oliveira, E.C.: TraSMAPI: an API oriented towards multi-agent systems real-time interaction with multiple traffic simulators. In: 13th International IEEE Conference on Intelligent Transportation Systems, pp. 1183–1188 (2010)

40. W Axhausen, K., Horni, A., Nagel, K.: The multi-agent transport simulation MATSim. Ubiquity Press (2016)

41. Zardini, G., Lanzetti, N., Pavone, M., Frazzoli, E.: Analysis and control of autonomous mobility-on-demand systems. Ann. Rev. Control Robot. Auton. Syst. **5**, 633–658 (2021). publisher: Annual Reviews

42. Zhang, H., Sheppard, C.J., Lipman, T.E., Zeng, T., Moura, S.J.: Charging infrastructure demands of shared-use autonomous electric vehicles in urban areas. Transp. Res. Part D: Trans. Environ. **78**, 102210 (2020)

43. Zwick, F., Kuehnel, N., Moeckel, R., Axhausen, K.W.: Agent-based simulation of city-wide autonomous ride-pooling and the impact on traffic noise. Transp. Res. Part D: Transp. Environ. **90**, 102673 (2021)

Towards Engineering Explainable Autonomous Systems

Michael Winikoff[✉][ID]

Victoria University of Wellington, Wellington, New Zealand
michael.winikoff@vuw.ac.nz

Abstract. Explanation is important to supporting appropriate levels of trust in autonomous systems. However, work in XAI (eXplainable AI) is focused on explanation of single system components, such as a machine learning algorithm or decision-making module. This paper: (1) argues that we need to develop ways to engineer explainable systems consisting of multiple components, and identifies this as a challenge for the community; (2) proposes an approach for explaining multi-component autonomous systems; (3) identifies integration issues that need to be addressed to make this vision a reality; and (4) poses a number of research challenges and questions that need to be addressed.

Keywords: Explanation · XAI · Engineering · Integration · Trust · Autonomous Systems

1 Introduction

Scenario: The video footage was clear: the self-driving car had collided with the pedestrian. But why? The investigator queried the system: "why didn't you stop?". After a pause, the response came back: "I could not stop (or slow down significantly) because there was a car close behind me, and I could not perform an alternative manoeuvre". The investigator selected the second part of the response and queried it, eventually determining that the system had prioritised avoiding collisions with cars behind and beside it, due to a failure by the image processing module to classify the pedestrian as human, because they were obscured by packages they were carrying.

Autonomous systems need to be explainable for a range of reasons [13,22,37, 40]: to be understandable [36], to help establish appropriate levels of trust [13,16, 31], and to be accountable [7]. Explanations are used for a range of purposes [3, 14,26], by a range of different stakeholders [21]. Stakeholders vary in their level of expertise and familiarity with the domain and with the system, and in their goals. For example, a software engineer trying to debug a system [39] has different needs than a lawyer seeking to construct a civil liability case in relation to a malfunctioning autonomous system [4].

This paper's contribution is to identify and articulate the challenge of engineering explainable multi-component systems, and to propose an approach to addressing this challenge, along with research challenges that we pose.

© The Author(s), under exclusive license to Springer Nature Switzerland AG 2025
D. Briola et al. (Eds.): EMAS 2024, LNAI 15152, pp. 144–155, 2025.
https://doi.org/10.1007/978-3-031-71152-7_9

There is a whole body of work on explainable AI (XAI) [2]: techniques that allow explanations to be provided for the behaviour of AI modules. For example, why did a machine learning system recommend to decline a given loan application? However, XAI is typically focused on techniques for explaining individual (often machine learning) components, not whole systems [2, §5.3]. This paper argues that XAI is necessary, but not sufficient, and that we need to extend explanation from single components, to whole multi-component systems, and also consider engineering issues. This will allow realistic autonomous systems (with multiple components) to be explainable. Rodriguez[1] et al. [32,33] also call for an engineering focus on XAI, and they also identify, but do not address, the issue of explaining multi-component systems. Kuznietsov et al. [20] also propose a high-level architecture for explainable autonomous driving, building on earlier work [30]. Both these papers are broader surveys, and they do not go into details on the proposed high-level architecture.

We next present and justify a proposed architecture for explainable autonomous systems (§2), including consideration of the sorts of questions that can be asked (§2.1), and the sorts of answers that can be given (§2.2). We then consider how the components in the proposed architecture integrate and interact (§3), and close (§4) with discussion of some broader issues and a summary of the research challenges that need to be addressed to enable the engineering of explainable autonomous systems.

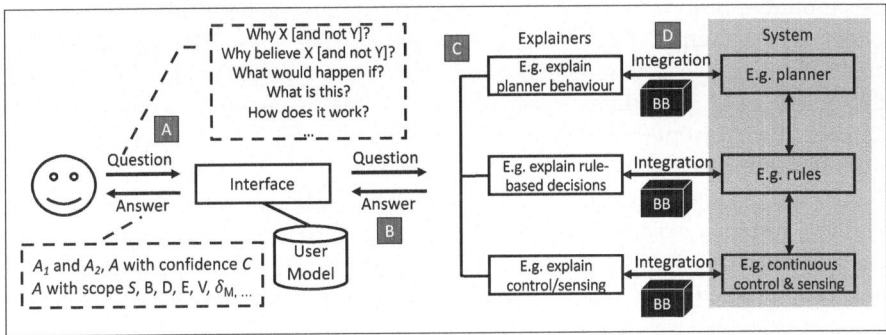

Fig. 1. Architecture (B=Belief, D=Desire, E=Emotion, V=Valuing, δ_M=user model change, BB = Black Box)

2 Architecture

Figure 1 shows the proposed architecture for an explainable multi-component autonomous system. The explainable system can be naturally viewed as a

---

[1] The papers by Rodriquez et al. and Kuznietsov et al. were not available when this paper was written.

multi-agent system. The original autonomous system (grey shaded on the right) consists of a number of components. Different systems might have a different number of components, but the architecture is generic: it can accommodate changes to the number of components in the autononous system by simply adding corresponding explainers. The rest of the architecture does not change.

In our example scenario we might have three components [12, §4.5]:

1. a component ("continuous control & sensing", bottom of Fig. 1) that deals with continuous data from sensors and controlling actuators, and is able to recognise and classify obstacles and intersections, and control actuators to follow the road while managing speed to avoid collisions;
2. a component ("rules", middle of the Figure) that has rules for dealing with common situations, and is able to decide on the route and make decisions on what to do at an intersection, issue lane change commands in line with the navigation, and decide on a range of manoeuvres including pulling over or changing lane to avoid obstacles and moving out of the way of emergency vehicles; and
3. a component ("planner", top of Figure) that deals with unusual situations using planning based on the following principles: (i) avoiding damage to pedestrians (most important), (ii) avoiding damage to vehicles containing humans, and (iii) avoiding damage to unoccupied vehicles and property.

Each system component is associated with a corresponding explainer agent that applies appropriate XAI technique(s) to explain the behaviour of that component. For example, explaining a component that uses BDI (Belief-Desire-Intention) plans to generate behaviour could be done following the approach of Winikoff et al. [41]. This aspect of the architecture is required because each component might operate using quite different principles, and therefore require a different approach to generating explanations.

In order to generate explanations, a "black box" that captures relevant details from the system's execution is used. For example, to explain a component that uses rule-based reasoning, the black box would likely need to capture the facts that were believed to be true at a given point in time that were the basis for the choice of rule that was made.

The user ("☺" on the left) interacts with an interface. Having a single interface agent is required because we want to be able to hide the internal structure of the system from the user: as far as the user is concerned, there is a single autonomous system that is exhibiting behaviour that needs to be explained[2]. This interface maintains a model of the user (e.g. what does the user already know?) that is used to filter answers.

When the user asks a question, the interface agent passes on the question to one or more of the explainer agents. This process is iterative: as seen in the scenario, an answer may prompt the user to ask follow-up questions. In

---

[2] Mualla et al. [28] and Calvaresi et al. [6] also propose a single interface agent, but differ in context, and lack the details of our architecture, as described in the remainder of this paper.

some situations (see §2.1) the system's reply might take the form of a question, with the user providing an answer. Argumentation [1,8,23,34] can be a good approach for structuring the dialogue, and there has also been some work on dialogue for explaining BDI agent behaviour [10,11]. In addition to providing an answer, there might be situations where the interface may need to respond with a request or question seeking clarification. For example, if the user asks "why did you do X instead of Y?", but Y is not actually an alternative to X, then the system might respond with "did you really mean 'instead of Y'?".

The interactions within the system (e.g. between user and interface, and between interface and explainer agents) are done by asking questions, and receiving answers. We therefore need to define what sorts of questions can be asked, and what constructs are used to provide answers. Although this may vary from system to system, for a given system we need to define this so the interface is able to indicate to the user what sorts of questions can be asked.

In defining the forms of questions and answers that are used we are guided by the extensive literature that aims to inform XAI researchers about relevant work in social sciences [5,25]. Key findings include that the explanations that humans naturally use are *contrastive* (see §2.1), *selective* (i.e. incomplete, covering only (some) relevant factors), and *social* (presented relative to what the explainer believes the listener already knows).

There are a few design decisions that need to be made to realise an instance of our architecture. The first design decision is whether the system is designed so that the interface can determine from the question which explainer agent to send it to, or whether it simply sends it to all the explainer agents, and explainer agents can reply with a response of "don't ask me" (we return to this in §6). The second design decision is whether to have a single black box for the whole system, or to have each system component have its own black box. We propose to have a black box for each component, since each component's requirements for the black box might be quite different to other components.

2.1 Questions . . .

In this section we consider what forms of questions the user should be able to ask. The most basic and obvious form is "Why?", for example "Why did you do this?" [18] or "Why did you *believe* this?" [39]. Additionally, when the system does something other than what the user was expecting, it can be useful to ask "Why did you *not* do *(something else)*?". However, in fact evidence from the social sciences shows that as humans we tend to use a more general form of *contrastive* questions [25]: "Why did you X (fact) instead of Y (foil)?" (although the foil is sometimes implied and omitted). Another (related) question form is the *counter-factual*: "What would happen if . . . ?" [29, Page 23][3]. Additionally, it

---

[3] This is different from a contrastive question in that the question includes a *difference* and the answer is the (alternative) outcome (the foil), whereas a contrastive question provides the actual outcome and (optionally) the alternative outcome, and gives the difference as the answer.

may be useful to allow the system to answer more basic informational questions such as "what is this?", "how does this work?" and "how do I use this?", which Haynes *et al.* [15] define respectively as ontological, mechanistic, and operational, and provide patterns for how to engineer systems that can answer these sorts of questions.

Finally, in addition to posing a question, it may also be useful to provide some information on what is desired in a good answer. For instance, how complete does the answer need to be? What is the aim of the person asking the question - are they a novice trying to clarify why something slightly unexpected occurred, i.e. to learn, or are they an expert seeking to dig deep to ascribe blame for something that should not have occurred?

2.2 ... and Answers

We now turn to consider how answers are formed: what concepts can be used in answers, and what other features are important to have to support our approach to explaining multi-component autonomous systems.

We begin with generic features. Firstly, answers need to be *decomposable*: when the system says "I could not stop because ... and I could not perform an alternative manoeuvre", the user needs to be able to decompose the answer to select the second part and ask "But why couldn't you perform an alternative manoeuvre?". This can be realised by defining a number of general-purpose combining forms for answers (e.g. "and", "but"). Additionally, answers need to be able to include references to indicate where the explanation for something involving a module depends on another module. For example, a rule-based module chose to perform a certain action because of information that it had earlier received from a video-processing module. These links allow the interface agent to direct follow-up questions. Secondly, it can be desirable to be able to include levels of confidence in answers. For example, the system might indicate that it believed a particular key fact held with roughly 75% probability, or it might indicate that it was "very" confident of a particular classification of an image. Additionally, when explaining machine learning it has been argued that we need to have a way to indicate the "scope" in which the explanation is relevant and reliable [26].

Turning to consider the concepts that can be used to form answers, these obviously depend on the component: a system component that uses image processing will have different explanatory concepts than, say, one that uses BDI plans to realise goals. There are a range of approaches for explaining various machine learning approaches by providing examples. For instance [27] annotating an image to highlight the parts that were most influential in a particular decision, or indicating that had certain features been different, an alternative behaviour would have occurred (e.g. a higher salary would have led to the loan application being approved). Turning to cognitive agents, it has been argued [41] that the concepts of "belief" and "desire", as used in BDI architectures, match directly with the same concepts that humans naturally use to explain their behaviour in similar contexts, and therefore that these concepts, along with the additional concept of "valuing" [24] form a natural basis for explaining autonomous systems. Furthermore, Kaptein *et al.* [17] argue that in addition to beliefs and desires, explanations sometimes are in terms of emotions, for instance: "I called the hospital because I was **scared** (emotion) that I might have a hypo (too low blood sugar level)" [17, p.304, emphasis in original]. Another form of explanation is a correction to the human's mental model, for example, noting that a particular action has a pre-condition that the user appears to be unaware of, and which justifies the need for an action to establish the pre-condition [35].

Figure 1 summarises the range of constructs that might be used as explanations, including generic ones ("and", confidence, and scope), and component-specific building blocks (beliefs, desires, valuings, emotions, and human model changes).

3   Integration

We now turn to a number of issues that relate to the integration of the system.

The first issue corresponds to the arrow labelled C in Fig. 1: how does the interface know where to send a given question? One option, which may be the simplest in some cases, is to simply send it to all explainers, if it is easy to have each explainer identify whether it is able to answer a given question. Another approach is to capture information that allows the interface to determine which explainer agent can answer a given question. This might be a static index. For example, if each system component has a distinct set of actions it can perform, then from the action one can determine which explainer agent to ask about it. Another option, if this is not the case, is to tag each action when it is performed with an indication of which system component generated that action. So, for example, when a rule is applied to decide to change lanes to avoid an obstacle, then the action would be tagged with "rules". However, there can be more complex cases (we return to these in §4). For instance, a decision to not stop might involve decision-making in all three system components: the continuous sensing component might detect an obstacle but, due to a car close behind, decide against stopping and invoke the rules component to consider whether to change lanes. In turn, the rules component might decide against a lane change and invoke the planner component to consider alternative approaches to avoid the obstacle. Finally, the planner component might decide that reducing speed and hitting the obstacle is the least bad option available.

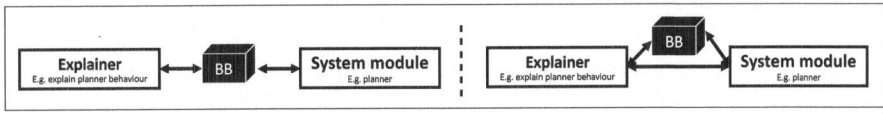

Fig. 2. Integration designs: indirect (via black box only) on left, direct on right

The second issue corresponds to the arrow labelled D in Fig. 1: how does each explainer interact with its corresponding system component to generate explanations? One option, which may be the simplest in some cases, is to have the interaction be *solely* using the black box (left side of Fig. 2): the system generates a trace in the black box as it runs, and the explainer constructs explanations using (only) this trace, without interacting with the system components. The advantage of this approach is that the system is cleanly separated from the explanation. However, it might require storing large amounts of data in the black box that could be reduced by allowing an explainer agent to interact with its corresponding system component. The alternative (right side of the Figure) is to also have direct interaction between the explainer and the module it is explaining. For example, to explain why a given image was not classified as having a pedestrian, the system might present the image (and perhaps some variants of it) to the component. Furthermore, in situations where the user has an implicit foil, the system component may need to be used to generate the plausible alternatives for the situation.

4   Research Challenges

In order to be able to engineer explainable multi-component autonomous systems a range of research challenges need to be addressed. We group the challenges into three groups: those relating to the broader context, those relating to the research process itself, and specific research questions.

Our first group of challenges concerns the broader context of use. To use explanation in a particular context, for example a civil liability lawsuit, there may be a range of information that is relevant and useful other than explanations of behaviour. Buiten *et al.* [4] flag a range of such information. These include the development process, what steps were taken to mitigate risk, "second order explanations" (i.e. what explanations were previously provided to the user), the situations in which the system tends to fail, and how common are system failures. The research challenge is how to effectively collect and meaningfully present this information. Some of the information is about human social processes (e.g. development process), but some pose specific engineering research questions. For example: how can we identify and communicate the situations in which a system tends to fail, or the probability of system failures? Furthermore, this needs to be done in a way that cannot be manipulated.

More broadly, we also need to investigate how to link the underlying user's goal (e.g. building trust) to the questions that the system is able to answer. For example, how to use a system that can answer "why did you do ..." questions to ultimately address the user's underlying question: "why should I trust this system?" [3]. This may have implications for the sort of questions that may need to be able to be asked.

The second group of challenges concern the endeavour of research: how to help the research community develop and evaluate solutions? More specifically: what scenarios would be useful? What test beds and benchmarks would help the research community to meaningfully and usefully evaluate ongoing work to assess and guide progress? Is there a role for standardisation? For competitions?

How should explanation provision be evaluated? (e.g. see [29]) These sorts of issues are ones where the XAI community could benefit from the experience and expertise of the EMAS community. These sorts of issues are ones where the XAI community could benefit from the experience and expertise of the EMAS community.

The third group of challenges is more specific research questions that relate to specific aspects of the architecture proposed in this paper. We believe these are perhaps the most useful to the EMAS community, and so close our paper with these questions, in the hope that they will spur further work to address them.

1. Regarding the first issue in §3: how can we manage the tagging of actions with the system component that is responsible?

   In complex cases, the decision to perform a certain action may have involved multiple system components. This raises a number of questions for how the architecture functions. Can the decision-making process be extended to keep a record that allows one module to be identified as the one making the final decision? Or instead can we just send questions to all explainer agents, and if so, how does an explainer agent determine whether the question is one that it can answer? And what should the interface do if it does not get exactly one meaningful answer? More broadly, what if there isn't a single responsible component (e.g. multiple agents interacting following a protocol)?

   One additional challenge here is dealing with contrastive questions: if the question is "why did you do X?" then it can be possible to track which modules were involved in selecting action X. However, for the question "why did you *not* do Y?" we need to be able to identify how Y might have been selected. This implies either that the black boxes capture information on possible alternatives (see questions 2 and 3 below), or that we need to have a way for explainer agents to explore what might have been with their corresponding module (see second part of question 2 below)

2. Regarding the second issue in §3: how do the explainer agents interact with the blackboxes? More specifically, what protocol is followed, and what interface (API) do the blackboxes need to provide?

   Furthermore, if explainer agents interact directly with the module that they are explaining, what protocol would be followed, and what interface (API) needs to be provided by the module?

3. What information is captured in the black box (e.g. [38])? How do we determine (in advance and/or at runtime) what needs to be captured, and how do we extend the system to do so?

   One issue is the management of storage: a complete trace of everything could be very large. There are approaches (e.g. [19]) for capturing system execution that manage to capture only key information and significantly reduce storage need, while permitting system execution to be "rewound" to any given point in the execution.

   Another issue is ensuring that the information captured allows explanations to be generated that include references where needed, i.e. where another module played a role in the observed behaviour, and follow-up questions relating to that factor (e.g. a belief held) should be directed to that module.

4. How can we ensure that provided explanations can be verified to be authentic and honest [9]? A key factor is how to ensure that the black box is tamper proof. A number of approaches are possible, depending on the system's operating environment and the amount of information captured. Approaches can include having a separate hardware component that provides the black box, and using encryption.

5. Are there situations where the interface agent may need to share information from the user model with explainer agents? For example, instead of generating explanations and then having the user agent filter them using the user model, it may be more efficient to share relevant parts of the user model with the explainer module, so it can not use them to guide to explanation generation process to avoid generating things that would subsequently be filtered out.

In addition to the above research questions, that are more focussed on EMAS-related topics, there are also XAI-oriented questions such as how to specify the parameters of a desired answer (e.g. level of detail, preferred explanatory factor types), how should confidence be expressed, how should the scope of validity of an explanation be indicated, and whether other question types or answer types are needed.

References

1. Amgoud, L., Prade, H.: Using arguments for making and explaining decisions. Artif. Intell. **173**(3–4), 413–436 (2009). https://doi.org/10.1016/J.ARTINT.2008.11.006
2. Anjomshoae, S., Najjar, A., Calvaresi, D., Främling, K.: Explainable agents and robots: results from a systematic literature review. In: Elkind, E., Veloso, M., Agmon, N., Taylor, M.E. (eds.) Proceedings of the 18th International Conference on Autonomous Agents and MultiAgent Systems, AAMAS '19, Montreal, QC, Canada, May 13-17, 2019, pp. 1078–1088 (2019). http://dl.acm.org/citation.cfm?id=3331806
3. Biran, O., McKeown, K.: Justification narratives for individual classifications. In: ICML 2014 AutoML Workshop, p. 7 (2014)
4. Buiten, M.C., Dennis, L.A., Schwammberger, M.: A vision on what explanations of autonomous systems are of interest to lawyers. In: Schneider, K., Dalpiaz, F., Horkoff, J. (eds.) 31st IEEE International Requirements Engineering Conference, RE 2023 - Workshops, Hannover, Germany, pp. 332–336. IEEE (2023). https://doi.org/10.1109/REW57809.2023.00062
5. Byrne, R.M.J.: Good explanations in explainable artificial intelligence (XAI): evidence from human explanatory reasoning. In: Proceedings of the Thirty-Second International Joint Conference on Artificial Intelligence, IJCAI 2023, 19th-25th August 2023, Macao, SAR, China, pp. 6536–6544. ijcai.org (2023). https://doi.org/10.24963/ijcai.2023/733
6. Calvaresi, D., et al.: EXPECTATION: personalized explainable artificial intelligence for decentralized agents with heterogeneous knowledge. In: Calvaresi, D., Najjar,

A., Winikoff, M., Främling, K. (eds.) EXTRAAMAS 2021. LNCS (LNAI), vol. 12688, pp. 331–343. Springer, Cham (2021). https://doi.org/10.1007/978-3-030-82017-6_20

7. Cranefield, S., Oren, N., Vasconcelos, W.W.: Accountability for practical reasoning agents. In: Lujak, M. (ed.) AT 2018. LNCS (LNAI), vol. 11327, pp. 33–48. Springer, Cham (2019). https://doi.org/10.1007/978-3-030-17294-7_3

8. Cyras, K., Rago, A., Albini, E., Baroni, P., Toni, F.: Argumentative XAI: A survey. In: Zhou, Z. (ed.) Proceedings of the Thirtieth International Joint Conference on Artificial Intelligence, IJCAI 2021, Virtual Event/Montreal, Canada, 19-27 August 2021, pp. 4392–4399. ijcai.org (2021). https://doi.org/10.24963/IJCAI.2021/600

9. Dazeley, R., Vamplew, P., Foale, C., Young, C., Aryal, S., Cruz, F.: Levels of explainable artificial intelligence for human-aligned conversational explanations. Artif. Intell. **299**, 103525 (2021). https://doi.org/10.1016/j.artint.2021.103525

10. Dennis, L.A., Oren, N.: Explaining BDI agent behaviour through dialogue. In: Dignum, F., Lomuscio, A., Endriss, U., Nowé, A. (eds.) AAMAS '21: 20th International Conference on Autonomous Agents and Multiagent Systems, Virtual Event, United Kingdom, May 3-7, 2021, pp. 429–437. ACM (2021). https://doi.org/10.5555/3463952.3464007

11. Dennis, L.A., Oren, N.: Explaining BDI agent behaviour through dialogue. Auton. Agents Multi Agent Syst. **36**(1), 29 (2022). https://doi.org/10.1007/S10458-022-09556-8

12. Fisher, M., Mascardi, V., Rozier, K.Y., Schlingloff, B., Winikoff, M., Yorke-Smith, N.: Towards a framework for certification of reliable autonomous systems. Auton. Agents Multi Agent Syst. **35**(1), 8 (2021). https://doi.org/10.1007/s10458-020-09487-2

13. Floridi, L., et al.: AI4People–an ethical framework for a good AI society: opportunities, risks, principles, and recommendations. Mind. Mach. (2018). https://doi.org/10.1007/s11023-018-9482-5

14. Gregor, S., Benbasat, I.: Explanations from intelligent systems: theoretical foundations and implications for practice. MIS Q. **23**(4), 497–530 (1999). http://misq.org/explanations-from-intelligent-systems-theoretical-foundations-and-implications-for-practice.html

15. Haynes, S.R., Cohen, M.A., Ritter, F.E.: Designs for explaining intelligent agents. Int. J. Hum Comput Stud. **67**(1), 90–110 (2009). https://doi.org/10.1016/j.ijhcs.2008.09.008

16. High-Level Expert Group on Artificial Intelligence: The assessment list for trustworthy artificial intelligence (2020). https://digital-strategy.ec.europa.eu/en/library/assessment-list-trustworthy-artificial-intelligence-altai-self-assessment

17. Kaptein, F., Broekens, J., Hindriks, K.V., Neerincx, M.A.: Evaluating cognitive and affective intelligent agent explanations in a long-term health-support application for children with type 1 diabetes. In: 8th International Conference on Affective Computing and Intelligent Interaction, ACII 2019, Cambridge, United Kingdom, September 3-6, 2019, pp. 1–7. IEEE (2019).https://doi.org/10.1109/ACII.2019.8925526

18. Koeman, V.J., Dennis, L.A., Webster, M., Fisher, M., Hindriks, K.: The "why did you do that?" Button: answering why-questions for end users of robotic systems. In: Dennis, L.A., Bordini, R.H., Lespérance, Y. (eds.) EMAS 2019. LNCS (LNAI), vol. 12058, pp. 152–172. Springer, Cham (2020). https://doi.org/10.1007/978-3-030-51417-4_8

19. Koeman, V.J., Hindriks, K.V., Jonker, C.M.: Omniscient debugging for cognitive agent programs. In: Sierra, C. (ed.) Proceedings of the Twenty-Sixth International Joint Conference on Artificial Intelligence, IJCAI 2017, Melbourne, Australia, August 19-25, 2017, pp. 265–272. ijcai.org (2017). https://doi.org/10.24963/IJCAI.2017/38

20. Kuznietsov, A., Gyevnar, B., Wang, C., Peters, S., Albrecht, S.V.: Explainable AI for safe and trustworthy autonomous driving: A systematic review. arxiv:2402.10086 (2024)

21. Langer, M., et al.: What do we want from explainable artificial intelligence (XAI)? - A stakeholder perspective on XAI and a conceptual model guiding interdisciplinary XAI research. Artif. Intell. **296**, 103473 (2021). https://doi.org/10.1016/j.artint.2021.103473

22. Langley, P., Meadows, B., Sridharan, M., Choi, D.: Explainable agency for intelligent autonomous systems. In: Singh, S., Markovitch, S. (eds.) Proceedings of the Thirty-First AAAI Conference on Artificial Intelligence, February 4-9, 2017, San Francisco, California, USA, pp. 4762–4764. AAAI Press (2017). http://aaai.org/ocs/index.php/IAAI/IAAI17/paper/view/15046

23. Madumal, P., Miller, T., Vetere, F., Sonenberg, L.: Towards a grounded dialog model for explainable artificial intelligence. CoRR **abs/1806.08055** (2018). http://arxiv.org/abs/1806.08055

24. Malle, B.F.: How the Mind Explains Behavior. MIT Press (2004). ISBN: 9780262134453

25. Miller, T.: Explanation in artificial intelligence: Insights from the social sciences. Artif. Intell. **267**, 1–38 (2019). https://doi.org/10.1016/j.artint.2018.07.007

26. Mittelstadt, B.D., Russell, C., Wachter, S.: Explaining explanations in AI. In: danah boyd, Morgenstern, J.H. (eds.) Proceedings of the Conference on Fairness, Accountability, and Transparency (FAT*), Atlanta, GA, USA, January 29-31, 2019, pp. 279–288. ACM (2019). https://doi.org/10.1145/3287560.3287574

27. Montavon, G., Samek, W., Müller, K.R.: Methods for interpreting and understanding deep neural networks. Digit. Signal Proc. **73**, 1–15 (2018). https://doi.org/10.1016/j.dsp.2017.10.011

28. Mualla, Y., et al.: The quest of parsimonious XAI: a human-agent architecture for explanation formulation. Artif. Intell. **302**, 103573 (2022). https://doi.org/10.1016/j.artint.2021.103573

29. Mueller, S.T., Hoffman, R.R., Clancey, W.J., Emrey, A., Klein, G.: Explanation in human-AI systems: A literature meta-review, synopsis of key ideas and publications, and bibliography for explainable AI (2019). CoRR **abs/1902.01876**, http://arxiv.org/abs/1902.01876

30. Omeiza, D., Webb, H., Jirotka, M., Kunze, L.: Explanations in autonomous driving: a survey. IEEE Trans. Intell. Transp. Syst. **23**(8), 10142–10162 (2022). https://doi.org/10.1109/TITS.2021.3122865

31. Robinette, P., Li, W., Allen, R., Howard, A.M., Wagner, A.R.: Overtrust of robots in emergency evacuation scenarios. In: Bartneck, C., Nagai, Y., Paiva, A., Sabanovic, S. (eds.) The Eleventh ACM/IEEE International Conference on Human Robot Interation, HRI 2016, Christchurch, New Zealand, March 7-10, 2016, pp. 101–108. IEEE/ACM (2016). https://doi.org/10.1109/HRI.2016.7451740

32. Rodriguez, S., Thangarajah, J.: Explainable agents (XAg) by design (blue sky ideas track). In: Alechina, N., Dignum, V., Dastani, M., Sichman, J. (eds.) Proceedings of the 23rd International Conference on Autonomous Agents and Multiagent Systems (AAMAS). ACM (2024)

33. Rodriguez, S., Thangarajah, J., Davey, A.: Design patterns for explainable agents (XAg). In: Alechina, N., Dignum, V., Dastani, M., Sichman, J. (eds.) Proceedings of the 23rd International Conference on Autonomous Agents and Multiagent Systems (AAMAS). ACM (2024)

34. Sklar, E.I., Azhar, M.Q.: Explanation through argumentation. In: Imai, M., Norman, T., Sklar, E., Komatsu, T. (eds.) Proceedings of the 6th International Conference on Human-Agent Interaction, HAI 2018, Southampton, United Kingdom, December 15-18, 2018, pp. 277–285. ACM (2018).https://doi.org/10.1145/3284432.3284470

35. Sreedharan, S., Srivastava, S., Kambhampati, S.: Using state abstractions to compute personalized contrastive explanations for AI agent behavior. Artif. Intell. **301**, 103570 (2021). https://doi.org/10.1016/j.artint.2021.103570

36. Verhagen, R.S., Neerincx, M.A., Tielman, M.L.: A two-dimensional explanation framework to classify AI as incomprehensible, interpretable, or understandable. In: Calvaresi, D., Najjar, A., Winikoff, M., Främling, K. (eds.) EXTRAAMAS 2021. LNCS (LNAI), vol. 12688, pp. 119–138. Springer, Cham (2021). https://doi.org/10.1007/978-3-030-82017-6_8

37. Winfield, A.F.T., et al.: IEEE P7001: A proposed standard on transparency. Front. Robot. AI **8**, 665729 (2021), https://doi.org/10.3389/frobt.2021.665729

38. Winfield, A.F.T., van Maris, A., Salvini, P., Jirotka, M.: An ethical black box for social robots: a draft open standard. CoRR (2022). https://doi.org/10.48550/arXiv.2205.06564

39. Winikoff, M.: Debugging agent programs with why?: Questions. In: Larson, K., Winikoff, M., Das, S., Durfee, E.H. (eds.) Proceedings of the 16th Conference on Autonomous Agents and MultiAgent Systems, AAMAS 2017, São Paulo, Brazil, May 8-12, 2017, pp. 251–259. ACM (2017). http://dl.acm.org/citation.cfm?id=3091166

40. Winikoff, M.: Towards trusting autonomous systems. In: El Fallah-Seghrouchni, A., Ricci, A., Son, T.C. (eds.) EMAS 2017. LNCS (LNAI), vol. 10738, pp. 3–20. Springer, Cham (2018). https://doi.org/10.1007/978-3-319-91899-0_1

41. Winikoff, M., Sidorenko, G., Dignum, V., Dignum, F.: Why bad coffee? Explaining BDI agent behaviour with valuings. Artif. Intell. **300**, 103554 (2021). https://doi.org/10.1016/J.ARTINT.2021.103554

Enhancing Confidence of the *vGOAL* Interpreter Using SAT Solving

Yi Yang$^{(\boxtimes)}$ and Tom Holvoet

imec-DistriNet, KU Leuven, 3001 Leuven, Belgium
{yi.yang,tom.holvoet}@kuleuven.be

Abstract. Agent programming languages and their interpreters are crucial in autonomous decision-making. While formal methods are extensively utilized to ensure the correctness of agent programs, their application for verifying the implementation correctness of interpreters remains infrequent. To formally specify and verify autonomous decision-making, we proposed *vGOAL* and implemented its interpreter. The implementation correctness of the *vGOAL* interpreter is crucial for users to gain trust in the *vGOAL* approach. Using program verification is one option, yet this would require a huge effort to verify the correctness of the *vGOAL* interpreter.

In this paper, we propose integrating an SAT-solving component into the *vGOAL* interpreter to enhance confidence in its core component: minimal model generation. The SAT-solving component consists of two subcomponents: an SAT-encoding component and an SAT solver. Leveraging PySAT for its interface to advanced solvers, our main contribution lies in the SAT encoding. We devise an algorithm to encode the inputs and outputs of the core component into a satisfiable CNF formula. Importantly, we justify that this algorithm generates a satisfiable CNF formula only if the result is correct. We demonstrate the practicality and efficiency of this SAT-solving approach using a case study involving an autonomous transportation system with three mobile robots.

Keywords: Autonomous Decision-Making · Implementation Correctness · *vGOAL* interpreter · SAT Solving

1 Introduction

Autonomous systems, defined as entities capable of independent task completion without continuous human instructions, hold immense potential for saving lives and mitigating risks in hazardous environments like nuclear power plants and space exploration. It is important to convince the public that autonomous systems will correctly execute tasks as desired without any violations of safety requirements. The development of safe autonomous decision-making is a challenging task in developing autonomous systems.

For many years, agent programming languages (APLs) and their interpreters have been extensively researched to develop autonomous decision-making [12]. More precisely, an APL is a specification language to specify an autonomous decision-making mechanism, and an APL interpreter serves as an autonomous decision-making component. Therefore, we can increase confidence in the autonomous decision-making process using APLs from two aspects: APL programs and APL interpreters.

Formal verification is built on a rigorous mathematical foundation. Hence, it is a reliable tool to provide high confidence for autonomous systems, especially in safety-critical applications. Many efforts have been made to prove the correctness of an APL program using formal verification, enhancing the confidence of the APL program. Particularly, model checking is the most successful and influential verification method in verifying APLs, including AgentSpeak [2], Gwendolen [4], and GOAL [7], owing to the automated verification process [1,5,9,13]. On the other hand, there is a noticeable gap in verifying the implementation correctness of APL interpreters. To the best of our knowledge, the implementation correctness of APL interpreters has only been briefly discussed in [5], and the authors believe it is important but requires significant effort.

In our previous work, we proposed *vGOAL* [17], a specification language specifically designed to formally specify and verify safe autonomous decision-making, and implemented its interpreter [16]. To verify the correctness of *vGOAL* specifications, we have implemented an automated model-checking process for *vGOAL*, and its preliminary version is described in [15]. The *vGOAL* interpreter is a tool to generate autonomous decisions. Consequently, its implementation correctness is crucial for users to trust the *vGOAL* approach. This paper aims to enhance the confidence of the *vGOAL* interpreter using an efficient and automated formal method.

It is truly a significant task to specify all preconditions and postconditions of thousands of code lines to verify the implementation correctness of the *vGOAL* interpreter. Instead of verifying the generation process, we propose demonstrating the correctness of the generated outputs, thereby enhancing confidence in the *vGOAL* interpreter. To achieve this, we turn to Boolean Satisfiability Problem (SAT) encoding and solving. SAT is the problem of determining if there exists an interpretation that satisfies a given Boolean formula [10]. SAT solvers have been researched and developed for many years, there are many well-known efficient SAT solvers such as Chaff [11]. If software verification problems are converted into Boolean Satisfiability Problems, the SAT Solvers can make the automated execution of software verification possible [6]. Therefore, SAT solving is a feasible solution to increase the confidence of an APL interpreter while adhering to the efficiency and automation requirements.

The *vGOAL* interpreter implements the semantics of *vGOAL*, whose core component is the minimal model generation. Consequently, the implementation correctness of the minimal model generation component plays a crucial role in the implementation correctness of the *vGOAL* interpreter. One distinguishing feature of *vGOAL* is its direct conversion of specifications into equivalently expressive propositional logical specifications. This characteristic facilitates the integration of an SAT-solving component into the *vGOAL* interpreter, particularly into its core component, the minimal model generation.

To practically enhance the confidence of the $vGOAL$ interpreter, we developed and integrated an SAT-solving component into its core component: minimal model generation. The SAT-solving component encompasses two subcomponents: an SAT-encoding component and an SAT solver, leveraging PySAT [8] as a simple interface to numerous state-of-the-art SAT solvers.

Our main contribution lies in SAT encoding. Specifically, we devise an algorithm to encode the inputs and outputs of the core component into a satisfiable conjunctive normal form (CNF) formula. Moreover, we justify that this algorithm generates a satisfiable CNF formula only if the result is correct. Each output generated by the minimal model generation process is checked by the SAT-solving component. In the event of any inconsistencies detected during this process, the $vGOAL$ interpreter halts execution. The SAT-solving component enhances the confidence of the $vGOAL$ interpreter because no incorrectly inferred autonomous decision will be generated. We demonstrate the practicability and efficiency of the SAT-solving component through an autonomous transportation system including three autonomous mobile robots.

The rest of the paper is structured as follows. Section 2 briefly introduces $vGOAL$, including its definitions and reasoning cycle. Section 3 describes how to integrate the SAT-solving component into the $vGOAL$ interpreter. Section 4 presents the formulation of the encoding problem, the description of an encoding algorithm, and the justification of the SAT-encoding algorithm. Section 5 describes a case study where we empirically test the differences of using the $vGOAL$ interpreter with or without the SAT-solving component. Finally, we draw conclusions on our work.

2   Preliminaries

This section aims to explain why the minimal model generation component is the core component of the $vGOAL$ interpreter. We clarify all key concepts in the paper, and we refer interested readers to [17] for more details of $vGOAL$.

2.1   vGOAL

Definition 1. *(vGOAL Specifications) [17] A* vGOAL *specification is defined as*

$$vGOALSpec ::= (MAS, K, C, A, S, P, E, D)$$
$$MAS ::= (id, B, goals, M_S, M_R)^*$$

A $vGOAL$ specification specifies autonomous decision-making. The first main component is agents' specifications, MAS. Each agent's specification comprises a unique identifier, a belief base, a set of goals, sent messages, and received messages, denoted as id, B, $goals$, M_S, and M_R, respectively. The other specifications are system specifications. K represents the knowledge base; C denotes the rules on enabled constraints generation; A denotes the rules on feasible action generation; S denotes the rules on sent message generation; P denotes the rules on event processing, including modifying agent goals and beliefs, and processing received messages; E denotes action effects; and D represents the domain of all variables.

Table 1. Semantics of *vGOAL* Specifications

Specification	Syntax	Semantics
B	$[b_1, ..., b_n]$	ground atoms: $I(B) = \{b_1, ..., b_n\}$
goals	$[[g_{11}, ..., g_{1m}], ..., [g_n]]$	ground atoms: $I(goals) = \{a\text{-}goal\text{-}g_{11}, ..., a\text{-}goal\text{-}g_{1m}\}$
M_S	$[s_1, ..., s_n]$	atoms: $I(M_S) = \{s_1, ..., s_n\}$
M_R	$[r_1, ..., r_n]$	atoms: $I(M_R) = \{r_1, ..., r_n\}$
K	$[k_1, ..., k_n]$	a first-order theory: $I(K) = \{k_1, ..., k_n\}$
C	$[c_1, ..., c_n]$	a first-order theory: $I(C) = \{c_1, ..., c_n\}$
A	$[a_1, ..., a_n]$	a first-order theory: $I(A) = \{a_1, ..., a_n\}$
S	$[s_1, ..., s_n]$	a first-order theory:$I(S) = \{s_1, ..., s_n\}$
P	$[p_1, ..., p_n]$	a first-order theory: $I(P) = \{p_1, ..., p_n\}$
id	*id*	$I(id) = id$
D	D	$I(D) = D$
E	E	$I(id) = E$

Table 1 illustrates the semantics of *vGOAL* specifications, detailing their syntax and corresponding interpretations: B and *goals* are interpreted as sets of ground atoms; M_S and M_R are interpreted sets of atoms; K, C, A, S, and P are interpreted as first-order theories; *id*, D, and E maintain their identity as specified. This table demonstrates that all *vGOAL* specifications, except for *id*, D, and E, are expressed within first-order logic. Additionally, D plays a crucial role in the transformation of first-order logical expressions to their logically equivalent logical formulae by removing all variables.

Definition 2. *(vGOAL States) [17] A* vGOAL *state is formalized as follows:*

$$state ::= (substate)_{\times n},$$
$$substate ::= id{:}(I(B), I(goals)).$$

The *vGOAL state* of a system is formally defined as a composition of substates, $(id{:}(I(B), I(goals)))_{\times n}$. Each substate represents an agent with a unique identifier and the semantics of its beliefs and goals, denoted as $I(B)$ and $I(goals)$.

Definition 3. *(Operational Semantics of* vGOAL*) [17]*

$$(substate)_{\times n} \xrightarrow{(id:(M_R,Act))_{\times n}} (substate')_{\times n}.$$

The operational semantics of $vGOAL$ is established by the reasoning cycle, which involves the minimal model generation of first-order theories and function updates based on the interpretation of $vGOAL$ specifications. After each reasoning cycle, a substate can only be updated by the action effects and the processed results of the event processing, including processing the received messages, subsequently updating the $vGOAL$ state.

2.2   *vGOAL* Interpreter

$vGOAL$ is a specification language for autonomous decision-making mechanisms, and it requires an interpreter to generate decisions based on the given $vGOAL$ specification. The $vGOAL$ interpreter implements the operational semantics of $vGOAL$, serving as an agent-based decision-making component for autonomous systems [16].

Table 2. State Update in $vGOAL$ Interpreter

Stage	Input	Output	Process
1	MAS	$state$	Interpretation
2.0	$id : (B, goals)$	$substate$	Start substate update
2.1.a	$K, B, goals, D$	$K',B, goals$	Logical Equivalence Transformation
2.1.b	$K', B, goals$	$subP$	Minimal Model Generation
2.2.a	$subP, C, D$	$subP, C'$	Logical Equivalence Transformation
2.2.b	$subP, C'$	GC	Minimal Model Generation
2.3.a	$subP, GC, A, D$	$subP, GC, A'$	Logical Equivalence Transformation
2.3.b	$subP,GC,A'$	GA	Minimal Model Generation
2.4.a	$subP , GC, S, D$	$subP , GC, S'$	Logical Equivalence Transformation
2.4.b	$subP , GC, S'$	GS	Minimal Model Generation
2.5.a	$subP, M_R, P, D$	$subP, M_R, P'$	Logical Equivalence Transformation
2.5.b	$subP, M_R, P'$	PR	Minimal Model Generation
2.6	MAS	MAS'	Communication
2.7	$substate, PR, E, D$	$substate'$	Substate Update
3	$(substate')_{\times n}$	$state'$	Substate Combination

Table 2 presents an overview of the state update implemented in the *vGOAL* interpreter. As an agent-based autonomous system consists of agents in a modular manner, a state consists of substates in a modular manner. The state update involves three stages. At first, *state*, the current state, is directly interpreted by *MAS*, agent specifications. Each substate of *state* needs to go through the second stage: substate update. After each substate of the *state* goes through the second stage, the state will be updated by the combination of the updated substates.

As presented in Table 2, the second stage is the key implementation of the *vGOAL* interpreter. The reasoning cycle involves six stages. The first five stages are implemented by the logical equivalence transformation and minimal model generation, and the last stage is implemented by communication among agents. The logical equivalence transformation is used to transform a given first-order theory under *vGOAL* syntax to its logically equivalent first-order theory without variables, specifically, from K and D to K', from C and D to C', from A and D to A', from S and D to S', and from P and D to P'. Hence, the converted first-order theories are expressible in propositional logic. The minimal model generation is used to generate the substate properties($subP$), the generated constraints (GC), the generated actions (GA), the generated sent messages (GS), and the processed results (PR). The communication is implemented by exchanging messages among agents. Compared with the implementation of logical equivalence transformation and communication, the implementation of the minimal model generation is much more complex and error-prone. The confidence of the *vGOAL* interpreter will be significantly enhanced if the implementation correctness of the minimal model generation is guaranteed.

3   SAT Solving Integration

This section elaborates on the data flow and the workflow concerning the integration of SAT solving into the *vGOAL* interpreter. As explained in Sect. 2.2, the *vGOAL* interpreter implements the operational semantics of *vGOAL*, particularly through the implementation of the reasoning cycle that enables substate updates. The SAT-solving component is used to check the correctness of the generated results of the minimal model generation, thereby enhancing the overall confidence in the *vGOAL* interpreter. The implementation of the *vGOAL* interpreter embedded with the SAT solver is available at [14].

Table 3. Dataflow between the Reasoning Cycle and the SAT-Solving Component

Component	Precondition	Input	Output	Guarantee	Termination
2.1.a	No	$K, B, goals, D$	$K', B, goals$	\	No
2.1.b	No	$K', B, goals$	R_1	$R_1 = subP?$	No
SAT Solving	No	K', B, G, R_1	SAT	$R_1 = subP$	No
SAT Solving	No	K', B, G, R_1	$UNSAT$	$R_1 \neq subP$	Yes
2.2.a	SAT	$subP, C, D$	$subP, C'$	\	No
2.2.b	No	$subP, C'$	R_2	$R_2 = GC?$	No
SAT Solving	No	$subP, C', R_2$	SAT	$R_2 = GC$	No
SAT Solving	No	$subP, C', R_2$	$UNSAT$	$R_2 \neq GC$	Yes
2.3.a	SAT	$subP, GC, A, D$	$subP, GC, A'$	\	No
2.3.b	No	$subP, GC, A'$	R_3	$R_3 = GA?$	No
SAT Solving	No	$subP, GC, A', R_3$	SAT	$R_3 = GA$	No
SAT Solving	No	$subP, GC, A', R_3$	$UNSAT$	$R_3 \neq GA$	Yes
2.4.a	SAT	$subP, GC, S, D$	$subP, GC, S'$	\	No
2.4.b	No	$subP, GC, S'$	R_4	$R_4 = GS?$	No
SAT Solving	No	$subP, GC, S', R_4$	SAT	$R_4 = GS$	No
SAT Solving	No	$subP, GC, S', R_4$	$UNSAT$	$R_4 \neq GS$	Yes
2.5.a	SAT	$subP, M_R, P, D$	$subP, M_R, P'$	\	No
2.5.b	No	$subP, M_R, P'$	R_5	$R_5 = PR?$	No
SAT Solving	No	$subP, M_R, P', R_5$	SAT	$R_5 = PR$	No
SAT Solving	No	$subP, M_R, P', R_5$	$UNSAT$	$R_5 \neq PR$	Yes
2.6	SAT	MAS	MAS'	\	No

Table 3 outlines the data flow between the reasoning cycle of the $vGOAL$ interpreter and the SAT-solving component. The table provides information on components, along with their preconditions, inputs, outputs, guarantees, and termination. Components include all stages in the reasoning cycle that interact with the SAT-solving component, involving from Stage 2.1 to Stage 2.6 and the SAT-solving component. Preconditions are the preconditions to enter the component. Inputs and outputs are the inputs and outputs of the component. Guarantees are the guarantees provided by the SAT-solving component. Termination gives information on whether the reasoning process should immediately terminate due to the erroneous results generated by the minimal model generation.

For the details of the inputs and outputs of the stages in the $vGOAL$ interpreter, we explained in Sect. 2.2. The SAT-solving component takes the inputs and outputs of its previous stage as the inputs, and it generates the satisfiability result of inputs: either SAT or $UNSAT$.

The SAT-solving component is used to check the correctness of the results generated by the minimal model generation for the given input, involving stages 2.1.b, 2.2.b, 2.3.b, 2.4.b, and 2.5.b. If the SAT-solving component generates *UNSAT*, the *vGOAL* interpreter will immediately terminate. The preventive termination guarantees that the *vGOAL* never executes any erroneous decisions due to the erroneous minimal model generation. Only when the SAT-solving component generates *SAT*, the *vGOAL* interpreter proceeds to its subsequent reasoning stage, including 2.2.a, 2.3.a, 2.4.a, 2.5.a, and 2.6.

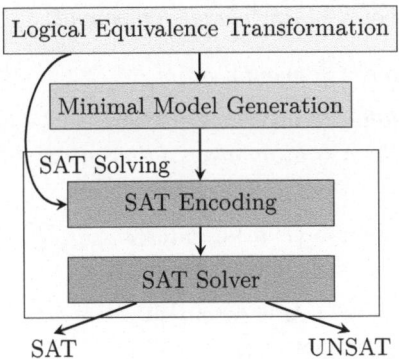

Fig. 1. Integration of the SAT Solving Component into the *vGOAL* Interpreter

Figure 1 illustrates the workflow of integrating SAT solving into the *vGOAL* interpreter. As shown in Table 1, the first five reasoning stages involve logical equivalence transformation and minimal model generation, where the SAT-solving component is integrated. The SAT-solving component comprises two subcomponents: an SAT-encoding component and an SAT solver. The inputs of the SAT encoding component are both inputs and outputs of the minimal model generation. The SAT-encoding component transforms these inputs into their logically equivalent formulas in CNF. The SAT solver takes the generated CNF formula as input and outputs its satisfiability result. The output *SAT* indicates the satisfiability of the inputs, verifying the correctness of the results of the minimal model generation for the given inputs. Conversely, an output of *UNSAT* denotes unsatisfiability, suggesting issues with the minimal model generation process in achieving the minimal model for the given inputs. We use PySAT [8] as the SAT solver for its simple access to numerous state-of-the-art SAT solvers. Consequently, our main work on the SAT-solving integration is the SAT-encoding component.

4   SAT Encoding

This section explains the SAT-encoding component in detail. First, we formula the encoding problem. Second, we describe the SAT-encoding algorithm. Finally, we justify the SAT encoding algorithm.

Definition 4 formally defines the inputs of the SAT-encoding component. The inputs of the SAT-encoding component are the inputs and outputs of the minimal model generation. T denotes the inputs of the minimal model generation, and M denotes the outputs of the minimal model generation.

Definition 4. *(Inputs of SAT-Encoding Component)*

$$atom :: = ground\_atom$$
$$atoms :: = \{atom\} \cup atoms | \emptyset$$
$$lhs :: = atom | atom \wedge lhs | \neg atom \wedge lhs$$
$$rule :: = lhs \rightarrow atom$$
$$rules :: = \{rule\} \cup rules | \emptyset$$
$$T :: = rules \cup atoms$$
$$M :: = M \cup \{atom\} | \emptyset$$
$$Input :: = T \cup M$$

The inputs, T, are the first-order theory that is constrained by the $vGOAL$ syntax [17] with no variables and no quantification. The inputs of the $vGOAL$ interpreter is a $vGOAL$ specification that follows the $vGOAL$ syntax. The logical equivalence transformation converts a first-order theory to its logically equivalent first-order theory by removing all qualifications and variables. The outputs, M, are the consequence of the minimal model generation during the reasoning cycle. Therefore, it only contains ground atoms.

Definition 5 formally defines the output of the SAT-encoding component as a formula in CNF. A CNF formula is commonly represented in a set of sets. For example, a CNF formula, $(a_1 \vee a_2) \wedge b_1 \wedge (c_1 \vee c_2)$ is represented as $\{\{a_1, a_2\}, \{b_1\}, \{c_1, c_2\}\}$. The input of PySAT uses the common representation of a CNF formula.

Definition 5. *(Output of the SAT-Encoding Component)*

$$atom :: = ground\_atom | \neg ground\_atom$$
$$Disjunction :: = atom | atom \vee Disjunction$$
$$CNF :: = Disjunction \wedge CNF | Disjunction$$
$$clause :: = \{atom\} \cup clause | \emptyset$$
$$output :: = \{cluase\} \cup output | \emptyset$$

Our goal is to prove the model generated by the minimal model generation process is the minimal model for the given *vGOAL* specification. Specifically, we need to encode the inputs of the SAT-encoding component into a formula in CNF that encodes the condition of the minimal model. As CNF formulae can be directly processed by an SAT solver, we can take advantage of the existing efficient SAT solvers. To achieve the goal, we design and implement Algorithm 1, which is the core of the SAT-encoding component.

Algorithm 1 takes the input of the SAT-encoding component as the input, denoting *input*. The algorithm generates a formula in CNF as the output, denoting CNF. Following Definition 4, *input* consists of a first-order theory (T) and a set of atoms (M). Following Definition 5, CNF is a CNF formula represented as a set of sets.

Lines 1–10 describe the initialization of G, A, *Check*, CNF, and Min_G. G denotes the set of the generated atoms by the minimal model generation process, initialized with $M \setminus atoms$. A denotes a set of negative atoms, initialized with an empty set. *Check* denotes a set of the generated atoms that need to be checked if they are generated by at least one rule in T, initialized with G. CNF denotes a formula in CNF. Each atom in $atoms \cup M$ is included in CNF as a clause. Min_G denotes a dictionary that contains all possible conditions for the derivation of the generated atoms, initialized with an empty dictionary. The keys of Min_G are assigned with the generated atoms. Each value of the key in Min_G records all possible combinations of premises of the generated atom, initialized with an empty set.

Lines 11–31 extend CNF by encoding each rule in T into two conditions. *derived_atom* denotes the atom that can be generated by the given rule. *flag* denotes if *derived_atom* is an atom in the set of generated atoms, G. If *derived_atom* is an atom of G, *flag* is assigned with *True*. In this case, *derived_atom* is removed from the set *Check*, as there is at least one rule that can generate *derived_atom*. *Premise* is a set of atoms that includes all preconditions to generate *derived_atom*.

Lines 19–20 describe the first condition is the transformation from the given rule to its logically equivalent formula in CNF. Following Definition 4, a rule in T can be transformed to logically equivalent clauses of a formula in CNF as follows:

$$\bigwedge_{i=1}^{n} A_i \rightarrow atom \equiv \bigwedge_{i=1}^{n} (\neg A_i \lor atom),$$

where $A_i ::= atom | \neg atom$.

Algorithm 1: Encode the input of the SAT-solving component into a formula in CNF

Input: $input = T \cup M$, $T = rules \cup atoms$

Output: CNF

1   $G \leftarrow M \setminus atoms$, $A \leftarrow \emptyset$

2   $Check \leftarrow G$

3   $CNF \leftarrow \emptyset$

4   **for** *each atom* $\in atoms \cup M$ **do**

5      $\lfloor$ $CNF \leftarrow CNF \cup \{\{atom\}\}$

6

7   $Min\_G \leftarrow \emptyset$

8   **for** *each atom* $\in M$ **do**

9   **if** *atom* $\in G$ **then**

10         $\lfloor$ $Min\_G \leftarrow Min\_G \cup \{atom : \emptyset\}$

11   **for** *each rule* $::= lhs \rightarrow atom \in rules$ **do**

12      $derived\_atom \leftarrow atom$

13      $flag \leftarrow False$

14   **if** *derived_atom* $\in G$ **then**

15         $flag \leftarrow True$

16   **if** *derived_atom* $\in Check$ **then**

17            $\lfloor$ $Check \leftarrow Check \setminus derived\_atom$

18      $Premise \leftarrow \emptyset$

19   **for** *each* $a ::= atom|\neg atom \in rule$ **do**

20         $clause \leftarrow \{-a, derived\_atom\}$

21         $CNF \leftarrow CNF \cup \{clause\}$

22   **if** *atom* $\notin M \cup atoms$ **then**

23            $\lfloor$ $A \leftarrow A \cup \{atom\}$

24         $Premise \leftarrow Presmise \cup \{a\}$

25   **if** *flag* **then**

26   **if** $Min\_G[derived\_atom] = \emptyset$ **then**

27            $\lfloor$ $Min\_G[derived\_atom] \leftarrow \{Premise\}$

28   **else**

29            $\lfloor$ $Min\_G[derived\_atom] \leftarrow Min\_G[derived\_atom] \times Premise$

30   **for** *each atom* $\in Min\_G$ **do**

31      $\lfloor$ $CNF \leftarrow CNF \cup Min\_G[atom]$

32   **if** $Check \neq \emptyset$ **then**

33   **for** *some atom* $\in Check$ **do**

34         $\lfloor$ $CNF \leftarrow \{\{atom\}, \{\neg atom\}\}$

35   **else**

36   **for** *each atom* $\in A$ **do**

37         $\lfloor$ $CNF \leftarrow \{\{\neg atom\}\} \cup CNF$

38   **return** CNF

Lines 24–31 encode the second condition that every generated atom can be generated by at least one rule in T, which is the key to proving the generated model is the minimal model. First, all preconditions of the rule are added to

Premise. If *flag* is *True*, the Min_G is extended by two cases. If Min_G is an empty set, Min_G is assigned with *Premise*. If Min_G is not empty, Min_G is extended by all possibility that the original clauses multiply *Premise*. CNF will be extended by all clauses recorded in Min_G.

Lines 32–34 describe the case that at least one generated atom cannot be derived by T. In this case, the generated model is certainly not a minimal model of T. CNF is defined by two unsatisfiable clauses, $\{atom\}$ and $\{\neg atom\}$.

Lines 35–37 describe the extension of CNF. For each atom in A, its negative atom is added to CNF.

Following Definition 4, there are three kinds of relations between T and M: M is the minimal model of T; M is a model of T, but M is not the minimal model of T; M is not model of T. We illustrate how Algorithm 1 handles these three cases with three simple examples.

Example 1. Input: $T \cup M$, where $T = rules \cup atoms$,
$rules = \{rule_1, rule_2, rule_3\}$, $atoms = \{a_1, a_2\}$, $M = \{a_1, a_2, e\}$
$rule_1 = a_1 \wedge a_2 \rightarrow e$, $rule_2 = b_1 \wedge b_2 \rightarrow e$, $rule_3 = c \wedge \neg d \rightarrow f$
Step 1: Initialization
$G \leftarrow \{e\}$, $A \leftarrow \emptyset$, $Check \leftarrow G$, $CNF \leftarrow \{\{a_1\}, \{a_2\}, \{e\}\}$, $Min\_G \leftarrow \{e : \emptyset\}$.
Step 2: Expand CNF by handling $rule_1$
$derived\_atom \leftarrow e$, $flag \leftarrow True$, $Check \leftarrow \emptyset$,
$CNF \leftarrow \{\{a_1\}, \{a_2\}, \{e\}, \{\neg a_1, e\}, \{\neg a_2, e\}\}$,
$Premise \leftarrow \{a_1, a_2\}$, $Min\_G[e] = \{\{a_1, a_2\}\}$.
Step 3: Expand CNF by handling $rule_2$
$derived\_atom \leftarrow e$, $flag \leftarrow True$
$CNF \leftarrow \{\{a_1\}, \{a_2\}, \{e\}, \{\neg a_1, e\}, \{\neg a_2, e\}\}, \{\neg b_1, e\}, \{\neg b_2, e\}\}$
$A \leftarrow \{b_1, b_2\}$, $Premise = \{b_1, b_2\}$,
$Min\_G[e] = \{a_1, a_2\} \times \{b_1, b_2\}$,
$Min\_G[e] = \{\{a_1, b_1\}, \{a_1, b_2\}, \{a_2, b_1\}, \{a_2, b_2\}\}$.
Step 4: Expand CNF by handling $rule_3$
$derived\_atom \leftarrow f$, $flag \leftarrow False$,
$CNF \leftarrow \{\{a_1\}, \{a_2\}, \{e\}, \{\neg a_1, e\}, \{\neg a_2, e\}\}, \{\neg b_1, e\}, \{\neg b_2, e\}, \{\neg c, f\}, \{d, f\}\}$,
$A \leftarrow \{b_1, b_2, c, d, f\}$.
Step 5: Expand CNF by encoding the condition for minimal model generation
$CNF \leftarrow CNF \cup Min\_G[e]$
Step 6: Expand CNF by adding all negative atoms in A.
$CNF \leftarrow CNF \cup \{\{\neg b_1\}, \{\neg b_2\}, \{\neg c\}, \{\neg d\}, \{\neg f\}\}$.
Output: CNF

Example 1 presents how Algorithm 1 generates a satisfiable CNF formula if the generated model is the minimal model. Following Lines 1–10 of Algorithm 1, the first step is initialization. Following Lines 11–29, CNF is extended by handling each rule in *rules*. The expansion process is executed three times as *rules* contains three rules, presented from Step 2 to Step 4. Following Lines 30–31, CNF is extended by adding all premises of the generated atoms in Step 5. Following Line 32, *Check* is an empty set, the instructions described in Lines 33–34 are not executed. Following Lines 35–37, CNF is extended by all negative atoms in A in Step 6. The output is $\{\{a_1\}, \{a_2\}, \{e\}, \{\neg a_1, e\}, \{\neg a_2, e\}\}, \{\neg b_1, e\}, \{\neg b_2, e\}, \{\neg c, f\}, \{d, f\}, \{a_1, b_1\}, \{a_1, b_2\}, \{a_2, b_1\}, \{a_2, b_2\}, \{\neg b_1\}, \{\neg b_2\}, \{\neg c\}, \{\neg d\}, \{\neg f\}\}$. The output is satisfiable when $a_1 \leftarrow True$, $a_2 \leftarrow True$, $b_1 \leftarrow False$, $b_2 \leftarrow False$, $c \leftarrow False$, $d \leftarrow False$, $e \leftarrow True$, and $f \leftarrow False$.

Example 2. Input: $T \cup M$, where $T = rules \cup atoms$,
$rules = \{rule_1\}$, $atoms = \{a_1, a_2\}$, $M = \{a_1, a_2, e, f\}$
$rule_1 = a_1 \wedge a_2 \rightarrow e$
Step 1: Initialization
$G \leftarrow \{e, f\}$, $A \leftarrow \emptyset$, $Check \leftarrow G$,
$CNF \leftarrow \{\{a_1\}, \{a_2\}, \{e\}, \{f\}\}$, $Min\_G \leftarrow \{e : \emptyset, f : \emptyset\}$.
Step 2: Expand CNF by handling $rule_1$
$derived\_atom \leftarrow e$, $flag \leftarrow True$, $Check \leftarrow \{f\}$,
$CNF \leftarrow \{\{a_1\}, \{a_2\}, \{e\}, \{f\}, \{\neg a_1, e\}, \{\neg a_2, e\}\}$,
$Premise \leftarrow \{a_1, a_2\}$,
$Min\_G = \{e : \{\{a_1, a_2\}\}, f : \emptyset\}\}$
Step 3: Expand CNF by encoding conditions for minimal model generation
$CNF \leftarrow CNF \cup \{\{a_1, a_2\}\}$.
Step 4: Assign an unsatisfiable formula to CNF.
$CNF \leftarrow \{\{f\}, \{\neg f\}\}$
Return CNF

Example 2 presents how Algorithm 1 generates an unsatisfiable CNF formula if the generated model is a model but not the minimal model. Following Lines 1–10 of Algorithm 1, the first step is initialization. Following Lines 11–29, the second step is the extension of CNF by handling $rule_1$. As there is only one rule in $rules$, the expansion process only is executed once. Following Lines 30–31 of Algorithm 1, CNF is extended by encoding the minimal model condition in Step 3. Step 4 follows Lines 32–34. $Check$ contains f, which implies f cannot be derived by the given first-order theory, T. Therefore, CNF is assigned with an unsatisfiable CNF formula: $\{\{f\}, \{\neg f\}\}$, which is returned as the output. The CNF formula is inconsistent, therefore, it is unsatisfiable.

Example 3. Input: $T \cup M$, where $T = rules \cup atoms$,
$rules = \{rule_1\}$, $atoms = \{a_1, a_2\}$, $M = \{a_1, a_2\}$
$rule_1 = a_1 \wedge a_2 \rightarrow e$
Step 1: Initialization
$G \leftarrow \emptyset$, $A \leftarrow \emptyset$, $Check \leftarrow \emptyset$, $CNF \leftarrow \{\{a_1\}, \{a_2\}\}$, $Min\_G \leftarrow \emptyset$.
Step 2: Expand CNF by handling $rule_1$
$derived\_atom \leftarrow e$, $flag \leftarrow False$,
$CNF \leftarrow \{\{a_1\}, \{a_2\}, \{\neg a_1, e\}, \{\neg a_2, e\}\}$,
$Premise \leftarrow \{a_1, a_2\}$, $A \leftarrow \{e\}$.
Step 3: Expand CNF by adding all negative atoms in A.
$CNF \leftarrow \{\{a_1\}, \{a_2\}, \{\neg a_1, e\}, \{\neg a_2, e\}, \{\neg e\}\}$

Example 3 presents how Algorithm 1 generates an unsatisfiable CNF formula if the generated model is not a model. Following Lines 1–7 of Algorithm 1, the first step is initialization. Following Lines 11–29, the second step is the extension of CNF by handling $rule_1$. As there is only one rule in $rules$, the expansion process only is executed once. As Min_G is empty, the instructions described in Lines 30–31 are not executed. Step 3 follows Lines 32–37. CNF is extended by adding all negative atoms in A, as $Check$ is empty. The output is $\{\{a_1\}, \{a_2\}, \{\neg a_1, e\}, \{\neg a_2, e\}, \{\neg e\}\}$. The CNF formula is unsatisfiable, because no truth assignment can make it true.

Proposition 1. *Following Definition 4, an input for Algorithm 1 consists of a set of atoms, M, and a first-order theory, T, where T consists of rules and atoms. The output of Algorithm 1 is a CNF formula following Definition 5, denoting as CNF. CNF is satisfiable iff the atoms $\cup M$ is the minimal model of T.*

Proof. We briefly explain how Algorithm 1 generates CNF for the given input. CNF consists of three parts. The first part is the CNF formula that is logically equivalent to T, denoting F_1. The second part is the CNF formula that encodes all possibilities for the derivation of the generated atoms, denoting F_2. The third part is the CNF formula that encodes all negative atoms, denoting F_3.

There are three kinds of relations between $atoms \cup M$ and T. We prove Proposition 1 by cases.

Case 1 $atoms \cup M$ is the minimal model of T.

In this case, F_1 is satisfiable, as there is a model. $F2$ and F_3 are satisfiable, as $atoms \cup M$ is the minimal model of T. F_2 is satisfiable, which indicates each atom in $atoms \cup M$ can be derived by T. F_3 is satisfiable, which implies no more atoms can be derived by T.

Case 2 $atoms \cup M$ is a model of T, but $atoms \cup M$ is not the minimal model of T.

In this case, there is at least one atom that cannot be derived by T. Following Lines 32–34, the output will be an inconsistent CNF formula. Therefore, the output is unsatisfiable.

Case 3 $atoms \cup M$ is not a model of T.

In this case, $\exists c.T \vdash c$, and $c \notin atoms \cup M$. Following Lines 32–37, either an inconsistent CNF formula is generated, or the output contains $\{\neg c\}$. The output is unsatisfiable in both cases.

5 Empirical Analysis

In this section, we analyze the time cost brought by the SAT-Solving component integrated into the *vGOAL* interpreter, as introduced in [16]. To conduct the comparison, we use the same autonomous logistic system case study described in [16], comprising three autonomous mobile robots denoted as A_1, A_2, and A_3. There are four durative high-level actions, each subject to potential success or failure. Failures are classified as non-fatal or fatal, with non-fatal errors causing the agent to drop its current goal, while fatal errors result in goal redistribution among other agents and removal of the faulty agent.

The $vGOAL$ interpreter consistently generates the same decision for a given input. Following Definition 1, only agent specifications, MAS, can be different during the executions. Moreover, each agent is specified as $(id, B, goals, M_S, M_R)$. id are not modified during the execution, while $goals$, M_S, and M_R are modified due to the modifications of B. Therefore, it is sufficient to illustrate the time cost brought by the SAT-solving component using three representative experiments: (i) successful completion of all four delivery goals, (ii) successful completion of the first three goals with one non-fatal action failure in the fourth, and (iii) successful completion of the first three goals with one fatal action failure in the fourth.

We conducted these experiments using both versions of the $vGOAL$ interpreter, with and without the SAT-solving component. Each run lasted six to eight minutes, with ROS providing real-time sensor updates every 0.5 s, resulting in 720 to 960 updates per run for real-time decision-making. All experiments demonstrated safe robot behavior, with no exceptions raised by the SAT-solving component.

Notably, during action execution, sensor updates frequently duplicate previous information. When such duplication occurs, the interpreter does not generate any decisions for the agent. Consequently, the SAT-solving component, which is integrated into the decision-making process, remains inactive. Therefore, minimal time discrepancies were observed between the two versions of the $vGOAL$ interpreter during experiments. To precisely measure the time cost introduced by the SAT-solving component, we extracted sensor inputs from the original real-time data, modifying only the occurrence of repeated sensor information.

All experiments are conducted with a MacBook Air 2020 with an Apple M1 and 16GB of RAM. Detailed information regarding the complete $vGOAL$ specification of the case study, is available at [14]. Additionally, we have provided three demonstration videos on [14]: an error-free run, a run involving a non-fatal error, and a run involving a fatal error.

In summary, the three experiments undergo identical decision-making processes for the initial three delivery goals, and the $vGOAL$ interpreter makes different decisions if an agent encounters no errors, a nonfatal error, or a fatal error. Table 4 presents the results of experiments conducted. The "Repeated" column indicates whether repeated sensor information was present. The "System" column specifies the number of agents in the system, while "Active" denotes the number of agents that have goals to achieve. "Decision" describes the decisions made by the $vGOAL$ interpreter, and "Error" categorizes errors encountered during the experiment: no errors, fatal errors, or non-fatal errors. The columns labeled "$vGOAL$ without SAT solver" and "$vGOAL$ with SAT solver" represent the time taken for the $vGOAL$ interpreter without or with the SAT-Solving component. The column, labeled "SAT", denotes the call numbers of the SAT-solving components involved in the decision-making generation at the current

Table 4. Experimental Results

Repeated	System	Active	Decision	Error	$vGOAL$ without SAT (s)	$vGOAL$ with SAT (s)	SAT Calls	Overhead(s)
Yes	3	3	No	No	2 ∼ 4 E-5	2 ∼ 4 E-5	0	0
No	3	3	$A_1 : move$ $A_2 : move$	No	0.82	0.88	352	0.06
No	3	3	No	No	0.64	0.67	249	0.03
No	3	3	$A_1 : pick$	No	0.31	0.33	102	0.02
No	3	3	$A_2 : pick$	No	0.38	0.41	151	0.03
No	3	3	$A_1 : move$	No	0.59	0.63	217	0.04
No	3	3	$A_3 : move$	No	0.65	0.71	309	0.06
No	3	3	No	No	0.61	0.64	192	0.03
No	3	3	$A_1 : drop$	No	0.31	0.33	111	0.02
No	3	3	$A_1 : move$	No	0.67	0.71	227	0.04
No	3	3	$A_3 : pick$	No	0.32	0.33	87	0.01
No	3	3	$A_2 : move$	No	0.79	0.84	282	0.05
No	3	3	No	No	0.61	0.65	171	0.04
No	3	3	$A_1 : move$	No	0.59	0.61	180	0.02
No	3	3	$A_2 : drop$	No	0.32	0.34	99	0.02
No	3	3	$A_2 : move$	No	0.68	0.73	217	0.05
No	3	2	$A_3 : move$	No	0.61	0.65	246	0.04
No	3	2	No	No	0.44	0.46	135	0.02
No	3	2	$A_2 : move$	No	0.47	0.50	165	0.03
No	3	2	$A_3 : drop$	No	0.24	0.25	78	0.01
No	3	2	$A_3 : move$	No	0.50	0.54	177	0.04
No	3	2	No	No	0.44	0.45	105	0.01
No	3	1	$A_3 : move$	No	0.46	0.50	157	0.04
No	3	1	No	No	0.44	0.46	99	0.02
No	3	1	$A_3 : move$	No	0.48	0.52	182	0.04
No	3	1	$A_3 : pick$	No	0.21	0.22	54	0.01
No	3	1	$A_3 : move$	No	0.21	0.22	45	0.01
No	3	1	$A_3 : move$	No	0.21	0.22	54	0.01
No	3	1	$A_3 : move$	Non-Fatal	0.48	0.51	158	0.03
No	2	1	$A_1 : move$	Fatal	0.38	0.41	166	0.03
No	3	1	$A_3 : move$	No	0.47	0.50	156	0.03
No	3	1	$A_3 : move$	Non-Fatal	0.47	0.50	156	0.03
No	2	1	$A_1 : move$	Fatal	0.46	0.48	134	0.02

step. The last column labeled "overhead" describes the overhead introduced by the SAT-solving component when making decisions.

We briefly explain the case where the overhead of the SAT-solving component is zero. If the sensor information is repeated between the current step and the last step, the *vGOAL* interpreter will not make any decisions. Hence, the SAT-solving component will not be executed in this case. In our setting, the *vGOAL* interpreter receives the sensor information every 0.5 s, while it takes at least a few seconds to complete an action. Therefore, the sensor information is repeated in our experiments many times. It is important that the SAT-solving component does not introduce overhead for this common case.

The table reveals four key observations. First, there exists an almost positive linear relationship between the time required for SAT solving for each decision-making process and the number of calls made to the SAT-solving component. The more calls for the SAT-solving component, the more time cost is brought by the SAT-solving component. Second, the calls for the SAT-solving component are positively linear to the agent number of the autonomous system, and the number of generated decisions. Third, the *vGOAL* interpreter generates decisions without involving the SAT-solving component when handling repeated sensor information. As shown in Table 4, the calls for the SAT-solving component are zero when the column for "Repeated" is "Yes". Finally, the time cost brought by the SAT-solving component is at most 0.06 s for each decision-making generation.

6   Conclusion

This paper presents the integration of an SAT-solving component into the core implementation of the existing *vGOAL* interpreter: the minimal model generation. The SAT-solving component consists of two subcomponents: an SAT encoding component and an SAT solver. Leveraging PySAT for its interface to advanced SAT solvers, our main contributions lie in SAT encoding. We introduce Algorithm 1, effectively encoding the inputs and outputs of the minimal model generation process into a CNF formula, accompanied by a proof sketch to establish its correctness. The empirical results obtained from experiments conducted in an autonomous logistic system illustrate the practical usability and efficiency of the SAT-solving component. The SAT-solving component can significantly enhance the confidence of the *vGOAL* interpreter.

The implementation correctness of the *vGOAL* interpreter is crucial for users to establish trust in the *vGOAL* approach. We face four challenges: complexity, guaranteed assurance, efficiency, and automation. The SAT-solving integration offers a practical solution by focusing on the error-prone minimal model generation, verifying the generated results rather than the entire process, and leveraging PySAT within the existing *vGOAL* interpreter.

Finally, we briefly discuss the potential applicability of the SAT-solving integration to other APL interpreters. Belief-Desire-Intention (BDI) APLs are the most popular paradigm of APLs encompassing BDI reasoning [3], which typically involves logical derivation. To show the correctness of the logical derivation component, we need to show every derived atom can be derived from the first-order theory, as outlined in Algorithm 1. Specifically, Algorithm 1 can be used to encode the logical derivation component by removing the encoding part from Lines 35–37.

Acknowledgements. This research is partially funded by the Research Fund KU Leuven.

References

1. Bordini, R.H., Fisher, M., Pardavila, C., Wooldridge, M.: Model checking AgentSpeak. In: Proceedings of the Second International Joint Conference on Autonomous Agents and Multiagent Systems, pp. 409–416 (2003)
2. Bordini, R.H., Hübner, J.F.: BDI agent programming in AgentSpeak using *Jason*. In: Toni, F., Torroni, P. (eds.) CLIMA 2005. LNCS (LNAI), vol. 3900, pp. 143–164. Springer, Heidelberg (2006). https://doi.org/10.1007/11750734_9
3. Cardoso, R.C., Ferrando, A.: A review of agent-based programming for multi-agent systems. Computers **10**(2), 16 (2021)
4. Dennis, L.A., Farwer, B.: Gwendolen: a BDI language for verifiable agents. In: Proceedings of the AISB 2008 Symposium on Logic and the Simulation of Interaction and Reasoning, Society for the Study of Artificial Intelligence and Simulation of Behaviour, pp. 16–23. Citeseer (2008)
5. Dennis, L.A., Fisher, M., Webster, M.P., Bordini, R.H.: Model checking agent programming languages. Autom. Softw. Eng. **19**(1), 5–63 (2012)
6. Gong, W., Zhou, X.: A survey of sat solver. In: AIP Conference Proceedings. vol. 1836. AIP Publishing (2017)
7. Hindriks, K.V.: Programming rational agents in GOAL. In: El Fallah Seghrouchni, A., Dix, J., Dastani, M., Bordini, R.H. (eds.) Multi-Agent Programming, pp. 119–157. Springer, Boston, MA (2009). https://doi.org/10.1007/978-0-387-89299-3_4
8. Ignatiev, A., Morgado, A., Marques-Silva, J.: PySAT: a python toolkit for prototyping with SAT oracles. In: SAT, pp. 428–437 (2018)
9. Jongmans, S.-S.T.Q., Hindriks, K.V., van Riemsdijk, M.B.: Model checking agent programs by using the program interpreter. In: Dix, J., Leite, J., Governatori, G., Jamroga, W. (eds.) CLIMA 2010. LNCS (LNAI), vol. 6245, pp. 219–237. Springer, Heidelberg (2010). https://doi.org/10.1007/978-3-642-14977-1_17
10. Marques-Silva, J.: Practical applications of Boolean satisfiability. In: 2008 9th International Workshop on Discrete Event Systems, pp. 74–80. IEEE (2008)
11. Moskewicz, M.W., Madigan, C.F., Zhao, Y., Zhang, L., Malik, S.: Chaff: engineering an efficient sat solver. In: Proceedings of the 38th Annual Design Automation Conference, pp. 530–535 (2001)
12. Shoham, Y.: Agent-oriented programming. Artif. Intell. **60**(1), 51–92 (1993)
13. Weiss, G.: Multiagent Systems. The MIT Press, Cambridge (2013)
14. Yang, Y.: Supplementary Documents (2024). https://drive.google.com/drive/folders/16xXEqjg41GWF2zMeR2phpqCuiCKo8m5L?usp=share_link
15. Yang, Y., Holvoet, T.: Making model checking feasible for goal. Ann. Math. Artif. Intell. **92**(4), 1–17 (2023)

16. Yang, Y., Holvoet, T.: Safe autonomous decision-making with vGOAL. In: Advances in Practical Applications of Agents, Multi-Agent Systems, and Cognitive Mimetics. The PAAMS Collection. Guimarães, Portugal (2023)

17. Yang, Y., Holvoet, T.: vGOAL: A GOAL-based specification language for safe autonomous decision-making. In: Ciortea, A., Dastani, M., Luo, J. (eds.) Engineering Multi-Agent Systems. EMAS 2023. LNCS(), vol. 14378. Springer, Cham (2023). https://doi.org/10.1007/978-3-031-48539-8_3

Agents for DDD – Back and Forth

Alessandro Ricci[1]([✉]), Samuele Burattini[1], Andrei Ciortea[2],
and Matteo Castellucci[1]

[1] Dipartimento di Informatica - Scienza e Ingegneria, Alma Mater Studiorum -
University of Bologna, Cesena Campus, Cesena, Italy
{a.ricci,samuele.burattini}@unibo.it
[2] School of Computer Science, University of St. Gallen, St. Gallen, Switzerland
andrei.ciortea@unisg.ch

Abstract. Domain-Driven Design (DDD) emerged in the last two
decades as an effective approach adopted especially in agile software
development to tackle "the complexity at the heart of software", to quote
one of its main mottos. In this paper, we are interested in exploring the
bi-directional conceptual interaction between DDD and Agent-Oriented
Software Engineering (AOSE)—and the synergies stemming from their
fruitful integration.

Keywords: Domain-Driven Design · Agent-Oriented Software
Engineering · Agents & Artifacts · JaCaMo

1 Introduction

Domain-Driven Design (DDD) was introduced about two decades ago by Eric
Evans with the so-called "Blue Book" [12]—and since has become a reference
approach for a large community of designers and developers in mainstream software development [34]. The original main motto of DDD, i.e. *tackling complexity
in the heart of software,* sounds familiar to researchers in Agent-Oriented Software Engineering, where the capability of tackling the complexity of software
systems is a main tenet for introducing agent-based approaches [19]. Complexity, though, can be tackled from different perspectives: DDD mainly concerns
what is defined as *structural* complexity i.e. challenges that emerge from the
inherent complexity of the entities within a domain [21]. AOSE mainly concerns
dynamic complexity, thus modelling and designing systems for domains that call
for autonomy, reactivity, adaptability, and distribution.

In this paper, we focus on the fruitful interaction and integration between
these two worlds—discussing how, on the one hand, agents can be integrated
with DDD to deal with complex dynamic domains, and, on the other hand,
DDD is relevant for enhancing the applicability of agent-based approaches to
mainstream software development.

In the next section, we start by briefly recalling the main concepts of DDD.
We then analyse the bi-directional benefits that both the DDD and the AOSE

D. Briola et al. (Eds.): EMAS 2024, LNAI 15152, pp. 175–188, 2025.
https://doi.org/10.1007/978-3-031-71152-7_11

communities can gain from one another and tie them to related works that motivate this exploration (Sect. 3). Following this analysis, we discuss the main scenarios that we see for integrating agent-oriented modelling in the context of DDD, including some examples based on existing (agent-based) technologies (Sect. 4). We conclude the paper with an overview of future work that we see in this direction.

2   Domain-Driven Design: An Overview

Since the early 2000s, DDD has emerged as a mainstream practice in software development: it is widely adopted for engineering complex systems based on domain models, which are meant to facilitate a shared understanding between technical and business teams. We present the key concepts underlying DDD in Sect. 2.1. One such concept is that of a Bounded Context, which allows breaking down complex systems into simpler subsystems. We discuss integration across Bounded Contexts in Sect. 2.2.

2.1   Key Concepts

As summarized by Evans in [13], DDD is an approach to the development of complex software in which designers and developers:

- Focus on the *core domain*.
- Explore *models* in a creative collaboration of domain practitioners.
- Speak a *ubiquitous language* within explicitly *Bounded Contexts*.

A **domain** is a sphere of knowledge, influence, or activity, that is the subject area to which the user applies a program is the domain of the software. A **model** is a system of abstractions that describes selected aspects of a domain and can be used to solve problems related to that domain. The concept of model is the heart of DDD. Actually, this is a main similarity with other well-known approaches in software engineering, such as Model-Driven Software Engineering (MDSE) [30]. In MDSE models are used to drive the software development process, representing different aspects of the software systems, with an emphasis on automation, i.e., the automatic generation of code and other artifacts from these models. In DDD, the focus instead is more on using models for aligning the software design with the business domain, through a shared understanding and robust modelling of the domain logic. As Evans pointed out in [12], *the Model-Driven Design approach adopted in DDD aims at discarding the dichotomy of analysis model and design to search out a single model that serves both purposes.*

A domain is typically broken down into several **Bounded Contexts**. They represent the description of a boundary (typically a subsystem) within which a particular model is defined and applicable. The **Ubiquitous Language** (UL) is the linguistic counterpart of the model, that is, the language structured around the domain model and used by all team members working within a Bounded

Context to discuss the model and connect all the activities of the team in a pervasive way, even into the code itself. Like contexts in general, Bounded Contexts are also the setting that determines the meaning of a word or statement of the UL, that is: statements about a model can only be understood in relation to a specific context and should not be considered globally defined.

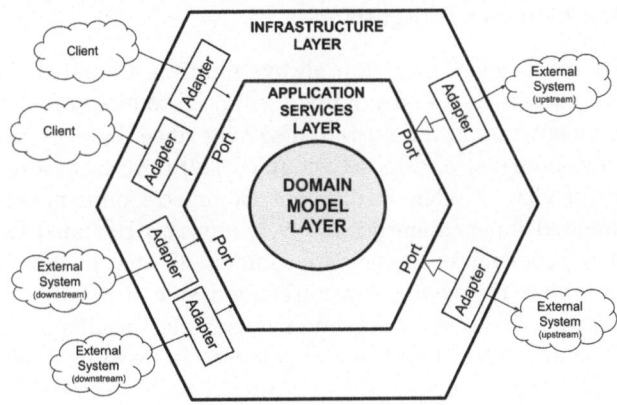

Fig. 1. Hexagonal (Ports-&-Adapters) Architectural Pattern. It uses *adapters* to decouple from the external world, and *ports* to decouple the infrastructure layer from the application layer. All dependencies go inwards, which makes the domain core stable.

Historically, DDD has adopted an object-oriented meta-model for representing any domain model, based on a set of core modelling building blocks composing a domain pattern model, including Entities, Value Objects, Aggregates, Domain Events as well as Services, Modules, Repositories, Factories [12,34].

At the architectural level, DDD calls for a strong separation of the technical concerns from the business concerns by adopting layering. Outer layers should depend on inner layers and the *domain layer* is the heart of the application, isolated from technical complexities (i.e., the *infrastructure layer*) by the application layer, which is in the middle (as depicted in Fig. 1).

The **domain layer** (or model layer) is responsible for representing concepts of the business information about the business situation together with business rules. State that reflects the business situation is controlled and used here, even though the technical details of storing it are delegated to the infrastructure layer. As Evans pointed out, this is the heart of business software.

The **application layer** wraps the domain layer: it defines the jobs the software is supposed to do and directs the expressive domain objects to work out problems. The tasks for which this layer is responsible are meaningful to the business or necessary for interaction with the application layer of other systems. This layer does not contain business rules or knowledge, but only coordinates tasks and delegates work to collaborations of domain objects in the layer below. Its state only reflects the progress of a task for the final users who, although not domain experts, should be able to understand and follow the progress of the activities they want to perform.

The **infrastructure layer** provides the generic technical capabilities that support higher layers—e.g., message sending for the application, persistence of the domain, or drawing widgets for the UI.

2.2 Bounded Context Integration

In a project of significance, there are always multiple Bounded Contexts, and two or multiple of those Bounded Contexts will need to integrate [33]. The problem is then of integration in a distributed setting since, by definition, Bounded Contexts are autonomous[1] and loosely-coupled [22] both from a modelling and technical point of view. Models in different Bounded Contexts can evolve and can be implemented independently; however, any two Bounded Contexts may also have inter-dependencies—as they are components that have to interact with one another to achieve the system's overarching design objectives. The Bounded Contexts that have to be integrated may then use different ubiquitous languages, raising the problem of identifying the language to be used for their integration purposes [20]. This problem has to be evaluated and addressed at the design level before the technical (implementation) one.

In DDD, Context Maps are used to explicitly represent, at the design level, relationships among Bounded Contexts. Such relationships are represented in terms of high-level patterns driven by the nature of collaboration between teams working on Bounded Contexts. A main example is given by Customer-Supplier patterns, where a Bounded Context is the supplier of a service for other customer Bounded Contexts. Different specific patterns are used depending on the balance of power adopted (e.g., Conformist, Anticorruption Layer, Open Host).

3   From DDD to AOSE and Back

We believe that a synergy between DDD and AOSE can bring benefits to both communities. In this section, we elaborate on this bi-directional connection and highlight how different initiatives in both communities suggest there might be a growing need for a joint effort aimed at integrating and conceptually aligning the two worlds. We consider this paper as a first step towards this direction.

3.1 DDD Relevance for Agent-Oriented Software Engineering

A main success factor of DDD in the mainstream is its effectiveness as a method for building consensus with stakeholders and developing complex systems that can easily scale and evolve. This is, of course, important in general for software engineering and could have a positive influence on MAS engineering as well.

---

[1] The term "autonomous" here has the same meaning used in Service-Oriented Architecture, see e.g. [11].

From the point of view of MAS developers, DDD can serve as a valuable way to structure domain models within the MAS itself. Following the different dimensions of Multi-Agent-Oriented Programming (MAOP) [5], domain knowledge can be represented in elements that belong to either the agent, environment, interaction, or organization dimension. As these dimensions can be considered horizontally layered upon each other, complex domains can become hard to represent. DDD and its focus on identifying Bounded Contexts to break down complexity into manageable isolated portions could add a vertical separation between concepts across the different dimensions. Moreover, within the same context, the UL can help maintain a strong consistency in how knowledge is represented across layers, whether it is data managed by agents, encoding norms and policies, or representing external stimuli from the environment.

Finally, as DDD is a generic methodology that does not directly tackle a specific paradigm, it could serve as a common ground in developing integration of MAS with other mainstream software architectures and with mainstream software development in general. For instance, recent efforts in the MAS engineering community have been bridging towards microservices [9]—the software systems more commonly paired with DDD—but also exploring the adoption of other software engineering practices closely related to DDD in agent-based software development, such as Test-Driven Development (TDD) [1,32] and Behaviour-Driven Development (BDD) [8,27].

3.2   DDD Limitations that Call for Agents

Landre in [21] remarks that DDD is great for tackling *structural complexity* but not *dynamic complexity*, which appears as a main issue of dynamic systems. Recalling the concept of dynamic complexity and dynamic systems by Derek Hitchins [17], Landre highlights that "complexity is a function of variety, connectedness, and disorder", where we have two types of connections: stable connections, which lead to structural complexity, and arbitrary connections, which lead to dynamic complexity.

Structural domain complexity manifests in nested structures like component hierarchies in products (for example, home appliances, industrial machinery), retail assortments, or project plans. Complexity arises from intricate internal state models, rules, and the extent of connectedness and variability within these systems. In contrast, *dynamic domain complexity* stems from interactions among autonomous components or objects. While objects may possess high internal complexity, dynamic complexity arises from their constantly changing interactions and their arbitrary connectedness. Domain-driven design helps to mitigate structural domain complexity: it provides abstractions such as entities, value objects, aggregates, repositories, and services that bring order, reduce connectedness, and manage variability within and across Bounded Contexts.

However, as Landre remarked in [21], the complexity of the dynamic domain is not addressed really in DDD. One step in that direction has been the introduction of *domain events* [33]. Still, an open issue that remains is the introduction of proper abstractions specifying how such events are managed to accomplish tasks.

These remarks are even more relevant as soon as we aim at applying DDD for the design of autonomous systems, operating in contexts characterised by uncertainty, and concurrency—such as systems dealing with the physical world, as is the case in cyber-physical systems and the Internet-of-Things (IoT).

4   Empowering DDD with Agent-Oriented Modelling

Given the remarks expressed in Sect. 3 on the limitations of DDD, a clear benefit that AOSE can bring to DDD is the modelling power of agent-oriented abstractions [31], which we consider at two different levels:

- at the level of a single Bounded Context, that is using agent-oriented abstractions (and metamodels) to define the domain model in Bounded Contexts, beyond the OO domain model pattern typically adopted in DDD;
- at the level of the Context Map, that is defining interactions and relationships among Bounded Contexts at a more systemic level.

In this section, we analyse these two levels, which are orthogonal but could eventually be integrated into a single conceptual view for a methodology that integrates DDD and AOSE. The material associated with this paper [25] includes the source code of the examples discussed in what follows.

4.1   Single Bounded Context

Depending on the complexity of an individual Bounded Context, we can adopt agent-oriented metamodels of increasing complexity as well. In particular, we may consider incrementally the different dimensions typically used for engineering MAS [4,10], which may help to mitigate the complexity inherent to the Bounded Context.

Bounded Context as a Single Agent. The simplest case is to map a Bounded Context to a single agent, that is defining the domain model in terms of the concepts typically used to define autonomous, reactive, and proactive behaviour. A minimal set could include concepts to define the agent's objectives (e.g., goals, tasks), how the agent accomplishes such goals (e.g., plans, routines), and concepts defining how the agent interacts with its environment (e.g., perceptions, actions). Beyond this minimal set, we may consider richer (meta)models such as the BDI model, which allows refining the characterisation of objectives into desires and goals, as well as introducing beliefs, intentions, and plans. These concepts become the building blocks of an *agent-oriented domain model pattern*, extending (or replacing) the classic OO version typically used in DDD (and based on concepts such as entities, aggregates, etc.).

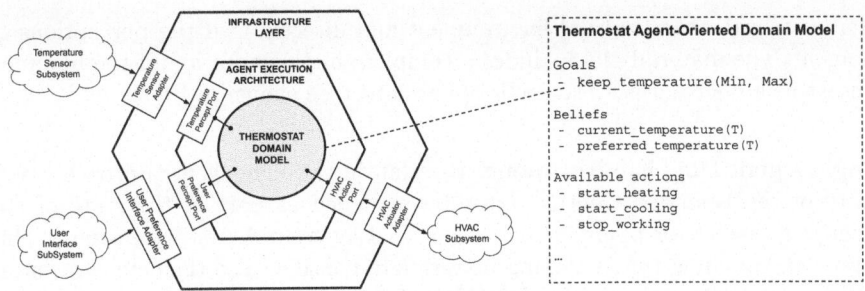

Fig. 2. Modelling a Bounded Context as a single agent: the Thermostat example. The domain model describes the thermostat behaviour in terms of (BDI) agent-oriented concepts. At the architectural level, the hexagonal/clean architecture is preserved: the infrastructure layer includes the adapters for integrating concrete sensing and actuating technologies, as well as technologies for interacting with other subsystems. The percept/action ports and corresponding adapters allow for decoupling the domain model from these specific technologies, yet enabling their effective integration.

As a simple but illustrative example, let's consider the case of a thermostat system modelled as a single agent, designed in a domain-driven perspective (see Fig. 2). The domain model modelled using BDI agent-oriented abstractions allows for describing the behaviour of the thermostat in terms of a goal (`keep_temperature(Min,Max)`), beliefs about current temperature as perceived through the temperature sensor subsystem (`current_temperature(T)`) and the preferred temperature as perceived through the user interface subsystem (`preferred_temperature(T)`), and actions to control the HVAC system (`start_heating`, `start_cooling`, `stop_working`).

In DDD, the domain model is "alive": it is meant to have a corresponding computational version that features the specified (or expected) behaviour. The same applies to the agent-oriented version—and, for that purpose, we can then use any agent-oriented programming technology (language, framework, platform) to implement the model. For example, an implementation of the thermostat domain model in Jason [6] is provided in the material associated with this paper [25].

At the architectural level, even when adopting agent-oriented abstractions, we still follow the clean architectural principles, as shown in 2: the agent-oriented domain model remains in the centre and does not depend on any aspect concerning, for example, the technology/infrastructural layer. Accordingly, both the dynamic knowledge about the world of the agent (i.e., its beliefs) as well as the knowledge about its tasks, including the practical knowledge about how to accomplish them or the policies to be used, can be considered part of the domain model at the centre. Around this layer, following the hexagonal architecture, we have the application layer and then the infrastructure layer. When an agent-oriented approach is adopted, the application layer corresponds to the agent execution architecture, which in this case is domain independent. The infrastructure layer concerns the implementation of sensors and actuators that enable interaction with the external environment and directly feed the perceptions of an agent. The material [25] includes a complete implementation of the bounded context as a microservice featuring the architecture shown in Fig. 2.

Single Agent Plus Environment. By adopting a single-agent approach, every entity of the Bounded Context must be modelled as part of the state of the agent (e.g., beliefs or plans in the case of BDI agents). A first extension to this approach, enriching the modelling power, is to consider also the environment as first-class modelling abstraction [35]: This allows for realising a separation of concerns between the entities encapsulating the locus of decision-making (agents), and resources and tools used to pursue its objectives (environment). Through this extension, a Bounded Context is mapped into an agent and an environment. In a minimal (meta)model, the environment can be conceived as a single monolithic entity with an observable state (to be perceived by the agent) and a set of actions (to be executed by the agent).

Beyond this minimal metamodel, different approaches have been proposed in the literature for modelling the environment as a first-class abstraction. An approach that was specifically conceived for cognitive/BDI agents is the Agents and Artifacts (A&A) metamodel [23]. A&A allows for modularising the environment in terms of *artifacts* (e.g., resources, tools) each exposing a usage interface composed of observable properties, operations, and observable events (or signals) [23]. On the agent side, artifact operations correspond to the actions that agents can do, and observable properties and events to their percepts, which in BDI agents can be mapped onto beliefs.

As a simple example, Fig. 3 shows the thermostat system based on a domain model including a thermostat agent—still described in terms of goals, beliefs, plans as before—and three artifacts, modelling the temperature sensor, the user preference subsystem, and the HVAC subsystem. In this case, the agent sensors/actuators are no longer bound to the external environment, but to the artifact-based environment, which is used to enable and mediate the interaction with the external environment. A full implementation based on the JaCaMo platform [3] is provided in the material [25].

At this stage, the logic governing the interaction with sensors and actuators represented at the infrastructure layer becomes part of the domain as well in the form of *artifacts*. They serve as DDD aggregate roots as the single entry point for a portion of the environment (and inherently of the domain of the bounded context). This option achieves a modularisation of such logic, improving the quality of the model. This also paves the way for more complex systems that may include many different entities in an environment, as well as possibly many different agents implementing the domain logic.

Multi-agent Systems and Agent Organisations. Finally, in a (complex) Bounded Context, the domain may be better modelled by considering multiple communicating agents sharing the same environment. This can be useful, for instance, to model explicitly at the domain level different loci of control or

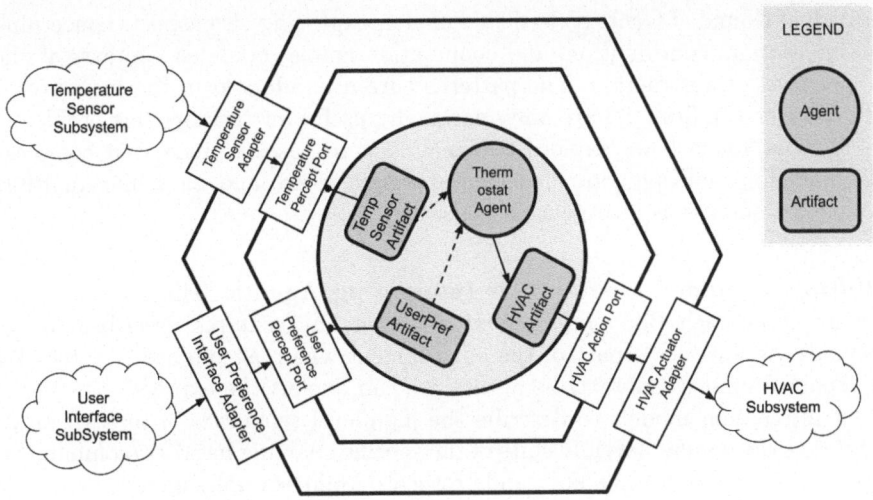

Fig. 3. Modelling a Bounded Context as a single agent plus environment: in this case, the domain model includes also environment abstractions. In the example, the A&A is used and artifacts as environment abstractions are used to explicitly model the temperature sensor, the user preference sub-system and the HVAC sub-system.

decision-making, eventually interacting in some way—either through direct communication (e.g., using agent communication languages) or indirectly through the environment. Organisation modelling approaches in this case can be further introduced to have first-class abstractions to specify the structure of the system as well as coordination activities (e.g., see [2]). Going further, even if in principle MAS and Organisation modelling can be useful for individual Bounded Contexts, their value is particularly important in scenarios involving multiple Bounded Contexts, as discussed in the next section.

4.2   Bounded Context Integration

Typically a project involves multiple "autonomous" Bounded Contexts, that need to be integrated to achieve the system's overarching goals. To this purpose, MAS and Organisation modelling can significantly enhance the approaches used in DDD to deal with this problem (see Sect. 2.2) while at the same time preserving the key principles and philosophy of DDD.

On the one hand, the integration problem among Bounded Contexts is clearly related to the interoperability problem, for example, in Service-Oriented Architecture (SOA) [11] or in (open) multi-agent systems. A general approach to deal with problems at the technical level accounts for defining an explicit *semantic* layer (i.e., semantic interoperability), in terms of shared ontologies formalising the meaning of concepts, including those specifying aspects concerning the interaction among parties (e.g., contracts). On the other hand, MAS and organisation modelling can be applied to extend the domain-driven principles beyond the individual Bounded Context, to define models capturing also aspects concerning the interaction, coordination, and cooperation among bounded contexts at the proper level of abstraction. The patterns currently adopted in the mainstream and described in Sect. 2.2 are only marginally useful for tackling this problem.

In what follows, we explore two main macro cases of increased complexity: modelling multiple Bounded Contexts as a MAS, and modelling multiple Bounded Contexts as an Agent Organisation.

Multiple Bounded Contexts as Interacting Agents. This case accounts for modelling each Bounded Context as either an agent (as described in the previous section) or as part of the environment where agents are situated. By designing Bounded Contexts as agents, we can exploit the expressive power of agent interaction models to describe the high-level semantics of interaction as defined at the domain level, in spite of the specific enabling network/communication/implementation technology and protocols. Main examples include high-level Agent Communication Languages such as FIPA ACL or KQML, or more recent information-oriented protocol specification languages such as BSPL [29].

A simple example extending the previous ones concerns a smart room scenario including a number of autonomous subsystems, in an Internet of Things perspective, each one properly designed as a distinct Bounded Context—and modelled as an autonomous agent. In that case, the request to the Thermostat to change/keep the temperature could be modelled, for example, as a request to achieve a goal `keep_temperature(Min,Max)`, possibly sent by the Bounded Context representing the smart room supervisor.

The MAS modelling includes also the case where one or multiple Bounded Contexts modelled as agents interact with one or multiple Bounded Contexts modelled as the (agent) environment, as described in Sect. 4.1. In the smart room scenario, for instance, the specific sensing and actuating subsystems used by the Thermostat Bounded Context may be designed as separate Bounded Contexts, modelled, for example, as artifacts (as in the A&A metamodel) used by the agent.

It is worth remarking that, in this case, the concepts of agent and artifact as well are used first of all as modelling abstraction for modelling the domain, not as technologies for implementing the system. So we may have Bounded Contexts modelled as agents (and artifacts) implemented using technologies and frameworks used in the mainstream to implement, for example, (micro)services and enterprise applications.

Multiple Bounded Contexts as an Agent Organisation. Finally, organisation modelling as developed in the MAS literature may provide a proper abstraction layer to tackle the structural and behavioural complexity of systems composed of a dynamic (and possibly large, open) set of interrelated Bounded Contexts. The concepts of groups and roles as provided, for example, in AGR [14] and Moise [18] can be effective to model domains where the structure is dynamic. In the smart room case, for instance, the configuration and facilities of the room may adapt and change dynamically depending on the users that enter, possibly having different preferences but also different capabilities, related to their roles.

5   Concluding Remarks

The bi-directional conceptual integration of DDD and AOSE could be beneficial for both worlds: on the one hand, it can extend DDD with the proper level of abstraction for building dynamic, adaptive, and complex systems that exhibit relevant levels of autonomy; on the other hand, it can help structure the development of domain models in AOSE. This paper provides a first conceptual framework to conceive and understand such integration, discussing in particular how agent-oriented modelling could be exploited both at the individual Bounded Context level and for the integration of Bounded Contexts.

This contribution is clearly related to existing work in literature exploring the adoption of agile methodologies for agent-based systems [7,26], including Test-Driven Development (TDD) and Behaviour-Driven Development (BDD) [28]. Domain-Driven Design provides us the background approach and reference, in terms of general modelling and design principles, in which also TDD and BDD can be properly conceptually situated.

The conceptual framework depicted in this paper is meant to provide a baseline for future work. One direction to be explored further is the development of a concrete agent-oriented DDD methodology, one that is based on an agent-oriented domain pattern. In line with the DDD philosophy, defining such a pattern would have to start from domain practice and a set of relevant use cases. For example, in the building automation domain, domain experts are the ones who define libraries of automation programs (i.e., procedural knowledge) that are then assembled to meet the technical requirements of the automation system for a specific building. Mapping such domain concepts and their relations to agent-oriented abstractions could bring insight into what would be a suitable agent-oriented domain pattern in this area.

A second research direction, which we explored less in this paper, is the development of a DDD-inspired agent-oriented methodology. The influence of DDD on AOSE could bring additional structure to the way MAS are designed and built. For example, adopting existing DDD modelling patterns (*tactical patterns* as known in DDD) and integrating them within agent-oriented methodologies could be one of the core challenges for a fruitful integration—and may allow developers to have more structurally sound domain models for MAS. A line of work on engineering MAS relevant to this research direction is the use of domain ontologies for model-driven engineering (e.g., see [15]). If domain models are expressed formally as domain ontologies, then ontology engineering methodologies (e.g., SAMOD [24], ACIMOV [16]) could further inform this investigation.

A third direction for future work is to investigate the design and development of new tools that would provide proper conceptual support for exploiting the integration of DDD and agent-orientation. Such tools may be based on existing ones for DDD and AOSE, but would likely require rethinking the development process from the ground up to provide for a streamlined integration of the two.

References

1. Amaral, C.J., Hübner, J.F., Kampik, T.: TDD for AOP: test-driven development for agent-oriented programming. In: Agmon, N., An, B., Ricci, A., Yeoh, W. (eds.) Proceedings of the 2023 International Conference on Autonomous Agents and Multiagent Systems, AAMAS 2023, London, United Kingdom, 29 May 2023 - 2 June 2023, pp. 3038–3040. ACM (2023). https://doi.org/10.5555/3545946.3599165
2. Boissier, O., Bordini, R., Hubner, J., Ricci, A.: Multi-Agent Oriented Programming: Programming Multi-Agent Systems Using JaCaMo. Intelligent Robotics and Autonomous Agents series, MIT Press (2020). https://books.google.it/books?id=GM_tDwAAQBAJ
3. Boissier, O., Bordini, R.H., Hübner, J.F., Ricci, A., Santi, A.: Multi-agent oriented programming with JaCaMo. Sci. Comput. Program. **78**(6), 747–761 (2013)
4. Boissier, O., Bordini, R.H., Hübner, J.F., Ricci, A.: Dimensions in programming multi-agent systems. Knowl. Eng. Review **34**, e2 (2019). https://doi.org/10.1017/S026988891800005X
5. Boissier, O., Bordini, R.H., Hübner, J.F., Ricci, A., Santi, A.: Multi-agent oriented programming with JaCaMo. Sci. Comput. Program. **78**(6), 747–761 (2013). https://doi.org/10.1016/J.SCICO.2011.10.004
6. Bordini, R.H., Hübner, J.F., Wooldridge, M.: Programming multi-agent systems in AgentSpeak using Jason. Wiley, Hoboken (2007)
7. Carrera, Á., Iglesias, C.A., Garijo, M.: Beast methodology: an agile testing methodology for multi-agent systems based on behaviour driven development. Inf. Syst. Front. **16**, 169–182 (2014)
8. Carrera, Á., Iglesias, C.A., Garijo, M.: Beast methodology: an agile testing methodology for multi-agent systems based on behaviour driven development. Inf. Syst. Front. **16**(2), 169–182 (2014). https://doi.org/10.1007/S10796-013-9438-5
9. Collier, R.W., O'Neill, E., Lillis, D., O'Hare, G.M.P.: MAMS: multi-agent microservices. In: Companion of The 2019 World Wide Web Conference, WWW 2019, San Francisco, CA, USA, May 13-17, 2019, pp. 655–662 (2019). https://doi.org/10.1145/3308560.3316509
10. Demazeau, Y.: From interactions to collective behaviour in agent-based systems. In: European Conference on Cognitive Science. vol. 95 (1995)
11. Erl, T.: Service-Oriented Architecture: Concepts, Technology, and Design. Prentice Hall Professional Technical Reference, Upper Saddle River, NJ (2005)
12. Evans, E.: Domain-driven design: tackling complexity in the heart of software. Addison-Wesley Professional (2004)
13. Evans, E.: Domain-Driven Design Reference: Definitions and Pattern Summaries. Dog Ear Publishing (2014)
14. Ferber, J., Gutknecht, O., Michel, F.: From agents to organizations: an organizational view of multi-agent systems. In: Giorgini, P., Müller, J.P., Odell, J. (eds.) AOSE 2003. LNCS, vol. 2935, pp. 214–230. Springer, Heidelberg (2004). https://doi.org/10.1007/978-3-540-24620-6_15
15. Freitas, A., Bordini, R.H., Vieira, R.: Model-driven engineering of multi-agent systems based on ontologies. Appl. Ontol. **12**(2), 157–188 (2017). https://doi.org/10.3233/AO-170182
16. Hannou, F.Z., Charpenay, V., Lefrançois, M., Roussey, C., Zimmermann, A., Gandon, F.: The ACIMOV methodology: agile and continuous integration for modular ontologies and vocabularies. In: Proceedings of the 2nd Workshop on Modular Knowledge (MK 2023). CEUR Workshop Proceedings, vol. 3637 (2023), https://ceur-ws.org/Vol-3637/paper25.pdf

17. Hitchins, D.K.: Advanced Systems Thinking. Engineering and Management, Artech House (2003)
18. Hübner, J.F., Sichman, J.S.a., Boissier, O.: MOISE+: towards a structural, functional, and deontic model for mas organization. In: Proceedings of the First International Joint Conference on Autonomous Agents and Multiagent Systems: Part 1, pp. 501–502. AAMAS '02, Association for Computing Machinery, New York, NY, USA (2002). https://doi.org/10.1145/544741.544858
19. Jennings, N.R.: On agent-based software engineering. Artif. Intell. **117**(2), 277–296 (2000). https://doi.org/10.1016/S0004-3702(99)00107-1
20. Khononov, V.: Learning Domain-Driven Design. O'Really (2022)
21. Landre, E.: Domain-Driven Design: The First 15 Years Essays from the DDD Community, chap. Agents aka Domain objects on steroids, Lean Pub (2024)
22. Millett, S., Tune, N.: Patterns. Principles and Practices of Domain-Driven Design, Wrox (2015)
23. Omicini, A., Ricci, A., Viroli, M.: Artifacts in the A&A meta-model for multi-agent systems. Auton. Agent. Multi-Agent Syst. **17**(3), 432–456 (2008). https://doi.org/10.1007/s10458-008-9053-x
24. Peroni, S.: SAMOD: an agile methodology for the development of ontologies (2016). https://doi.org/10.6084/m9.figshare.3189769.v4, https://figshare.com/articles/journal_contribution/SAMOD_an_agile_methodology_for_the_development_of_ontologies/3189769
25. Ricci, A., Burattini, S., Ciortea, A., Castellucci, M.: Agents for DDD – Back and Forth – Material (2024). https://github.com/Agents-and-DDD/EMAS-2024-paper-material.git
26. Rodriguez, S., Thangarajah, J., Winikoff, M.: User and system stories: an agile approach for managing requirements in AOSE. In: Proceedings of the 20th International Conference on Autonomous Agents and MultiAgent Systems. p. 1064-1072. AAMAS '21, International Foundation for Autonomous Agents and Multiagent Systems, Richland, SC (2021)
27. Rodriguez, S., Thangarajah, J., Winikoff, M.: A behaviour-driven approach for testing requirements via user and system stories in agent systems. In: Agmon, N., An, B., Ricci, A., Yeoh, W. (eds.) Proceedings of the 2023 International Conference on Autonomous Agents and Multiagent Systems, AAMAS 2023, London, United Kingdom, 29 May 2023 - 2 June 2023, pp. 1182–1190. ACM (2023).https://doi.org/10.5555/3545946.3598761
28. Rodriguez, S., Thangarajah, J., Winikoff, M.: A behaviour-driven approach for testing requirements via user and system stories in agent systems. In: Proceedings of the 2023 International Conference on Autonomous Agents and Multiagent Systems, pp. 1182–1190. AAMAS '23, International Foundation for Autonomous Agents and Multiagent Systems, Richland, SC (2023)
29. Singh, M.P.: Information-driven interaction-oriented programming: BSPL, the blindingly simple protocol language. In: The 10th International Conference on Autonomous Agents and Multiagent Systems - Volume 2, pp. 491–498. AAMAS '11, International Foundation for Autonomous Agents and Multiagent Systems, Richland, SC (2011)
30. Stahl, T., Voelter, M., Czarnecki, K.: Model-Driven Software Development: Technology, Engineering. Management. John Wiley & Sons Inc, Hoboken, NJ, USA (2006)
31. Sterling, L., Taveter, K.: The Art of Agent-Oriented Modeling. The MIT Press, Cambridge (2009)

32. Tiryaki, A.M., Öztuna, S., Dikenelli, O., Erdur, R.C.: SUNIT: a unit testing framework for test driven development of multi-agent systems. In: Padgham, L., Zambonelli, F. (eds.) AOSE 2006. LNCS, vol. 4405, pp. 156–173. Springer, Heidelberg (2007). https://doi.org/10.1007/978-3-540-70945-9_10
33. Vernon, V.: Implementing Domain-Driven Design. Addison-Wesley (2013)
34. Vernon, V.: Domain-Driven Design Distilled. Addison-Wesley, Boston, MA (2016)
35. Weyns, D., Van Dyke Parunak, H., Michel, F., Holvoet, T., Ferber, J.: Environments for multiagent systems state-of-the-art and research challenges. In: Weyns, D., Van Dyke Parunak, H., Michel, F. (eds.) E4MAS 2004. LNCS (LNAI), vol. 3374, pp. 1–47. Springer, Heidelberg (2005). https://doi.org/10.1007/978-3-540-32259-7_1

Author Index